Jewish First Wife, Divorced

.

Jewish First Wife, Divorced

The Correspondence of Ethel Gross and Harry Hopkins

Edited by
Allison Giffen and June Hopkins

LEXINGTON BOOKS
Lanham • Boulder • New York • Oxford

LEXINGTON BOOKS

Published in the United States of America
by Lexington Books
A Member of the Rowman & Littlefield Publishing Group
4720 Boston Way, Lanham, Maryland 20706

PO Box 317
Oxford
OX2 9RU, UK

British Library Cataloguing in Publication Information Available

Library of Congress Cataloging-in-Publication Data

Gross, Ethel.
    Jewish first wife, divorced : the correspondence of Ethel Gross and
Harry Hopkins / edited by Allison Giffen and June Hopkins.
        p. cm.
Includes bibliographical references.
    ISBN 0-7391-0502-7 (alk. paper)
    1. Hopkins, Harry Lloyd, 1890–1946—Correspondence. 2. Gross,
Ethel—Correspondence. 3. Statesmen's spouses—United
States—Correspondence. 4. Statesmen—United States—Correspondence.
I. Hopkins, Harry Lloyd, 1890–1946. II. Giffen, Allison. III. Hopkins,
June, 1940– IV. Title.
    E748.H67 A4 2002
        973.917'092—dc21
                                    2002011610

Printed in the United States of America

♾™ The paper used in this publication meets the minimum requirements of
American National Standard for Information Sciences—Permanence of Paper
for Printed Library Materials, ANSI/NISO Z39.48–1992.

Contents

Acknowledgments

THIS BOOK HAS BEEN A LONG time in the making, and there are many people and institutions that have helped in the process. We would like to thank our academic institutions, New Mexico State University, Western Washington University, and Armstrong Atlantic State University for allowing us the time to work on this collection and for their financial support in the form of several grants. Nicholas Scheetz, manuscript librarian at Georgetown University's Lauinger Library, Special Collection, was extremely helpful in providing us with copies of the letters housed there. We owe a debt of gratitude to Dr. Roger Daniels for his detailed and enlightening oral history of Ethel Gross taken in 1964. Katherine Ferreira, graduate student at AASU, spent a great deal of time and effort in digitizing the letters, and we have Joy Watson to thank for providing a grant to allow her to do this. We thank our large and extended family for the encouragement and insight they have given us. We especially thank our partners, Bill Lyne and Dennis Bradley, who carefully read versions of this manuscript and offered helpful critiques and without whose love and support this project would never have been completed. And, finally, we thank Ethel Gross and Harry Hopkins for having kept all of their correspondence, a remarkable feat given the many times they moved.

Introduction

ON THE OCCASION OF President Franklin Delano Roosevelt (FDR) signing a new $1.5 billion relief bill, a 1937 issue of *Life* magazine presented a photographic biography of Harry Hopkins, subtitled: "The Story of Harry Hopkins's Rise to Power." Called by some "The Assistant President," Harry Hopkins was FDR's New Deal Relief Administrator and wartime emissary to Churchill and Stalin, and he continues to be the subject of numerous academic monographs and essays.[1] The *Life* magazine spread presented photos of Hopkins's childhood home, college tennis team, and assorted family members. Ethel Gross, his first wife of seventeen years, was conspicuously absent.[2] The only reference to her occurred indirectly in the caption beneath a photo of their son David Hopkins: "eldest of Harry Hopkins's three sons by his Jewish first wife, divorced." As the producer of male children, Ethel Gross could not be entirely erased from the biography. Instead, she was reduced to a generic label, "Jewish first wife, divorced," one that insisted on her scandalous otherness (intermarriage and divorce were still social taboos in 1937).

The lives and contributions of many American women have been passed over in the same way that readers of *Life* magazine probably glanced over this caption, which obscures seventeen years of work and marriage. By bringing to light the private documents of American women, we gain access to their engagement with their culture's ideology. Such insights permit us to restage their often-overlooked contributions to the American cultural drama. The correspondence of Ethel Gross and Harry Hopkins offers a record of one woman's response to a set of historical circumstances in the first half of the twentieth century that had a profound effect

1

on the material lives of American women. Ethel Gross was a Hungarian Jew whose family immigrated to New York City's Lower East Side when she was a child. A settlement worker at Christodora House when she met Hopkins, her work in social welfare and the women's suffrage movement placed her at the center of the Progressive Movement in New York City. She served as the secretary of the Equal Franchise Society and the Women's Political Union, and her progressive ideas exerted a significant influence on Harry Hopkins. These letters have much to tell us about the experience of a Jewish immigrant woman, the process of Americanization, and the construction of citizenship. They reveal the significant influence of Progressivism on the formation of Harry Hopkins's political ideology. They also offer insights into the complex tensions for early twentieth-century women between the requirements of domestic roles and their own intellectual and professional ambitions.

I. COURTSHIP: SUFFRAGE AND SETTLEMENT WORK, 1913

I think if she were not there to give definition to my personality it would vanish in the excessive vagueness of its contours. It is only around her that I concentrate myself

Andre Gide, *The Counterfeiters*
Recorded in Ethel Gross's journal

The correspondence between Harry Hopkins (1890–1946) and Ethel Gross (1886–1976) began in February 1913 when the two initiated a secret courtship while they both were employed at Christodora House, one of the largest settlement houses in New York City.[3] For the next nine months, until their marriage in October, they wrote to each other regularly, sometimes every day. A twenty-two-year-old Iowan Methodist, Hopkins was a graduate of Grinnell College where he had been steeped in the ideas of the Social Gospel Movement.[4] Gross, on the other hand, was a twenty-six-year-old Hungarian Jew, a social worker, and a suffrage activist. Given their differences in age, ethnicity, and class, the two had sufficient reason to keep their relationship quiet. The courtship letters (February to October 1913) represent nearly one-third of the total correspondence and are infused with the anxiety and thrill of their clandestine interfaith relationship, their commitment to social work, suffrage, and reform, and their growing passion for each other. When combined with the correspondence of their marriage, separation, and divorce and placed alongside excerpts from Gross's personal papers, they form a coherent narrative that traces the emotional arc of their relationship.

Christodora Settlement House provided the ideological as well as geographical locus for Hopkins's and Gross's relationship, though the two arrived there by radically different paths. In 1891 at the age of five, Ethel Gross immigrated with her family from Kaschau, Hungary, to New York City. Her father, Bencion Gross, had been educated at the Theological Seminary at Pressburg and worked as a manager in his family's glass factory in Hutta. Though he, his wife, Celia Rich Gross, and their five children were comfortably ensconced in the middle class, as Jews they endured the humiliation of social, legal, and economic restrictions. In Hungary in the mid-nineteenth century, Jews could not live in many big cites, were taxed unfairly, and suffered discrimination in the business world.[5] Bencion died of tuberculosis in 1891, and when Celia's nine-month-old son also died soon after, she decided to act on her husband's wish to migrate to America. The thirty-seven-year-old widow and her five surviving children joined the wave of over four million immigrants who came to America at the end of the nineteenth century, traveling by steerage class to New York City.[6]

Celia Gross and the children settled in New York's Lower East Side, in a densely populated Jewish ghetto.[7] Soon after she arrived, Celia endured yet another loss, when a daughter, Henrietta, died. The family now consisted of four children, ages three through sixteen—Benjamin, Ethel, Edward, and Francesca—living in a typical, dark and airless dumbbell tenement.[8] Upon arrival in New York City, Gross was immediately enrolled in the local public school but dropped out in the eighth grade because of anemia and fainting spells.[9] Luckily, by that time she had become acquainted with Christodora House and its founder and headworker, Christina MacColl, who became Gross's mentor for many years. MacColl arranged for Gross to spend the summer in the country, in Dalton, Massachusetts, to regain her health; upon Gross's return, MacColl employed the twelve-year-old Gross at Christodora House supervising recreational programs for young children. Gross was clearly ambitious and, in addition to her work at the settlement, learned to use the new typewriting machine and took lessons in shorthand. She also took extension courses at the local state university where she passed Regents examinations. At fourteen she secured a much coveted clerical job with the Engineering News and Publishing Company where she worked for two years, after which she moved to the M.P. Foster Electrical Company.

It is not clear from the documents how Celia supported herself and her children, since there is no occupation listed for her on the 1900 census report. She most probably did piece work for the garment industry in her home. This was one of the few jobs available to women like Celia, who, although educated, could not speak English and had few marketable skills.[10] While the Gross children worked hard to assimilate into American life,

Celia seemed never to have fully adjusted, and in 1911 or 1912, when all four children were in their twenties, Celia committed suicide by gassing herself in the oven. In what must have been an extremely traumatic experience, Ethel was the one who found her mother's body in the tenement kitchen. In the years when Gross was working at the settlement house, trying very hard to leave the Jewish ghetto and all that it connoted behind her, she and her mother, with whom she was very close, were on quite different paths. The tragedy of her mother's suicide must have strengthened Gross's ambition to enter into the American mainstream and indirectly propelled her toward Harry Hopkins.

Throughout her teenage years while holding various clerical positions, Gross also continued to work at the settlement house as counselor for the children and as MacColl's personal secretary. MacColl was a committed social worker dedicated to the tenets of the Social Gospel, which attributed social disorder to both environmental and spiritual causes. She fervently believed it was her spiritual imperative to relieve the sufferings of others and in 1897, responding to what she called "a sob of the spirit," resolved to build a settlement house in New York City's Lower East Side. She chose a site just blocks away from the Gross family's tenement apartment in New York's Sixth Assembly District, an area rife with social and economic problems. Fifty-five percent of the inhabitants were foreign born, and the neighborhood supported the greatest concentration of immigrants in the United States, about 4,000 per block. Such neighborhoods were the object of fascination for the middle-classes in the first decades of the twentieth century. Through the photographs of Jacob Riis and Lewis Hines, sketches of ghetto life in popular magazines and newspapers, sensationalist slum fiction, and the immigrant fiction of writers like Abraham Cahan and Anzia Yezierska, the ghetto became framed as a site both familiarized and exotic, dangerous but penetrable.[11]

Christodora, which means "gift of God," sought to bring social uplift through spiritual salvation. MacColl's brand of Protestantism preached hard work and service to others, which, for the young women of the neighborhood, translated into a celebration of their duties as wives and mothers. For MacColl, Protestantism became a vehicle by which she could convert her immigrant neighbors to an "American" way of life: an (impossible) middle-class ideal that dictated that women's responsibility lay within the home as "educated mothers."[12] Wed to constructions of both gender and national identity, MacColl's evangelical Protestantism played an important role in the life of the settlement, and documents indicate that the settlement workers rejoiced when a Catholic or Jew embraced Protestantism.[13] Always practical in her approach, however, MacColl also recognized that the young women of the neighborhood needed much more than religion. She declared that the settlement:

was not to be a mission. We are to have entertainments, musicals and social gathering—good jolly ones—and while we will, of course, have the word of God, we do not intend to get unconverted girls out of heated shops and filthy tenements to preach to them. We will meet them as our sisters, our friends and try to be a help and a blessing and God will do the rest.[14]

MacColl actively played the part of sister and friend to Ethel Gross. She offered her advice, contacts for work, and an important role model based upon her specific brand of Protestantism that idealized domesticity and hard work.

Yet MacColl was not Gross's only role model. In 1908 MacColl recommended Gross for a job as a private secretary to Katherine Mackay, wife of Clarence Mackay, founder of the U.S. Telegraph and Cable Company. Along with the commitments required of a wealthy socialite, Katherine Mackay involved herself in a number of reforms. When Gross began working for her, Mackay was interested in educational reform in Rosalyn, Long Island, where the Mackay mansion was located but soon after, directed her attention to women's suffrage. In 1908 Mackay founded the Equal Franchise Society (EFS), unique because it targeted women from the so-called "Four Hundred"; members of New York's wealthiest industrial families. Gross became the secretary for EFS and divided her time between the swank EFS Manhattan offices in the Metropolitan Life Building in Manhattan and the Mackay's Long Island mansion.

Mackay's world offered Gross access to a fascinating intersection of the wealthy and the radical in New York City, and she was exposed to new ideas that presented alternatives to MacColl's middle-class Protestant values. As Mackay's personal secretary, she was expected to accompany her everywhere, from lunch at Sherry's to two three-month European trips. Consequently, Gross had to learn the manners and dress of the upper classes. As secretary of EFS, Gross was also gaining an education in the strategies and tactics of women's political action: she marched in suffrage parades, organized speaking engagements for the Society's rallies, wrote press releases, and attended dinner parties with the elite of New York City. She interacted with such notables as Carrie Chapman Catt, Crystal and Max Eastman, and Harriet Stanton Blatch and in the process developed a strong commitment to women's suffrage.[15] From these years Gross gained not only an education in the etiquette of the wealthy but also a fervent interest in the right of women to participate in the public sphere. Yet, while Gross's sense of the possibilities for women must certainly have been broadened as a consequence of these experiences, she never let go of many of the central tenets of Christina MacColl's brand of social Christianity and maternalism.

The influence of MacColl's ideals are evident in the circumstances under which Gross left her position with Katherine Mackay and returned to work at Christodora House. In the autumn of 1912, Gross accompanied Mackay to Paris on their second European trip together. At this time, Mackay was having a rather public affair with a Dr. Joseph Blake, whose irate wife was suing Mackay for alienating the doctor's affections. Because of the Mackays' wealth and social status, the newspapers were boosting sales by giving the scandal full coverage. The blitz of media attention and the ensuing "sordid divorce" made Gross uncomfortable, and when she returned home for the Christmas holidays, she decided that, despite the lure of Mackay's affluence and connections, she could not return to her employ.[16] Instead, she went back to Christina MacColl and Christodora House where she worked in several capacities—as MacColl's personal secretary, as an administrator for the Haven Relief Fund, and as director of the drama program. It was at that time that Gross met Hopkins, who had recently arrived at Christodora House, and they quickly fell in love.

As an educated, middle-class midwesterner, Hopkins's path to Christodora House was radically different from Gross's. Together, these two journeys are exemplary of what historians have identified as a dual migration that occurred between 1880 and 1920 from America's heartland and from Eastern Europe to urban centers like Chicago and New York City. Hopkins grew up in a rural, middle-class household in Grinnell, Iowa. His father began work as a harness maker and later sold leather goods while his mother ran household affairs as well as the Methodist Home Missionary Society.[17] Hopkins graduated from Grinnell College where he had studied with Edward Steiner, one of the leading thinkers of the Social Gospel Movement. That first summer after graduation, accompanied by one of Grinnell's young professors of social reform, Louis Hartson, Hopkins worked as a counselor at Christodora's Northover Boys Camp in Bound Brook, New Jersey. At the end of the summer, he decided to remain in New York and became head of the boys' programs at the settlement's central location on the Lower East Side.

Settlement work at this time had developed into one of the new and few careers available to educated women, and Hopkins was one of only a handful of men to work at Christodora House. Most of the workers were young, educated, Protestant women from the middle-classes, many of whom were recruited from institutions like Smith and Wellesley. These women represented one of the first waves of female college-graduates, and settlement work permitted them to put their college training to practical use. The Jewish ghetto in New York City was a dangerous and exotic locale for these women. Most had never seen a slum, much less lived there before, and the settlement house offered a protective residential enclave from which they could offer social services to immigrant neighbors.[18]

Ethel Gross was not a typical settlement worker. In an extended oral history conducted by historian Roger Daniels in 1964 when Gross was seventy-eight years old, she recalled her experiences at Christodora House and the early stages of her relationship with Hopkins:

> And the thing that surprised me was when I found that he had taken any notice in me at all. Because at the settlement at that time there were all these young college people who had all these advantages, who had come from beautiful homes and were giving their time. I had him all paired off, first with one and then another and they all liked him, at least so it seemed to me.[19]

Gross's memory of her surprise at Hopkins's interest in her registers her perception of herself as different and somehow less appealing than the other workers, a perception that recurs throughout her recollections of Christodora House. In her private papers we find a similar sense of her status as different within the culture of American institutions. For example, in a journal entry, probably written when she was in her twenties, Gross recorded her memories of herself within the public schools:

> I could probably write a wonderful essay on the value of education—never having had any. The elementary school which I attended, entered at the age of five—feeling ashamed of the difference between myself and all the other children around me, because I was the only little foreigner, probably did more harm than good. Fear is the emotion that I remember most as I look back on that period. Fear of not doing what the teacher wanted. Fear of being and acting differently from my classmates. Fear of looking different because of my clothes. Fear seemed to predominate everything I did. It became the motive for doing nearly everything I did at school.[20]

Significantly, as a child, it was precisely the support that Christodora House provided that helped to allay her terrors related to her foreignness. Gross learned how to look and act like an American girl, and with ambition and hard work she crossed the boundary from settlement client to settlement worker. In effect, she was a model for the settlement house: a success story exemplifying the process of assimilation and job training that such institutions performed. Yet, Gross was never fully accepted by the other settlement workers and, as her oral history suggests, never saw herself wholly as one of them. An important mark of her difference from the other workers was the fact that, unlike her colleagues, she did not live in the graciously appointed settlement house, a bastion of white middle-class gentility in the ghetto. Instead, she returned home each evening to her family's tenement apartment on East Tenth Street.

Gross had left behind that terrified child and had become a cosmopolitan woman while working for Mackay. Interestingly, there are striking parallels between the position she occupied with Mackay and her position at the settlement house. In both places she was in their world but not of it, an outsider permitted a qualified insider-status. For both Christodora House and the Equal Franchise Society, she was a kind of "trophy"—living proof that the system worked and that America was, indeed, a land of opportunity. Such a model legitimizes upper- and middle-class privilege by (erroneously) demonstrating that social position is a consequence of ambition and hard work and, thus, is always earned.

At Christodora House, Gross occupied a conflicted site that reveals the limitations of the Americanization process at work in such institutions. As a model immigrant, she sought to inhabit an American identity (implicitly constructed as white Protestant) but also could never fully discard her identity of exotic otherness. Rather than becoming an American, she became an Americanized Eastern European Jew. Such institutions always make room for this kind of an identity, and she performed an important function as a kind of poster child for their enterprise. Ironically, her acceptance was predicated on the degree to which she supported and participated in those sociopolitical arrangements that implicitly construct an American identity as white and Protestant (and thus always marginalized her).

Gross's life, as it emerges in these documents, offers scholars the flesh and blood material from which they can think through some of the thorny debates about competing interpretations of the settlement house movement. Currently, scholars are divided between two paradigms, the "heroic model" exemplified in Allan Davis' influential study, *Spearheads of Reform*, which reads the settlement movement as the best and brightest of the progressive era and the "Social Welfare as Social Control" model, which challenges this assessment. This latter approach takes its cue from the New Social History and the New Left of the 1970s, which examines social reform from the point of view of working class and ethnic communities for whom this process of Americanization appears, at times, as an assault on these cultures. In her overview of the historiography of social welfare, Ruth Crocker notes the ways in which the institution of the settlement house, "while challenging basic problems in society, also unwittingly aids in the consolidation of corporate capitalism that rested on wide inequalities of wealth and power."[21] Of course, these "wide inequalities of wealth and power" are precisely what create the need for institutions like Christodora House, and Gross's relationship to the institution, as well as her relationship to Hopkins, offer scholars the concrete examples from which to think through such contradictory impulses.

When Gross and Hopkins met in January 1913, he must have represented everything most "American" to her. She was attracted not only to his Methodist Iowan background but also his "can do" ambition and energetic commitment to social welfare. In the correspondence, and in her recollections of Hopkins in the oral history, he emerges as a charming, sociable, and even light-hearted figure, qualities that all suggest a sure sense of one's place in the world. Hopkins embodied the American dream, and, given Gross's own ambitious nature and her desire to get a piece of that dream, he must have seemed a compelling choice for a partner. If Gross was attracted to Hopkins's rural Americanness, clearly Hopkins was attracted to Gross's exotic otherness.[22] Because of their differences, in particular because of anti-Semitism and social injunctions against interfaith marriage, the two kept their courtship a secret for many months. The thrill of their clandestine romance and the transgressiveness of intermarriage generate much of the emotion in the correspondence, especially in Hopkins's letters. Yet, Gross's place in Hopkins's affections was similar to her place at Christodora House. Although her difference was appealing to Hopkins (an underlying theme in a significant number of the love letters leading to their marriage), it was a difference made palatable by the assimilation process. She was exotic but safely exotic because her identity as an Eastern European Jew had been domesticated. She had become at home in America.

The courtship letters also offer some insights into the interesting negotiations required for strong, ambitious women like Gross, who were seeking to revise a conventional domestic identity to include a larger and more public scope of activity. In the early love letters, for example, we can identify the romantic script of that cultural moment and the ways that the two writers participated in courtship practices while self-consciously seeking to rewrite them. In an early letter from Hopkins to Gross written in February 1913, Hopkins struggled with his conventional notions of wifely behavior and his attraction to Gross as a modern woman:

> Let's see, how much did we spend last night? You seem to have forgotten what an awful smoker you are, but I've been thinking that we might raise chickens to pay for all such luxuries. I can see you bringing the eggs to market. Now I'm not fooling—you little dear—we're going to have a garden and raise potatoes—onions—radishes—lemons—but you are not a bit enthusiastic over it—you could practice suffrage speeches while you were planting a row of beans.[23]

Part joke, part threat, and an implicit admission of his own anxiety, this excerpt reveals something about the kind of pressure that internalized scripts about marriage can exert. Gross's reply is also telling:

> To answer your last letter—it was very thoughtful of you to remember about my cigarettes. Could I smoke as I carry the eggs to market? But there—I'm spoiling the pretty picture that you drew. I'd love to raise chickens—they'd be so lonesome all day with both of us away! Wouldn't they? But it's such a relief to know that I can have my cigarettes—and if you are very good I'll slip you a little one now and then![24]

Here, in one of her most assertive moments in the early letters, the lovers' banter permitted Gross a little space to lodge her resistance to some of the contours of the role of wife. Without overtly criticizing the "pretty picture," she playfully reminded him that she, too, would be working outside the home.

Throughout this correspondence, careful readers can determine Gross's understanding of the cultural requirements of her role as female lover. Her letters reveal a nuanced interplay between self-assertion and acquiescence, a kind of give and take that was always bounded by the norms of the day. We find evidence of this when, in March 1913, Gross began to work for the Women's Political Union (WPU) as personal secretary to its founder, Harriot Stanton Blatch. Daughter of Elizabeth Cady Stanton, Blatch was more radical than Mackay and modeled her activism on the militant suffragettes in England.[25] In a letter to Hopkins dated March 10th, 1913, Gross informed him of the possibility of this new work about which she was clearly excited and concluded, "So if I come down to break windows at Christodora House some day, don't be surprised."[26] Gently and humorously deprecating, Gross's comment suggests the ways in which she understood how radical activism, especially women's radical activism, would be received, even by a supportive lover who publicly aligned himself with the cause of suffrage.

Hopkins's response to Gross's activism and her political ideas about the role of women is interestingly ambivalent. Many letters reveal a young man exhilarated to be part of something "modern" and radical, and this exhilaration seemed to further amplify what were already very powerful romantic feelings: "I have thought about bigger and better things since you came into my life. I feel the thrill now of knowing that I won't have to live a lie with you but can shape my own life—influenced beyond words by the dearest of girls."[27] The "thrill" Hopkins felt was directly related to his ideas about what he called "woman's place in the world," which for Hopkins and Gross was a new place as equal partners. His letters suggest that part of that thrill came from the sense that, as a couple, the two were path breakers: "I had a long argument with Miss Ellis on woman's place in this world—fear that I shocked her—but dearest—we'll make it so ideal—that they will be converted to our way of thinking."[28] These comments also suggest that for this, still quite young, midwesterner merely the idea of being a little bit shocking contributed to the excitement. Yet at times, Hopkins also registered his discomfort with Gross's politics and independent nature through little jokes about the ways in which she was becoming "militant" in her work for Blatch. For example, in one letter he noted: "I can hardly picture myself as a dutiful 'hubby' and I'm not so sure that I always will obey, and I know that you won't."[29] And in another, he offered a subtle dig at Gross's insistence that she would work once they were married: "Am invited out to dinner tomorrow night. A Mr. McGuire, sec'y of the censor board, (whose wife does *not* work)."[30] Hopkins's ambivalence about Gross's work, along with her own careful self-representation of her activism, offer insight into the pervasive power of cultural prescriptions about gender, courtship and marriage, even for ambitious, idealistic young people self-consciously seeking to alter them.

II. MARRIAGE: WORLD WAR I AND CIVILIAN RELIEF, 1915–1918

A gifted woman can feel that the way she lives as a woman does not determine her value, nor her position, in her profession or art or business. The ordinary woman, though, has only one position that sets her apart from the uniform mass–that is her position as a wife.

Recorded in Ethel Gross's journal
Attribution unknown

What are merely hints of discomfort in the courtship letters grow more evident in the correspondence during their marriage (1913–1931).[31] The remaining letters fall neatly into three sections: 1915–1918, the early years of their marriage in New York; 1918–1928, when the family lived in the South and then returned to New York; and 1929–1945, when the marriage dissolved and they were divorced. The early New York letters were less frequent than the courtship letters and were typically occasioned by Hopkins's business trips. During these years, Hopkins worked for several social service agencies in New York City, where he gained an education in the less idealistic side of urban politics. Gross continued to work part-time doing secretarial work for Harriot Stanton Blatch's suffrage organization, the Women's Political Union. In October 1914, their first son, David, was born, and letters from family and friends suggest that these were happy years. Filled largely with the ordinary business of life, the couple's correspondence confirms these accounts.

The first significant body of marriage letters was written during an extended separation in 1918, after the family had moved to New Orleans. The couple decided it was best for Gross and their then three-year-old son David to spend the summer in Far Rockaway, New York, in order to avoid the heat of New Orleans. Far Rockaway was a popular beach resort at the eastern end of Long Island where Gross's sister and her husband, Francesca and Benjamin Kohn, had a house on the beach.[32] The letters between the two during that summer expose the beginnings of marital tensions related, in part, to Gross's growing anxiety about her husband's fidelity in her absence. More significantly, perhaps, these letters reflect tensions generated by Hopkins's increased absorption in his work, and his concomitant retreat from their youthful ideals about "woman's place in the world" and the new kind of partnership that their marriage would represent.

The family moved to New Orleans when Hopkins accepted a position with the American Red Cross Division of Civilian Relief—relief necessitated by America's entrance into the Great War. Before New Orleans, Hopkins had worked in New York City, first for the Association for Improving the Condition of the Poor (AICP) and then as head of the newly established Bureau of Child Welfare administering pensions to indigent single mothers. This latter job proved to be short-lived and tumultuous, and he resigned over very public and contentious disagreements with city officials about how to run the agency. Hopkins's new position as assistant director for civilian relief in the American Red Cross's Gulf Division in New Orleans was important to him for a number of reasons. First, it offered him a much-desired opportunity to contribute to the war effort. He had been drafted, but the subsequent physical exam revealed defective eyesight, and he was rejected for service. Second and more pertinently, this new position provided him with a chance to reestablish himself professionally and put his career back on track. Consequently, the stakes for Hopkins at this new job were high, and he became deeply engaged in the work.

The Far Rockaway letters suggest a shifting power dynamic in the marriage directly related to Hopkins's increased preoccupation with his career. For the first several weeks, their letters had a chatty and upbeat tone and were filled with expressions of longing and love. As Hopkins became embroiled in a number of crises, including emergency relief services for the Lake Charles flood victims, his letters became briefer and less frequent. In addition, he repeatedly pushed Gross's return date further and further into August and then into September and October, which set into action a series of complex negotiations between the two about the duration of her stay in Far Rockaway. Initially, Hopkins appeared to be concerned about the comfort and health of his family: "But my dear, it is hot as blazes down here—no place for the baby and I really wish you would keep him there for the summer—if you can be happy."[33] Yet, read in the context of Gross's resistance to extending her visit and to her repeated entreaties for more attention from him in the form of longer and more frequent letters, his insistence on postponing her return appears to be linked to more than her comfort. Ambitious and proud of what he was accomplishing, he subtly suggested in his letters that the presence of a wife and child might impede his progress.

The strong sense of partnership evident in the early Far Rockaway letters slowly eroded as the summer progressed. As Hopkins's letters became more laconic, Gross's became more plaintive and communicated a clear sense that she felt shuttled to the edges of what was developing into an exciting career. For example, in a letter filled with her longing to be reunited with her husband, Gross offered a telling comment that speaks to the role she wished to play in his life and work. Responding to his description about

ARC's services for crippled soldiers she wrote, "That seems like such a large piece of work in itself and a most interesting one. You must be getting your work fixed up in fine style. I wish I weren't so far away from it all."[34] And later, about the Lake Charles flood, she commented, " I am so homesick for you tonight and oh, so proud of what you are doing at Lake Charles . . . I wish I were with you—helping you."[35] Gross expressed her desire not just to be with her husband but to be part of the important work that he was doing. This desire seeps through a number of her letters more indirectly, as well. While filled with the requisite details of domestic life, her letters also offered commentary about the political climate and ARC shoptalk. Gross was being held at a distance from work to which she had always been committed, and her comments pointedly reminded Hopkins of her continued interest in social work. Such comments reflected an insistent effort to participate in the only way permitted her.

Because of pressing work in Lake Charles, coupled, perhaps, with Gross's epistolary demands for his attention, Hopkins's correspondence degenerated into a series of quick and testy telegrams. Gross answered these telegrams in a revealing letter that seemed to be responding to his negative characterization of her worry and impatience to return to him: "Your telegram came last night and I was much relieved to get it. It sounded as if you were a bit impatient at me for worrying over you again . . ."[36] Next, Gross's letter rhetorically transformed what was an implicit critique of her behavior into an implicit critique of his. She achieved this by representing her worrying as an example of wifely selflessness that suggested pettiness on his part for his impatience. She then shifted into a conciliatory mode, expressing her gratitude for any letter, however brief. As in the early courtship letters, this letter illustrates that give and take typical of much of her correspondence with Hopkins.

The letter's final paragraph exemplifies this rhetorical gesture. Gross began in an assertive mode by offering an aphorism that gives her point the weight of folk wisdom:

> Someone once said that women who love their men just a little get along much better than those who love them a lot—because instead of spending so much time fretting—they go blithely on and are fretted over instead. But I'm glad I love you a lot—and I'm going to keep right on doing it—even tho I know that you can't possibly miss me as much as I miss you. Now please don't be cross with me and please don't think I don't understand just how busy and anxious you have been about your work in the past two weeks.

This passage reveals Gross's attempt to match the light, humorous tone present in so many of Hopkins's letters, yet the underlying joke has a distinct edge to it. Gross represented herself as a martyr to matrimonial love, one who not only took on the burden of the relationship, but who welcomed it: "But I'm glad I love you a lot—and I'm going to keep right on doing it." The barb of this portrait of wifely selflessness becomes clear when the letter shifts from a general comparison between women (like herself) who love a lot and women who love "a little" to a comparison between the quality of her love and the quality of her husband's. At this point, the language returns to the personal and specific, and Gross effectually sneaks in a direct accusation, ". . . I know that you can't possibly miss me as much as I miss you." This represents an especially interesting moment in the correspondence in which Gross exploited the conventions of "true womanhood" as expounded at Christodora House. Model wives and mothers invest all their emotional energy into their husbands, exemplifying the ideals of Christian self-sacrifice. Read in the context of so many letters that expressed her desire to join her husband in his work and step outside the boundaries of the private, domestic sphere, this letter points to the contradictions inherent in the project of building a new partnership within an old institution.

While Gross relied on levity to lodge subtle critiques of Hopkins, Hopkins used it to diffuse Gross's concerns, especially her concerns about infidelity: "You ask who Miss Clifton is—46 years—a New York School teacher and friend of Miss Dunwiddie's—very much her style—please forgive me—she's terribly homely and I am partial to good looks."[37] This reassurance is typical of a number of responses in which Hopkins calmed Gross by reassuring her that the object of her jealousy was old and unattractive. In her oral history Gross offered a very different portrait of the women with whom Hopkins worked:

> In the South they had an entirely different group of people than the social workers in the North who were trained and were very serious minded. But these were often society girls, just beautiful Southern girls who were anxious to serve in some way during the war . . . There were several girls who were very much in love with him. I mean, I believe there was talk about that. He had a wonderful and personal way with them.[38]

Gross's recollection of New Orleans offers an explanation for her reiterated concern in the letters about Hopkins's female colleagues. Moreover, Hopkins's reassurances seem hardly consoling since his implication was that had the women been young and beautiful, Gross *would* have had something to worry about. He made this implication more explicit it a letter he wrote toward the end of the summer:

> This bachelor life is hell and when I tell you some of my experiences you never will leave home again. You may be sure I will never let you. You women—damn you—don't need to have men around but my dear I've had to bite my lips hard

several times to keep from going astray! You little dear—I miss you so much and I know how much I love you—tis ever thus when ever away—you will say.[39]

Though Hopkins was trying for comedy, the implication is rather grim: fidelity to his wife required serious effort on his part. Gross had been demoted to "you women" rather than the specific individual with whom he fell in love, and he seemed to be suggesting that almost any pretty girl would do. His "joke" relied on a sexual double standard: men, unlike women, have sexual desires that need to be satisfied, and the passage exemplifies how far he had departed from the more radical ideals about partnership and work that contributed to the passion of the couple's courtship.

Gross's often plaintive tone assumed a more bitter cast when Hopkins postponed her return home for another two weeks after she and David had already started the journey back to New Orleans. Responding to his telegram that reached her in New York City, Gross detailed the inconvenience such a change of plans caused her and her sister's family. In this long letter, she dropped any pretense of levity ("I could see we were not wanted at present") and accused Hopkins of indifference toward his family:

> I know too that you are busy and haven't time to bother too much with these things. But I'm sure you took care of the Guatemala refugees and the homeless at Lake Charles much better. Please forgive me if this letter is discouraging— or if you don't like it—*I must get these things off my chest.* Perhaps I'll feel better after I do. As it is now I feel no enthusiasm about staying here—and less about going back to N. O.—now.[40]

Gross tempered this naked expression of pain and concluded the letter by trying to appease Hopkins: "I do love you dear—and I'll try to be good from now on" suggesting that a "good" wife shouldn't express her anger as she had in the passage above. Gross also followed up a few hours later with another letter in which she demonstrated this good wifely behavior, telling Hopkins that she did not mind waiting two more weeks and that she was looking forward to the wonderful winter they were going to share in New Orleans. Yet, as in so much of her correspondence, Gross also exploited this gesture of appeasement by asserting her continued resistance to the contours of conventional marriage: "I am looking forward to this winter— more than I ever have before—I know it is going to be a wonderful one for us all. Even if you are busy we will be near enuf to the office for you to get home soon after your work is finished. And I am going to make an effort to be of some use—outside—if only a few hours a week."[41] Gross concluded with a portrait of a happy family reunited, but a family in which the wife and mother works "outside."

III. MARITAL TENSIONS: THE 1920s

Because your eyes
Are slant and slow
Because your hair
Is smooth to touch
My heart is high again
But oh, I doubt
If it will get me much

Oscar Wilde, *The Ballad of Reading Gaol:*
Harlot's House: Salome. Illustrated by John Vassos
Recorded in Ethel Gross's journal

Remember that nothing in your whole life will hurt you much after this.

Recorded in Ethel Gross's journal

The Hopkins family settled in New Orleans at the end of 1918, and Hopkins rose through the ranks of the American Red Cross (ARC), promoted first to Director of Civilian Relief, Gulf Division and then, after the war ended and the ARC reorganized, to head of the Southern Division headquartered in Atlanta. In April 1920, Gross gave birth to their second child, a girl who died of whooping cough at the age of one month. In 1921 several months after the family moved to Atlanta, a third child, Robert, was born, and the following year the family returned to New York City. During these years, Hopkins built a national reputation as a social worker, initiating the professionalization of Southern social workers and becoming one of the founders and then president of the American Association of Social Workers. In New York City, after a short stint with the AICP, Hopkins worked for the New York Tuberculosis Association (NYTBA) from 1922 until 1930 when he went to work for Governor Franklin D. Roosevelt. Professionally, these were successful and stable years for Hopkins. In 1925 their third and last surviving child, Stephen, was born, and the family, including David, age 11, Robert, age 4, and Stephen, the baby, moved out to the suburbs, first to Ludlow near Mount Vernon, and then soon after to Scarborough-on-Hudson where they remained until 1928, when the marriage began to fall apart.

The extant letters from these years are occasioned primarily by Hopkins's many business trips and, until 1927, depict a warm and loving marital relationship. In her oral history Gross asserted, "these letters will indicate that we had a close, happy family life, and I never had any reason to think that it would be any different . . ."[42] These ordinary yet loving letters, however, belie what must have been subterranean tensions within the marriage. Sometime in 1926 Hopkins met and fell in love with Barbara Duncan, a young woman who worked at the NYTBA. A trained nurse, she came from an upper-middle-class Protestant family in Port Huron, Michigan. This was not a light flirtation, and Hopkins spent as much time as he could with her, though the relationship posed a powerful personal conflict for him.[43] Indeed, some time in 1927, in an attempt to resolve the problems in his marriage and get over his strong feelings for Duncan, Hopkins consulted with Dr. Frankwood Williams, a psychoanalyst whom his close friend John Kingsbury had recommended.[44]

The first indication in the correspondence of this marital discord appeared in a series of letters in November 1927 when Gross left the family behind and took a boat trip down the Mississippi in order to give the couple some respite from marital tensions and from each other. The first in this series, from Hopkins, was a breezy, newsy letter that only referred to their difficulties in its conclusion: "Now Ethel—do have a good time—there is nothing to worry about so far as the children are concerned. And I am alright—this is the best move we have made in years and is sure to help—*And don't worry about it.*"[45] In Hopkins's emphasized appeal, "it," the object of Gross's worry, seems to have a number of referents: her concern about leaving the children, about leaving Hopkins, and her more general concern about the marriage. While appearing to reassure Gross, Hopkins deftly displaced the cause for their marital troubles onto her worry rather than the effects of his infidelity. This letter is notable, too, for a potentially chilling reference earlier in the letter. Buried in a paragraph filled with family news, Hopkins wrote "and last night to bed at nine after reading Oscar Wilde's *Salome!*—which was illustrated by my friend John Vassos." In this particular edition, the illustrator, John Vassos, had used Barbara Duncan as his model for an alluring pose of Salome. Hopkins certainly knew that the model was Duncan, and his interest in mentioning this detail to his wife, who had no direct knowledge of his relationship with Duncan, appears at best thoughtless, at worst somewhat mean-spirited.

Hopkins's generally light-hearted letter in no way prepares the reader for the bitter, sarcastic, and desperate tone of Gross's letter of the following week. Gross was upset because she had heard, through a mutual friend, that Hopkins wanted her to extend her stay another two weeks: "As far as I am personally concerned, prolonging my absence from home won't help me to solve my problems. I can only learn by doing, as I said to you before I left home."[46] This comment suggests that the trip was at Hopkins's insistence and that Gross would have preferred to stay home and more actively work to resolve what she identified as "my problems." She continued by asserting that she was unable to be a "professional visitor," floating from friend to friend, and then threatened Hopkins with two alternatives:

> But if you think I should stay away longer I can do it by doing one of two things—one is to get a job and the other is to start on a mad career of pleasure. I find I can still give pleasure to certain types of people, especially men,

and I'd get a real kick out of seeing how far I could string it out. If I could use my powers in this direction it would be sufficiently interesting and diverting so that I would worry less and less about getting back to the children.

I think too that in this way I could develop a hard-boiled quality that is quite an asset in many ways and that I could never develop living with someone I love.

I think Ben would send me some money for clothes if you continued the little legend about my nerves, but I don't want to do anything to tie me down to my family too much. I want to be free.

Though Gross began by suggesting that she might get a job, she spent most of this letter describing a very different vocation, what she called "a mad career of pleasure" which was, essentially, the life of a kept woman. This letter was radically out of character with everything she had previously expressed about her feelings for her family and her vision of herself. She desperately wanted to return home, so she turned to a readily available script, the one that she knew would frighten Hopkins the most. Gross offered a portrait of a hardened woman who uses her sexual attractions to gain what she needs and desires. In effect, she offered a vision of Salome, the dark-eyed, Eastern seductress, whom Hopkins so strangely alluded to in his previous letter. Gross seemed to be exploiting Hopkins's willingness to buy into this racialized portrait of female sexuality, one that she could play for Hopkins with much greater power than the Anglo, Midwestern Barbara Duncan.

This representation of herself was a defensive ploy that countered the narrative of their marriage that Hopkins seemed to be writing. Hopkins's patronizing admonitions to her to relax and not worry, his willingness to frame their marital difficulties as Gross's problem, and his belief that all would be resolved if she took a little vacation from her life, took their cue from a powerful cultural script about hysterical women and the efficacy of the rest cure. Gross seemed acutely and uncomfortably aware of this script, which had been codified in popular culture by such figures as S. Weir Mitchell and critiqued by Charlotte Perkins Gilman.[47] She referred to Hopkins's explanation for the trip as "the little legend about my nerves," and her sarcastic tone registered how much she resented the role in which Hopkins had cast her. Gross concluded the letter by threatening to pursue her "mad career of pleasure," not for two weeks, but for at least two months. Her threat worked. Hopkins replied with a brief telegram telling her that she should return home as originally planned.

There is no extant correspondence between Hopkins and Gross until eight months later, in July 1928, when Hopkins decided to travel to Europe with several colleagues to attend the First International Conference of Social Work in Paris. He was accompanied by John Kingsbury and his adult daughter, Jean, along with Katherine Lenroot, another social worker.

Kingsbury apparently believed that some distance between Hopkins and Gross would alleviate tensions between the two and had originally suggested the trip. En route, the two men discussed Hopkins's marital problems, and Kingsbury recorded his memory of the conversation in his notes for his unpublished autobiography: "S.S. Amsterdam En Route—Tale of estrangement from Ethel told in my cabin—Reasons for marriage—pity for poor struggling Jewish girl—to shock the good Methodists back in Iowa. Reason for estrangement—Jewish relatives and customs—story of family funeral. 'No woman in the case.' (Not consistent with Ethel's talk with me on Scarboro train some mos. before.)"[48] Apparently unwilling to admit to his affair with Duncan, Hopkins turned to a readily available explanation related to racial difference, one that sounds shockingly deceptive (even self-deceptive) in light of his passionate courtship and the past fifteen years of a tightly-knit married life together.

Ironically, the reasons Hopkins offered for the failure of the marriage—Gross's Jewishness, her ethnic identity—were the very factors that contributed to his attraction to her in the first place. A number of cultural critics have explored the underlying power dynamic of such an attraction noting the way in which the dark female body comes to be seen by white America as an enabling site for personal and political transformation.[49] Gross offered Hopkins what bell hooks calls the "seductive promise" of otherness.[50] Her difference—her ethnic body—became for the young and idealistic Hopkins the means through which he could inhabit a more radical identity and challenge the status quo. Once Hopkins "grew up" and refined and clarified his goals in terms of success within the system, Gross's difference ceased to appear enabling and the attractiveness of her exoticism lost its luster. This conversation between Kingsbury and Hopkins is significant because it reveals the latent racism of such an attraction to otherness by demonstrating how readily it can shift to repulsion. Of course, Hopkins neither married nor divorced Gross just because she was Jewish, and the story he told Kingsbury was an oversimplification of their relationship that testifies to the power of such racial scripts. Rather than engage the painful and complicated problems in their marriage, problems that Hopkins, himself, contributed to significantly, he turned to race, offering an easy explanation that his particular audience not only understood but seemed all too ready to believe.

Hopkins's comments to Kingsbury, along with the fact of his continuing relationship with Barbara Duncan, suggest that, emotionally, he was moving farther and farther away from Gross and their marriage. Read in this context, the letters he wrote home once he arrived in Europe are poignant for their casual intimacy and warmth. They suggest that the dissolution of this marriage must have been painful and complicated for Hopkins as well as Gross. In Hopkins's letters he appeared genuinely interested in describing his trip to Gross and eliciting her opinion, though compared to earlier correspondence, the tone is more formal and a bit defensive: "Will write you again on Sunday—not as a sense of duty but because I want to."[51] As in earlier letters, Hopkins continued to entreat Gross not to worry, "London is big and old and stolid. No stranger can ever get on the inside. But of love—think of you every day. Don't worry."[52] Hopkins also returned to his habit of reassuring her that he was "behaving" and that he found his women companions unattractive and uninteresting. (His unflattering descriptions of Katherine Lenroot, a noted social worker, are especially unfortunate.) About midway through the trip he wrote, "I think of you often Ethel and have wished many times you were with me. If it interests you at all—my virtue, such as it is, came thru Paris intact!"[53] Hopkins's European letters were the last to express any kind of warm marital feelings. He arrived home on August 15, 1928. By the end of the year the marriage was over. They officially separated in September 1929, and Hopkins married Barbara Duncan in 1931, two months after the divorce was finalized.

IV. DIVORCE: DIVERGING LIVES, THE GREAT DEPRESSION, AND WORLD WAR II, 1929–1945

> Ex-Wife
> He looked as if he understood
> That one did not love a man
> Because he was worth
> Loving, or because one
> Felt worthy of his love in
> Return, or for any reason
> That one's acquaintances
> Would think sound.
>
> Recorded in Ethel Gross's journal
> Attribution unknown

The last fifteen years of Hopkins's life mark the period of his greatest achievements in national social welfare and international diplomacy. When the Great Depression hit New York City, Hopkins was Director of the New York Tuberculosis and Health Association and, along with many social workers in the city, sought to mitigate the effects of the crisis by establishing emergency work bureaus and work relief programs. During the 1930 New York gubernatorial campaign, Hopkins met Franklin Roosevelt, who was seeking reelection, and the two began to develop an important professional relationship. In 1931, the year Hopkins divorced Gross and married Barbara Duncan, Governor Roosevelt called on Hopkins to administer the first of the so-called alphabet agencies, the Temporary Emergency Relief Administration (TERA). This was the beginning of some of Hopkins's most important work administering programs for the New Deal.[54] In 1932, the newly elected President Roosevelt called Hopkins to Washington, D.C. where, for the next seven years, he successively ran a number of agencies including the Federal Emergency Relief Administration (FERA), the Civil Works Administration (CWA), and the Works Progress Administration (WPA). From 1934 to 1935 Hopkins served on the Committee for Economic Security and participated in the creation of the Social Security Act, the legislative foundation for the American welfare system.

Hopkins left Gross at the central turning point in his career, when he shifted from the state to the national level. His new wife, Barbara Duncan, was well suited to the part of a Washington hostess, a useful quality for Hopkins who was becoming an increasingly powerful and public figure in Washington, D.C. Duncan helped Hopkins enter into the social world of the rich and powerful. She often gave small dinner parties at their Georgetown home, and the two were seen at the "21" Club in New York and Joseph Kennedy's home in Palm Beach, Florida. In addition, Duncan was extremely accommodating when it came to Hopkins's work and put few demands on his time and attention. In 1932 Duncan and Hopkins had a daughter, Diana, Duncan's first and Hopkins's fourth surviving child. While Hopkins loved his daughter, as he loved his sons, work consumed most of his attention. Duncan believed her job was to take care of all Hopkins's domestic concerns, freeing him up to immerse himself fully in the business of managing a national economic crisis. Tragically, in 1937, Duncan died of breast cancer. That same year, Hopkins was diagnosed with stomach cancer and underwent a surgery at the Mayo Clinic that removed the cancer along with two-thirds of his stomach and part of the duodenum. The severity of this procedure was hidden from the public, and the press only reported that Hopkins had had an operation to remove an ulcer. He recuperated for several months at Joseph Kennedy's home in Florida and returned to his office in March of 1938. While the cancer did not recur, Hopkins suffered from a medical condition that prevented his body from absorbing nutrition. He continued to experience frequent bouts of illness related to malnutrition and found himself in and out of hospitals for the rest of his life.

When Hopkins left Gross in 1929, their eldest son David was fifteen and the two younger boys, Robert and Stephen, were eight and four years old. The primary care of the children rested with Gross, a responsibility that increased when Hopkins moved to Washington, D.C. in 1933. Hopkins did offer financial support and faithfully contributed half of his monthly salary to the family until his death in 1946. During these years, Gross and the children moved a number of times. Immediately after the divorce they lived in

New York City; Gross then moved the family to Scarsdale, and finally settled in Northfield, Massachusetts from 1937 to 1940. The eldest son, David, attended Alfred College and then the University of Chicago, and married in 1937. Despite the divorce, Gross seemed to have continued to inhabit the role of Mrs. Hopkins. She was committed to creating a sense of family for her sons and encouraged their respect and love for their father, who became a kind of heroic, absent figure. After Barbara Duncan died, Gross made an effort to include young Diana in the family. In a letter expressing her condolences about Barbara's death she wrote:

> I should like you to feel that you can come here at anytime you want to make a plan. I can always go somewhere and visit. The children are devoted to Diana and I think she could have a very jolly time. Could something be planned over the Christmas holidays? Stephen and Robert both have eighteen days.
>
> I have made many unsuccessful attempts to write to you in the past month. Words are so inadequate to express my deep sympathy for all that you have been through, all that you are going through. Is it any comfort for you to know that Robert and Stephen have a very deep affection for you and that you can count on them for loyalty and devotion?[55]

Despite an underlying sense that she had been discarded, Gross continued to think of all of them as a family, of sorts. Though opportunities presented themselves, Gross had no romantic involvements until after Hopkins's death and was committed to keeping the family intact.[56]

For Gross, the role of Mrs. Hopkins meant not only carrying on the work of raising the children but also of contributing to the social welfare of whatever community she found herself in. During these years, when the boys were in school and no longer in need of constant care, Gross pursued the interests that she had developed while working at Christodora House. While in Scarsdale, she started the Children's Theater Arts Workshop, a large project that required a significant time commitment. She was also active in local community politics, performing such tasks as organizing voter registration. In addition, Gross began to pursue her interest in art more formally. In the late 1920s she studied for three summers with William E. Schumacher in Woodstock, New York and in 1940 she studied with Hans Hoffman in Provincetown, New York. Essentially, Gross remained consistently committed to the ideals of service and family that she and Hopkins articulated together as early as 1913.

The letters between Hopkins and Gross offer some of the inside story behind the very public and well-documented career of Hopkins during these years. Despite his great professional success, he struggled financially throughout his career, and the correspondence between the two after the divorce treated the issue of money repeatedly. These are the only letters that expressed any rancor, and the ill will seemed to be, in part, a product of their frustrations with their financial limitations rather than their bitterness toward each other. Most of their correspondence was characterized by a respectful and carefully polite tone and concerned itself with the children's health and education. Some of the most telling letters during these years offer insight into the ways that Gross felt that she and her children were unfairly shuttled to the margins of Hopkins's life. In 1938 when a *Time* article referred only to David Hopkins and omitted the existence of his two younger brothers, Gross wrote Hopkins, "This has happened on several occasions . . . It must be obvious to you how embarrassing this can become in time to Stephen and Robert, and to me."[57] This was not the first such letter that Gross had written, and she resorted to threats, asking him to deal with the matter directly or else she would write to *Time* herself: "I am enclosing a letter I have written, *but not mailed*, to the TIME magazine. I shall hold it for two or three days until I hear from you." Instead of responding himself, Hopkins had one of his assistants, Aubrey Williams, take care of the matter. Williams wrote back a formal, polite letter suggesting that Hopkins did not intend this oversight and could not be held accountable for what the press chose to print. Hopkins's failure to address the matter himself is a reflection, in part, of just how busy he was. Yet it also suggests something about his priorities. Hopkins's involvement in his work at the expense of his family reflected a pattern of behavior since the beginning of his career. Gross's accusation twenty years earlier in which she bitterly noted that he "took better care of the Guatemala refugees and the homeless at Lake Charles" than he did of his own family continued to have relevance for her.

As the crisis in Europe intensified and the United States drew closer toward involvement in World War II, Hopkins's political responsibilities grew. By this time he had developed a strong relationship with Roosevelt, whose concern with the situation in England and France began to take precedence over domestic economic concerns. Roosevelt tutored Hopkins in international relations and gave him a cabinet position as secretary of commerce in 1939 with the idea that he would groom him to run for president in 1940. Hopkins was just too ill for such an enterprise and instead moved into the White House and became the president's advisor and wartime emissary. Hopkins traveled extensively during the war years, and his work included arranging the Atlantic Conference between Churchill and Stalin and meeting with Stalin in Moscow to assess the advisability of Russia's participation in the Lend Lease program, which Hopkins unofficially administered. In 1941, he married for the third time, to a socialite named Louise Macy who was the Paris correspondent for *Harper's Bazaar*. Elegant and well-bred, Macy represented a world of sophistication that Hopkins seemed to have become enamored with during this period of his life. The two inhabited a social circle of the politically and socially elite comprised of figures like the Harrimans and the Whitneys.

Gross also contributed to the war effort, working for the American Red Cross, first in Fort Devens, Massachusetts, as senior recreational officer and later at the U.S. Naval Hospital in Newport, Rhode Island. All three boys enlisted as well: David joined the Navy and was stationed on an aircraft carrier in the Pacific. Robert, the middle son, joined the Army signal corps and was stationed in the European theater. In 1943, right after his high school graduation, their youngest son, Stephen, joined the Marines and in 1944, at the age of eighteen, was killed, shot by an enemy soldier in the Pacific. Because of Hopkins's high profile, Stephen's death received a good deal of media attention. A number of the news reports omitted any mention of Gross. Rather than contacting Hopkins as she had when this had happened on previous occasions, Gross sent a letter directly to the *New York World Telegram* correcting the mistake: "I am writing to you in order to call your attention to the fact that Stephen, Robert, and David are my three sons as well as the sons of Harry L. Hopkins, confidential advisor to the President Roosevelt. In all your news items and stories you either completely omit this fact or state it incorrectly."[58] This letter was picked up in a number of periodicals, including *Time* magazine, which included a photo of a serious Gross in her Red Cross Uniform with the caption under her name reading: "she identifies herself." This brief letter, coupled with her image, appears as an assertion of self, a reminder that she would not allow herself to be effaced or discarded, particularly when the subject was her son's death.

Gross's letter must have caused Hopkins some public embarrassment, and she wrote him a poignant letter immediately afterwards. She began by justifying her act of public assertion:

> I wouldn't hurt you for anything in the world, but after the heartbreaking news came about Stephen I wanted to shout it from the housetops, over and over again: "my son Stephen was killed." I had to say it over and over again to believe it. I could not bear to be further removed from him by not being identified with him. It's terribly important to me to be his mother at this time. Just as important as when he was born.[59]

Gross's desire to "shout it from the house tops" was a response that any mother might have had to such terrible news. Yet, it also suggests a response to the specific ways that she had been "removed" from the public image of Hopkins's family. She continued by recalling their years together when Stephen was a child, a gesture that reasserted the bond she and Hopkins shared as his parents. The memory of this bond, which became a bond of shared bereavement, led Gross to offer Hopkins consolation. In the next paragraph she offered a generous description of the important contributions that Hopkins made toward the enrichment of Stephen's short life:

Through your great achievements you were able to enrich his life with friend-ships and experiences with great—I want to say—all the great and important people who belong to this era. Some people—many people—live a whole life-time and never have such experiences. All this was highly exciting to him and stimulating. It gave him an insight and an understanding.[60]

Gross' compassionate gesture suggests that with the death of her son, she wanted to let go of some of the bitterness she had carried with her for fif-teen years. She concluded the letter by taking the opportunity to speak of her own feelings about Hopkins and their relationship. Clearly, this was not an easy paragraph for Gross to write, and she crossed out several phrases and revised them. Significantly, the revisions are characterized by the choice of a less conciliatory phrase. For example, she originally wrote "I see more clearly why it was difficult for you to live with me; and I don't blame you for leaving me." However, she revised this to read "I see more clearly why it was difficult for you many times; and I blame you less for leaving me."[61] Gross was unwilling to identify herself as the reason for Hopkins's leaving and unwilling to absolve Hopkins of all the blame. She continued with a subtle suggestion that Hopkins's choices were a consequence of his careerism: "You knew how and with whom you wanted to live your life and you have gone a long way." Gross concluded with a resonant final line: " It does me good to say these things to you. And I hope you won't mind." Gross needed to speak her mind, and when her son died, she would not al-low herself to be written out of the story. These letters and papers extend her efforts to "identify herself" by offering, with her own words, more of the story of the "Jewish first wife, divorced."

NOTES

1. See, for example, Henry Adams, *Harry Hopkins* (New York: G. P. Putnam, 1977); Searle F. Charles, *Minister of Relief: Harry Hopkins and the Depression* (Syracuse, N.Y.: Syracuse University Press, 1963); June Hopkins, *Harry Hopkins: Sudden Hero, Brash Reformer* (New York: St. Martin's Press, 1999); Paul A. Kurzman, *Harry Hopkins and the New Deal* (Fairlawn, N.J.: R. E. Burdick, 1974); George McJimsey, *Harry Hop-kins: Ally of the Poor, Defender of Democracy* (Cambridge, Mass.: Harvard University Press, 1987); Robert Sherwood, *Roosevelt and Hopkins: An Intimate History* (New York: Harper and Brothers, 1948); Matthew B. Wills, *Wartime Missions of Harry L. Hopkins* (Raleigh, N.C.: Pentland Press, 1996).

2. Ethel Gross married twice, first to Harry Hopkins and then, in her later years, to Morris Conant. She changed her name with each marriage. To avoid confusion, we have chosen to refer to her by her maiden name, Gross, throughout the text.

3. For information on settlement houses see Ruth Hutchinson Crocker, *Social Work and Social Order: The Settlement Movement in Two Industrial Cities, 1889–1930*

(Urbana, Ill.: University of Illinois Press, 1992); Mina Carson, *Settlement Folk: Social Thought and The American Settlement Movement 1885–1930* (Chicago: University of Chicago Press, 1990); Harry P. Kraus, *The Settlement House Movement in New York City 1886–1914* (New York: Arno Press, 1980); Alan F. Davis, *Spearheads For Reform; The Social Settlements and the Progressive Movement* (New York: Oxford University Press, 1967).

4. For information on the Social Gospel Movement see Susan Curtis, *A Consuming Faith: The Social Gospel and Modern American Culture* (Baltimore: Johns Hopkins University Press, 1991); Donald K. Gorrell, *The Age of Social Responsibility: The Social Gospel in the Progressive Era 1900–1920* (Macon, Ga.: Mercer University Press, 1988); Ronald C. White and C. Howard Hopkins, *The Social Gospel: Religion and Reform in Changing America* (Philadelphia: Temple University Press, 1976).

5. For more on Jews in Hungary see Charles Loring Brace, *Hungary in 1851* (New York: Charles Scribner, 1852); Aron Moskovits, *Jewish Education in Hungary 1848–1948* (New York: Black Publishing Co., 1964); Bela Kalman, *The World of Names: A Study in Hungarian Onomotology* (Budapest: Akademiai Kiado, 1978).

6. Coincidentally, 1891 is the same year that the U.S. Census Bureau declared the official closing of the Western Frontier. This line, which marked the distinction between (white) civilization and (dark) wilderness, disappeared only to reemerge in the nation's urban centers. Eastern European Jews, Irish and Italian Catholics, and African Americans living in urban ghettos became America's new symbols for "otherness," the new savage against which genteel middle-class America could define itself.

7. Strangely, there is no indication in the letters or journals that any of the relatives who had preceded them to America ever helped Celia when she arrived in New York. According to the 1900 Census for New York City, there was another Gross family from Hungary listed as living in their tenement, 356 E. Tenth Street. Gross is a common name, and it could be that they were not relatives at all. In the mid-eighteenth century, all Jews in Hungary were ordered to abandon their patronymics and adopt surnames. Those who could not afford to buy more elegant names were assigned such mundane names such as Gross, meaning "tall." See Kalman, *World of Names*.

8. Ethel's name in Hungary would have been Etelke.

9. Gross enjoyed robust health most of her life, and it seems likely that her physical reaction to school was related to her profound anxiety.

10. See Elizabeth Ewan, *Immigrant Women in the Land of Dollar: Life and Culture on the Lower East Side, 1890–1925* (New York: Monthly Review Press, 1985) and Donna Gabbacia, "The Transplanted: Women and Family in Immigrant America," *Social Science History,* 12 (Fall 1988): 243–253.

11. For more on popular representations of the ghetto see especially Sabine Haenni, "Visual and Theatrical Culture, Tenement Fiction, and the Immigrant in Subject in Abraham Cahan's *Yekl,*" *American Literature* 71, no.3 (Sept. 1999): 493–527.

12. This is what historian Sheila Rothman calls the "ideology of educated motherhood." Sheila Rothman, *Woman's Proper Place: A History of Changing Ideals 1870 to the Present* (New York: Basic Books, 1978).

13. Ethel Gross, of course, never did convert to Protestantism, though she did downplay her "Jewishness," and as a young adult embraced Ethical Culture.

14. See Christodora Papers, Columbia University, Butler Library, Manuscripts Collections.

15. See Harriot Stanton Blatch and Alma Lutz, *The Challenging Years* (New York: G. P. Putnam's Sons, 1940).

16. In 1964, Gross's memories of this event, more than fifty years earlier, were still tinged with the distaste she then felt for the scandal. Ethel Gross Hopkins Conant, transcript of taped interview by Roger Daniels, August 17–October 26, 1964, Oral History Archives, Powell Library, University of California at Los Angeles. (Hereinafter Conant Interview.) The tapes are available at UCLA's Powell Library; transcripts in authors' possession.

17. For more information on Hopkins's early years see Hopkins, *Sudden Hero* and McJimsey, *Ally of the Poor.*

18. For more on female college-graduates and settlement work see Crocker, *Social Work*, 19–22.

19. Conant Interview, 15.

20. Taken from an early journal written by Ethel Gross, in possession of authors.

21. Crocker, *Social Work*, 5.

22. Gross described their attraction in terms of opposites, framing it as city versus country. She recalled: "Now how country was he? He had his high ideals, which appealed to me. The fact that he cared so much about helping people who needed help. He was gay at the same time, and he used to go every place singing and whistling. He was the kind of person, I think, that most young girls would be attracted to." Conant Interview, 15.

23. Letter #2.

24. Letter #4.

25. The term "suffragette" refers to women in England who were actively involved in the fight for the vote. In the United States, such women were called "suffragists," largely to distinguish them from those involved in the more radical and violent movement in England. In the oral history, Gross stated: "Now you use the word 'suffragette.' Of course all of us suffragists objected to that word because that was what the English Suffragettes were called, and they were identified with . . . strapping themselves to the gates of the House of Parliament . . . and that kind of aggressive thing." Conant Interview,14.

26. Letter #10.

27. Letter #31.

28. Letter #38.

29. Letter #26.

30. Letter #14.

31. Hopkins and Gross were married at the Ethical Culture Society in New York City by John Lovejoy Elliot in October 1913. Ethical Culture offered a kind of institutionalized, and thus, a socially sanctioned, site for their interfaith marriage. See Samuel Frederick Bacon, *An Evaluation of the Philosophy a Pedagogy of Ethical Culture* (Washington, D.C.: Catholic University of America Press, 1983); Felix Adler, *Atheism: A Lecture* (New York: Co-Operative Printers Association, 1879). There was a question as to whether marriages in Ethical Culture were actually legal. In 1909 Elliot married two people (settlement workers) and the *New York Times* ran an article asserting that it had been ruled that they were legally married. ("Settlement Head

'Ethically' Married," *New York Times,* January 11, 1909, 1:7.) The fact that Harry Hopkins and Ethel Gross chose to get married in the Ethical Culture Society in 1913 underscores their impulse toward the radical.

32. Fanny Gross and Benjamin Kohn were first cousins and never had children.

33. Letter #110.

34. Letter #117.

35. Letter #122.

36. Letter #131.

37. Letter #153.

38. Conant Interview, 38.

39. Letter #150.

40. Letter #154.

41. Letter #155.

42. Conant Interview, 109–110.

43. Dr. James Halsted, untitled, typed manuscript in authors' possession. (Hereinafter Halsted TMs.) Dr. Halsted had been married to Eleanor and Franklin Roosevelt's daughter Anna and later (in the mid-1970s) married Diana Hopkins Baxter, daughter of Harry Hopkins and Barbara Duncan. The two met while Halsted was researching a biography of Hopkins. The manuscript cited is a draft of that unpublished biography. Some of the manuscript is unpaginated; in authors' possession. 122–133.

44. John Kingsbury was a prominent New York City social worker who had mentored Hopkins in his early years after Christodora House. Kingsbury and his wife Mabel were close friends with Hopkins and Gross throughout the 1920s.

45. Letter #180.

46. Letter #182.

47. S. Weir Mitchell (1829–1914) created the "rest cure" for nervous women. His most famous pronouncements on the ailments of "neurasthenics," also known as "hysterics," appear in *Wear and Tear, or Hints for the Overworked* (Philadelphia: *Lippincotts* [1887] 1904) and *Doctor and Patient* (Philadelphia: *Lippincotts* [1887] 1904). See also 'The Evolution of the Rest Cure" in *The Journal of Nervous and Mental Disease* 31.6 (June 1904): 368–73. Charlotte Perkins Gilman underwent the rest cure herself, and nearly went mad as a consequence. Her short story, "The Yellow Wallpaper" first published in 1892 offers one of the most celebrated critiques of the treatment.

48. John A. Kingsbury, "Autobiography Notes," Library of Congress, Manuscripts Division, B84: Reference Materiel," 2. Taken from Kingsbury's notes for an autobiography he was writing but never completed.

49. See especially Coco Fusco, "Whose Doin' the Twist: Notes Toward a Politics of Appropriation" in *English is Broken Here: Notes on Cultural Fusion in the Americas.* (New York: The New Press, 1995) and bell hooks, "Eating the Other: Desire and Resistance" in *Black Looks: Race and Representation* (Boston: South End Press, 1992).

50. In her essay "Eating the Other" hooks explores what she calls the "commodification of otherness" in popular culture which relies on the assumption that sexual agency expressed within the context of a racialized sexual encounter is a conversion experience that alters one's place and participation in contemporary cultural politics. The seductive promise of this encounter is that it will counter the

terrorizing force of the status quo that makes identity fixed and static, a condition of containment and death. (22)

51. Letter #186.

52. Letter #188.

53. Letter #190.

54. These years have been well documented by scholars of the New Deal. See especially, Kenneth Davis, *The New Deal Years 1933*–1937 (New York: Random House, 1986); Hopkins, *Sudden Hero;* William Leuchtenburg, *Franklin D. Roosevelt and the New Deal, 1932–1940* (New York: Harper & Row, 1963); Robert McElvaine, *The Great Depression: America 1929–1941* (New York: Times Books, 1984); McJimsey, *Ally of the Poor;* Arthur Schlesinger, Jr., *The Coming of the New Deal* (Boston: Houghton Mifflin, 1958).

55. Letter #224.

56. Gross's letters and papers suggest that a colleague, Don Oscar Beque, was in love with her during the 1930s, but she seems to have resisted engaging in a romantic relationship with him.

57. Letter #230.

58. *Time* 28 Feb.1944, 44.

59. Letter #266.

60. Letter #266.

61. Letter #266.

Ethel Gross, c. 1912.

Harry Hopkins, 1912.

Harry Hopkins, c. 1916.

Ethel Gross, marching in a suffrage parade, 1913.

Suffrage parade, 1913. From left to right: unidentified, Mrs. John Cabot, Mrs. Townsend, Miss Elizabeth Cook, Harriet Stanton Blatch (seated), Ethel Gross.

From left to right: David Hopkins, Adah Hopkins Aime, Harry Hopkins, Stephen Hopkins, Ethel Gross Hopkins, Dick Aime, Robert Hopkins, 1926.

Ethel Gross Hopkins and her first son, David Hopkins, c. 1920.

Harry Hopkins in Washington, D.C., working as head of the Federal Emergency Relief Administration, 1934.

Harry Hopkins, second from right. Seated to his left, Franklin Delano Roosevelt, and seated to his right is Harold Ickes, September 1935.

Ethel Gross Hopkins at the christening of the liberty ship, SS Stephen Hopkins, May 10, 1944.

Ethel Gross Hopkins in her Red Cross uniform, 1943.

Ethel Gross Hopkins Conant in her painting studio at home in California, 1962.

Chapter One

Courtship: Suffrage and Settlement Work, 1913

THESE NINETY-EIGHT LETTERS FOLLOW Ethel Gross and Harry Hopkins through what began as a secret courtship for eight months, beginning in February and continuing through October 1913 when the two were married. The bulk of these letters were handwritten and were often mailed and received on the same day, the following day at the latest. At times a messenger either mailed the letters or even hand delivered them.

Gross and Hopkins met at Christodora Settlement House, possibly at a suffrage meeting held there in January 1913 by the State Woman Suffrage Party. Gross had recently been working as private secretary for Katherine Mackay and as secretary of the Equal Franchise Society and had just returned from her second trip to Paris with the Mackay family. In February, when the courtship began, Gross was working part time at Christodora House, located on Tompkins Square Park at 147 Avenue B in New York's Lower East Side. In March she began working as secretary of the Women's Political Union, a suffrage organization founded by Harriot Stanton Blatch, daughter of Elizabeth Cady Stanton.

During this time, Hopkins was living and working at Christodora House while Gross was living with her sister and brother-in-law, Francesca and Benjamin Kohn, at 60 St. Nicholas Avenue, in Harlem, a significant subway ride from the Lower East Side and Christodora House. Some of Hopkins's duties took him to the settlement house's Northover Camp in Bound Book, New Jersey, which entailed a ferry ride across the Hudson River. Anticipating marriage, Hopkins sought a better paying job and in April was hired by John A. Kingsbury, Director of the Association for Improving the Condition of the Poor (AICP), located in the United Charities

Building, 105 E. Twenty-second Street. Organized in 1854, The AICP was one of the oldest, largest, and most influential agencies in NYC providing help for the needy. Hopkins worked as a district visitor in the Lower West Side and then as supervisor of the association's Bureau of Employment.

Gross's two brothers, Edward and Benjamin, were both living in New York City at this time and were most likely just beginning their diamond business. Hopkins's older brother, Lewis, worked in New York City as assistant secretary to the National Board of Censorship of Moving Pictures (later the Hays Office). His mother, Anna, and sister, Adah, both of whom lived in Grinnell, Iowa, visited from time to time.

Ethel Gross and Harry Hopkins were married on October 21, 1913 in the Ethical Culture Society's headquarters at 2 W. Sixty-fourth Street by Dr. John Lovejoy Elliot.

1.

MY DEAR ETHEL:

I came home to find Miss Austin* calmly working for me, not in the least peeved nor inquisitive so I take my own little place at the roll-top desk to talk to you before my debating team comes in – the debaters have come and gone and I think you have just been on the wire talking to Miss MacColl. Did you think I would answer that phone? I am afraid that would be altogether too pointed as you would say.

I am ending this day with a miserable headache and together [with] the more or less five thousand people who are hanging around this desk, I can't say that conditions are particularly encouraging for letter writing especially to you.

Just why we find ourselves so intensely interested in each other on so short an acquaintance and in a Settlement office at that, is more or less of [a] mystery to me. We have lived absolutely different lives up till now – while you have been working, I have been playing at school – you were brought up in a city where you could follow your natural inclinations. I have always been surrounded by conservative narrow-mindedness – we have been somewhat separated socially and it would be hard for you to come down to my means. Thank the Lord I do not feel at all bound by tradition or anything else and like you for what you are. I think our interests are common, which is absolutely essential to happiness. I have thought of you so much since Sunday that I have been more or less of a failure as a Settlement worker for some days. Am looking forward to Sunday!

A boy just told me that Miss Austin was the most even tempered woman he ever saw – "she's mad all the time."

The dinner bell is ringing so good bye till Sunday.

Yours

HARRY

Written on Christodora House letterhead.

*Edith Austin was a settlement worker at Christodora.

2.

[February 24, 1913]
Monday afternoon

*Written on
Christodora House
letterhead.*

DEAREST ETHEL:

Let's see, how much did we spend last night? You seem to have forgotten what an awful smoker you are but I've been thinking that we might raise chickens to pay for all such luxuries. I can see you bringing the eggs to market. Now I'm not fooling – you little dear. We're going to have a garden and raise potatoes – onions – radishes – lemons – but you are not a bit enthusiastic over it – you could practice suffrage speeches while you were planting a row of beans.

And I'm so happy Ethel – for I always felt there must be some girl like you on this earth somewhere but I must confess that I didn't expect to find her working in a Settlement. It was Miss MacColl's fault for she had no business letting us on the same floor. I wonder if she will view her handiwork with exceeding great joy. But you know Ethel the happiest people that I know in N.Y. are two workers that met at the Eastside House and are living on $1,500* a year!

*A salary of $1,500 a year would be the equivalent of approximately $26,000 in today's dollars.

But, girl, there is going to be an awful row when your family learns how you have fallen from grace. That is why we had better get it over with as soon as possible and let them get it out of their systems once and for all. Oh! But my father! Ye Gods – it is lucky that he hasn't any money for he certainly would leave me out. I love to think how it will rock the very foundations of our dining room. The poor old dears are badly in need of something to talk of and they are going to get enough to last for at least a week.

Believe me Ethel you are more than I ever deserve – but I will try to make you happy dear for I love you if I ever loved anyone in my life.

Good bye dear.

Your Own

HARRY

3.

DEAREST:

The mail brought no letter from you this morning – nor to-night – although one came from little Frances T. Your young friend is probably still carrying it around in his pocket. If he only knew how much I wanted it – I am sure he would have mailed it – or even carried it up to me! Hope you feel all right and that you will get to bed early to-night. I skated for two solid hours this morning and had a wonderful time. Miss Austin met me down at the rink. Pretty soon I'll know how. Then this afternoon I darned stockings! Gave my sister an awful shock.

I suppose when you call up tomorrow morning you'll tell me where and how to meet you tomorrow afternoon. Hope the museum is open.

Spent a lot of time to-day thinking about you –

Good-night –

Much love –

ETHEL

4.

DEAREST:

I looked for you on the opposite station last night – but I couldn't see you – You must have taken a car down to your ferry. I hope you got there all right and that you got back all right. I shall be glad to hear from you that you did because I find myself worrying just a little bit – which I suppose is silly.

Do you know that I'm coming down to dinner on Thursday evening and afterward coach the Aloha's in their play? Miss MacC. called me up late last night about it.

I told Sis that you were coming up on Sunday – so that's all settled.

Yesterday was such a perfect day!

** "Goldie" or "Goldy"
refers to Miss
Goldstein, a friend of
the Gross family.*

When I reached Goldie's* she put me to work making fudge. The "newly-wed" came and put an awful lot of airs to us poor girls – but we made her come down a peg or two.

I am not coming down this afternoon. I've got some shopping to do – and some people to see – but I may get down earlier than just dinner-time to-morrow.

Dearie – when I think how hurt you looked when I said what I did to you yesterday – it makes me feel like such a wretch. But I never have any doubts about *anything* while I am with you – you *do* understand why I said it – don't you? Good-bye – sweetheart for now. To answer your last letter – it was very thoughtful of you to remember my cigarettes. Could I smoke as I carry the eggs to market? But there – I'm spoiling the pretty picture you drew. I'd love to raise chickens – but they'd be so lonesome all day with us both away! Wouldn't they? But it's such a relief to know that I can have cigarettes – and if you are very good I'll slip you a little one now and then! If this letter ever gets misplaced where you live – I hate to think of the consequences! Perhaps you better burn it right away.

Hope you're having a nice day.

I send you much love –

ETHEL

5.

*[February 26, 1913]
Wednesday*

*Written on
Christodora House
letterhead.

*Frank S. was most
likely a settlement
worker.*

ETHEL DEAR:

Can you imagine me writing this with Frank S.* sitting a few feet away? If he knew who it was to – it makes me feel sort of queer I guess.

Why didn't you come down today – looked for you all afternoon but no Ethel.

Got home from Jersey about 12 – never again.

Ethel dear, you won't doubt any more that I care for you, will you? My ideal is more than realized – more than I ever deserved.

The best I have will be for you and our home.

Did you get home alright from "Goldy's" or rather from Miss Goldsteins? And what did your sister say for you running off to "Aunt Clemmy's" with that man from the Settlement?

Must get this mailed before dinner so good bye dear.
Your
HARRY

6.

[March 5, 1913]
Wednesday morning

MY DEAREST:

I've tried to start this a dozen times but either Miss C. I.* or Miss Austin have been inconveniently around.

I certainly was all in last night – must have been a frightful bore –

Can you imagine your picture perched up on my dresser? Well it is there to stay.

P.M.

Oh Ethel I've found your gloves resting peacefully in my pocket along with your spool of thread. But listen – I pulled them both out in front of everybody before I was fully aware of just what I might be doing. You said they were all worn out – they are not. I am afraid you are altogether too extravagant dear.

I may have to be in this week end after all because of a concert here Sunday night which I am trying to forget but I need help.

I have been counting the months over this morning, sweetheart, and it does seem too long – it will be all the better when the time does come.

See you Thursday.
With all my love
HARRY

Written on Christodora House letterhead.

*C. I. or C. I. M. refers to Christina Isobel MacColl.

7.

[March 5, 1913]
Wednesday evening

DEAR BOY:

*Hanna was a friend of the Gross family.

I am waiting for Hanna* and her father who are coming here to call on us this evening. They are not really due for another hour – and I have been looking forward to this time when I could sit down and talk to you.

I wish you were right here – in this same room – but there, I suppose you must work sometimes. I hope you had a good rest this morning – you ought to have had the *full* morning off since you worked yesterday. Don't get too tired out dear – because I'll think it's all my fault – which it is – but the time we have together seems so short for all the things we have to talk about. Doesn't it?

I went down to Vautines today to buy a wedding present and I bought the most charming old Chinese vase! I wanted to keep it.

†Hopkins's older brother, Lewis Hopkins, worked as assistant secretary to the National Board of Censorship of Moving Pictures.

I've been thinking about my party for the concert today – some more – I shall ask Goldie – and I am enclosing herewith a ticket for your brother.† Will you ask him if he would like to come? As for the other two people, I haven't quite made up my mind. If you happen to think of anyone you would like, just tell me tomorrow.

You're probably getting ready for your Virginians now. I can just see you moving around down there. How do you suppose C. I. M. knew I was at the Equal F. office yesterday? She called me up directly there and I thought of course she got the number from home but my sister says no. It seems queer. Spooky. Where did you put my picture? And who has seen it? You don't know what a lot of buzzing there will be as soon as someone does.

Yesterday was so nice. "Nice" doesn't express it at all. Every minute of it was perfect – only I think we spend too much money – where do you suppose I'll get a job? Some days I feel very hopeful – other days I don't.

Good-night dearest. I dreamed about you all last night – and the queerest dream it was too.

Tomorrow afternoon seems a long way off – sweetheart –

ETHEL

8.

[March 7, 1913]
Friday afternoon

DEAREST:

"Our little family joke" got me home at 1:30 but I am sure I am better for it today. We had such a good talk didn't we dear? And I do understand Ethel, girl – the differences between you and other girls is that you are absolutely honest and frank, which doesn't usually go with love affairs. I love you more after last night than ever before and am sure that my ideal is realized in you, sweetheart. I don't see where I ever invented the conceited notion that you would ever wait three years for anybody let alone me – poor devil that I am. I confess that you did take a little of the wind out of my sails but as long as it is the truth – it doesn't hurt.

Miss C. I. didn't have a word to say – she was as nice as pie this morning. Poor dear – how she will regret wrecking your life for a Methodist settlement worker – and a poor Methodist at that. Ten years from now we'll show her it wasn't so bad – won't we Ethel?

Oh! But it's cold Ethel – don't freeze anything. Am afraid that it will be pretty cold at camp but I'm going anyway – be back Sunday about 3.

I hope you have a good time Saturday dear – till Sunday at 4 dearest.

Your

HARRY

Written on Christodora House letterhead.

9.

[March 7, 1913]
Friday afternoon

DEAREST BOY:

I have just come in from a very strenuous walk in the park – and oh it was cold – but nice. One of the girls came to spend the afternoon with me – and that is one of the things we did.

Hope you reached home all right last night and that you were not too tired, dear, this morning. I know I should just *make* you go earlier – but it's so hard when I don't want you to. I must make some good resolutions. I slept like a rock last night – and this morning I wended my way to the Underwood office and saw the manager – whom I know. I've registered myself down there and he promises great things – but what will come of it, I do not know. I also had a letter this morning which sounds encouraging – from Mrs. Miller. I'm to see her Saturday.

If this weather keeps up it will be freezing cold out at camp tomorrow. Be sure and take care of yourself.

When I got home this morning, I found a woman with a baby in her arms, begging in the street. She seemed like a fairly young woman – and as she came right up to me – I asked her why she had to do that. She said her husband left her – that she could not find him – that she had five children on her hands – that she herself could not find work – but that she could work at dressmaking. Now – is the Charity Organization Soc. the place to send that woman? She has an older daughter – 15 – who can take care of the baby while she works. Wish I could do something for her – she seemed so helpless and destitute and cold. I gave her the address of the Charity Organization and a letter to a dressmaker I know – but I am going to call on her again in a couple of days. Where do you think is the place to send her if these other things are not right? Tell me Sunday – it makes me want to go out to meet you – but I know I mustn't. Shall we go to the Ethical Culture* Sunday night? Have you asked your brother about Wednesday night. I am enclosing the ticket this time. Can you call me up at home here tomorrow morning and tell me whether or not he can come? Sometime – when the office is empty? Did anyone tease you about last night? You were so dear – and it was so nice to have you with me – because I had quite made up my mind that I was going home alone.

Won't it be a wonderful time when "going home" will mean the same place for us both – I'm not going to put a question mark after that last sentence – because it is no question – is it – dear –

*Founded by Felix Adler, the Ethical Culture Society promoted social reform and was closely associated with the Settlement House Movement. Gross and Hopkins were married in the Ethical Culture Society's headquarters on NYC's West Side by Frank Lovejoy Elliot, Adler's close associate.

I hope you'll have a good rest at camp – and that you will let nothing prevent your going. Wish you would come here right from the train! But I suppose your grip would be a nuisance – except you wouldn't have to carry it around but just take it home with you when you leave me – last thing – Harriet Fischel just telephoned and asked if she could come up here to-night – so I said "yes" – you never told me what Julia Weber said to you when she saw you. My what a long letter – and so many questions and answers!

Good-night dearest.

I think about you such a lot – wish you weren't so far away! Next time you see me – ask me what it is I've been saving up for you.

What I said about "3 years" last night – seems so crude when I think about it now. Besides – three or even two months from now, it won't seem possible that I could have said such a thing. I shall gradually take back all I said.

Another good-night and a great deal of love from
Your
ETHEL
Friday evening

10.

[postmarked March 10, 1913]
Monday

HELLO DEAR!

I've just been writing many letters and I thought it would be kind-o-nice to send you one too. Had a call from the Plaza this morning. Am going to see the lady at 5:30 this evening. In the meantime I'm going to see Miss King about some *business.*

Hope you got a good rest last night. Harry dear – I wonder if you always tell me everything that's on your mind about you – and – I – Wish you would.

If you can think of any way that I can find my "lady" work, I wish you would tell me. Is there a bureau of employment in connection with any of the charitable organizations listed in the Charity Directory? She is Catholic, you know.

Now that I have talked to you – I shall be on my way. Am going downtown.

Mrs. Blatch is Harriot Stanton Blatch

Mrs. Blatch* just called me up. Said she heard I was looking for some new work and asked me to come down to see her at 12 o'clock Wednesday. So if I come down to break windows at Christodora someday – don't be surprised.

Good-bye dearest – until tomorrow.

ETHEL

11.

[postmarked March 13, 1913]
Thursday morning

Written on Christodora House letterhead.

DEAREST:

Wednesday slipped by someway with no letter to you, dear – but I did talk to you twice over the phone which was almost as good.

I don't seem to be able to forget about what you said Tuesday night Ethel – perhaps we were both tired and out of sorts – yet I know there is something in your mind which must come out – because you doubt don't you dear? But when you talk of going out of my life – dear – it can't be – unless –

You still believe that I don't know my own mind (I'm too young you say – pooh you) – you have a foolish notion that things are moving along too fast for me (always me) – who started this anyway. Did you ask me to marry you – I would have waited till dooms day if I had waited for you – although I admit I wasn't discouraged. Then you insist that if things do not turn out right, it will be your fault – it certainly is unselfish of you to take all the blame but sweetheart you never will have to take any because I won't give you a chance. Now Ethel you won't talk about those foolish things again will you dear? You must know, girl, what you mean to me – so good and strong – and I love you so. It isn't an ideal marriage from any point of view but our own – I'm through doing what other people think I ought to do. But Ethel it is going to be a thousand times harder for you than it is for me – but enough –

Am anxious to see you about the job – what did Miss King think of you calling *me* up?

Hope this reaches you this p.m. Good bye my girl.
HARRY

12.

[postmarked March 14, 1913]
Thursday night 11 P.M.

MY DEAREST:

I love you so – I can't bear to think that what I said the other night – hurts – and that you are still worrying about it.

I haven't anything more on my mind besides what I told you – and that came one day when I thought of all that I was getting you in for – wondered whether it was fair to you. – But dearie – I realize now that none of these troubles will be lasting – and that our great happiness in each other *is* – and we mustn't let other people's theories which they have never tested – mar it for one minute when we are so sure of the road before us.

I'm not at all worried about my end of it, about the attitude of my friends and my family. Whatever the first shock will be – it won't last and when they see how happy we're going to be and how fine and big – and altogether ideal you are – they will say it is what they always wanted for me. For oh, Harry – you are everything I want and I am such a lucky girl.

So don't let's worry about any of those other things any more. We won't climb any of the hills or mountains – until we get to them. Besides I can't imagine there being any mountains – with you – they will *all* look like hills.

And dearest – I don't doubt you for one minute – ever – the thought of you keeps surging in my heart until this seems like a beautiful world. And the part that makes me happiest is that I know how you care. And life without you now – well, it just *couldn't be* that's all. Yes, dearie – I do give you the credit for asking me the question – but I was a pretty close second – wasn't I – and it was the fact that I encouraged you so – right from the start that made me wonder whether I had any right to – for your sake.

But sweetheart – there are no doubts now and those were only passing clouds – I was so happy – I wanted to be sure I wasn't selfish and so I cross-examined myself – and then passed it on to you so brokenly – no wonder it hurt. But I'm glad it's out now – and I love you all the more and I feel that I know you better now that it is. I don't suppose I can ever keep from telling you what's on my mind.

Good-night dearest – write to me soon again. Every word of your letter is so dear and sweet – and my "subway special" was such a treat! It isn't nearly so lonesome now that I have them.

I send you all my love –
ETHEL

13.

[postmarked March 15, 1913]

Written on Christodora House letterhead.

DEAREST:

I'm that excited! Miss MacColl knows I am going to get married! But she was so nice – only Ethel girl, I didn't tell her who to – and she didn't ask so that is still left for you. And then – she did just what you said she'd do – offered to raise my salary – looking right through me all the time – and wouldn't take a definite decision from me – I am to tell her sometime within a week. When I know all the time what I am going to do – and now listen, dear – I lost my nerve when she wanted to know how soon it was coming off and lied to her – told her within a year or *two*. All this time she was telling me what a boy I was and that it was one of those things which she had no control over. I simply couldn't tell her this *fall*. She said some awfully nice things about me – I don't know whether she meant them or not.

This is a frightful letter Ethel girl but I've just come from seeing her and am nervous as the devil.

It seems to be up to you now so get up your nerve – I know she is going to be perfectly dear about it.

Oh, Ethel – I love you so this afternoon – my ideal – and we will make each other happy!

I don't see how I can wait till Sunday – dearest.
Good Bye My Sweetheart
HARRY
I won't dare look at C. I. at the dinner table – am going out and get some air before my club.

14.

[postmarked March 17, 1913]

ETHEL DEAR:

I wish I were riding beside you on the subway instead of ambling my time away at Christodora. We were to-gether just long enough to be tantalizing – and then dear little Miss Ellis had to butt in – she knew I wanted to see you – alone.

Sunday seems so far away dear – I am coming up early and we can take a walk before going up to Miss Goldstein. Am invited out to dinner tomorrow night – a Mr. MacGuire, sec'y of the union board, (whose wife does *not* work). Sat. night I had a chance to go to a card party but must stay by the ship.

Hasn't your sister said anything about me being up so often – well she will don't worry –

Did I tell you Ethel I have had my young and inno-cent life insured for $1500 – costs $48 a year – get $936 back at end of *20* years and insurance of $1000 when I pass beyond.

The boys are beginning to come down – I don't want them to see do I?

Ethel darling sleep tight. Here comes C. I. Mac!

Good night.
With a Kiss
HARRY

Written on Christodora House letterhead.

15.

[postmarked March 19, 1913]
Wednesday morning
At the office
First one in
9:00 A.M.

GOOD-MORNING DEAREST.
I love you.
ETHEL

2 minutes afterward –

Enter every body.

16.

[postmarked March 19, 1913]
Wednesday

DEAREST:

There are so many things running around my brain
this morning, Ethel. That I don't know where to start
and probably never will finish. A boy has just been run
over by an Ave. B. car in front of the house – nothing
serious but the usual crowd has collected.

I had another talk with Miss MacColl this morning
but nothing was said about *us*. She hinted at my "*new*
responsibility" and wanted to know if I would rather
stay in the city this summer than go to Northover – I
asked her if there might be any chance of me living at
Christodora this summer and working for my board
certain evenings in the week – She would see – you
know Ethel it would mean a difference of about $40 a
month and that would help some – wouldn't it dear?
The only thing my evenings would be more or less
tied up – and I wouldn't get to see you much more
than I do now.

Your sister and brother-in-law made a very good impression – Miss Ames thought Mr. Kohn good looking!

Miss MacColl said "You know he is very religious." This at the breakfast table with me trying to hide behind a half slice of toast! Sorry I didn't get back to see them – I came just after the dance was over – 11:30.

You know sweetheart – it does bother me a lot about your brother and sister – I wish they might know all about it so that we might know just where we are at – Now dear, don't think I blame them for objecting to me – it is a perfectly natural prejudice which can only be dispelled when they see how ideally happy we will be – I am not doubting for a minute but that we will hear mumblings from out West before long but they will have to wait and see how perfectly dear and sweet you are.

Is confession good for the soul? – here goes. I am not big enough to overlook that inventory of names you went over in Goufaroni's – and my *little, small* mind is frightfully jealous. I don't suppose you understand do you? But, dear, I care for you so much now that I hate to think anyone else ever cared like I do – am I not selfish? Now that I have that off my mind – I feel better.

I understand your play was a howling success – your ears would burn if you heard the nice things they were saying about you this morning.

Lewis met me at Haslam's last night and asked me about you – I said I saw Miss Gross occasionally – which is the truth.

It is lunch time now dear – so good bye – I am going to post this right away so it will reach you tonight I hope –my darling –
Yours
HARRY
Be sure you pay back that money you borrowed yesterday! What a "scrimp" I am.

17.

[March 17, 1913]
Monday

SWEETHEART:

I don't feel at all like work this morning – and there's so much to do! Wish I was going to see you to-night. I miss not having you on the premises but I must buckle down and get to work.

A distant elderly cousin is on here from Philadelphia – my sister informed me over the 'phone this morning – also my brother sent word that he would arrive on Tuesday – but that he does not want to spend a single night in the city – going right out to New Jersey.

His wife is evidently worse again from what he says.

Good-bye dearest – be good –
Much much love –
ETHEL

18.

[March 17, 1913]
Monday night

Volume I

MY DEAREST:

I seem to be a trifle tired to-night because of my "unaccustomed" labors to-day. I have joined the "working class" again and it's good to be back.*

*Gross had probably just started working for Harriot Stanton Blatch at the Women's Political Union.

I bought my desk this a.m. way up on 138th Street – a secondhand roller-top with typewriter-drop – quartered oak for $23 in good condition. I don't know whether it was a bargain or not – but I didn't have much time to run around much. It's as nice as that $37.50 one we saw on Saturday – only that it isn't [undecipherable]. The janitor is scrubbing it out for me to-night for 30 cents! I was too weary to do it myself.

I had a very nice day. Everybody was so nice to me – they let me have whatever I want and I think I'm going to like it very much. It's work every minute – and much running up and downstairs – but after I get things started I won't do so much of that. I have a desk phone and that ought to save me some steps.

So much for that. My boy must know all there is to know.

Now – about you and I. I wonder if you saw Miss MacColl to-day and if you are writing me about it? Because I have something to write.

This morning a letter came from my kid brother. It was for all of us and in it he answered one of my sister's letters to him. Well, it seems that she wrote him that she was worried about you and I – because – although I had not said anything to her – she felt sure that I cared about you. Well the sum and substance of it is that from her letter Ben's got a very imperfect and unsatisfactory idea about you and it's up to me to write and tell him about you and about it *all* – myself – for I have simply got to answer his letter and I can only answer it one way. You see – my sister's attitude is this: – at least this is what she said when I talked to her about it – (I didn't *tell* her anything – just that I asked her why she wrote what she did) She says that she would always welcome and like anybody that I chose for a friend – but she 'does not believe in inter marriages because that born prejudice against the jew might be slumbering sometimes but it is never dead no matter how broad-minded they are" – I am quoting from a letter she wrote today to my brother.

Letter #2. She brought it in here for me to read. She goes on the say "perhaps I can't do anything for or against – but the only reason I write you about it is because it worries me – even if he is a perfect ideal of a man."

I write you all of this so that you may know just how she feels. She's a dear sister and after all she is considering my happiness – and I mustn't be too hard on her. But I wish she had let me tell my brother myself as I asked her to.

Dearest – I don't worry about my happiness. If I could only make them all feel how assured it would be with you! I just can't imagine you with that kind of prejudice "slumbering" anywhere about your person – I don't feel any toward you – and I know I couldn't love you as I do if you had the least scrap of if in you – I've been with you such a lot. You would unconsciously make me feel it if you had – and you haven't.

Why can't people get away from stereotyped phrases and understand how two people can be in perfect harmony and absolutely suited to each other – in spite of the fact that they were born to different faiths. You have your theory and I have mine – and they are much more alike than my sister's and mine or my brother's and mine although we were born and brought up under the same roof. I know you are saying to yourself that we don't think exactly about all things and I'm very glad we don't. It's stimulating for the mind not to – isn't it? For after all, we are two individuals.

My – but I talk a lot. I know just how your debaters feel. But I shall have to write my brother and tell him *everything*. I can't see my way out. And that means I shall have to tell my sister everything.

Harry, are you going out to dinner tomorrow night – or only afterwards – or have you made other plans – and if you haven't – can you meet me at 5 o'clock – and can we go to the Italian restaurant and have dinner so that I can tell you just what I am going to say to my family and how? Then I could go on to my club and you to your call. Please don't hesitate to say if you have planned to do anything else. If you haven't you could meet me in the lobby of the Martha Washington Hotel* – at 5 o'clock and we could go down to Goufaroni's on 10th St. 9880 Madison Square is my telephone number – and you could get me there any time after nine and tell me. I know that yesterday was a long session and that it ought to last for more than 2 days – but I should like to talk to you – across the table – about some things.

I don't feel nearly so weary now that I've had all this out. I hope you won't try to read this before breakfast!

Good-night – sweetheart –

Much love –

Ethel

P.S. Now please remember that if you can't manage tomorrow afternoon – 5 o'clock – that is all right – it doesn't have to be – E

*The Martha Washington Hotel, located at 30 E. Thirtieth Street, was a residence for single women and a regular meeting place for Hopkins and Gross.

19.

[postmarked March 20, 1913]
Thursday afternoon

MY DEAR LITTLE ETHEL:

The mail has just (3:00) has just brought the dearest of letters from the dearest of girls – and I am hastening to get even.

Your abbreviated note made me whistle all day – dear – this was yesterday – but I have had the blues all day to-day until your letter came.

This has been a terribly long week Ethel – Sunday is still three days off! It won't always be that long between visits will it dear? I wish I might get off Friday night but no – why can't I be one of the lucky devils who don't have to work when they should be "recreating?" Are you going – or rather did you go to the social workers' dance last night?

I wrote a long letter home yesterday but didn't say anything about being engaged to you sweetheart. Why should they be disturbed – do you? I can hardly wait to see the letter your brother will write – may I? And what will your sister say to me Sunday – tell her to be as easy as possible on me won't you dear? Am going to settle everything with Miss MacColl tomorrow so I may have something exciting to write in my next – she will never forgive me for stealing her pride and joy – and right under her own watchful eyes at that. But just the same she is undoubtedly the best friend we have between us and if she doesn't give us her "blessing" – who will?

Have been reading "Damaged Goods" today – you might enjoy it – but you are not very *old* Ethel and I'll have to protect you from all this wicked literature.

Ethel, dear, I must stop thinking about you – for I can't do any work.

Good night darling

HARRY

Let's tell people we're the same age dear – then you won't have to apologize for me all the time.

Written on Christodora House letterhead.

20.

[March 20, 1913]
Thursday night

DEAREST:

No letter from you to-night. And it's so lonesome. Perhaps I'll get one in the morning.

A girl cousin came and called on us this evening with her mother. Haven't seen her since before I went away last summer. It's now after 11 and they have just gone.

I practically told my brother-in-law and my sis to-night. At least they know how I feel about you – but they don't know that you know – we discussed every phase of it.

Must write to my bro tomorrow night.

Good-night sweetheart. Wonder what you've been doing to-day and what you've been thinking –

Had a busy day as usual. Had to get an extra stenographer to help out.

Hope you've written to me.

My love to you –

ETHEL

P. S. We close at one o'clock Saturdays all the year around, so I shall always be free Saturday afternoons.

Am sleepy now.

Good night dear –

21.

[postmarked March 21, 1913]
Friday afternoon

*Written on
Christodora House
letterhead.*

DEAREST:

This is Good Friday you know and everyone is going to church this afternoon but *wicked* me – Ethel I came very near to sending you some Easter lilies – wouldn't that have been an awful break!

Your sleepy little note just arrived – you're just as dear as ever aren't you sweetheart.

Do you know what I did last night? – foolish question – Mr. Mason called me up and wanted me to go to the

Boston Symphony with him. Miss A* offered to take the office so I took a vacation. The music was heavenly – had supper at the Astor afterwards. He is a queer chap with queer ideas yet charming to be with. Can we have him and Miss Ellis to our wedding – or is it to be in the City Hall? Listen, dear, somebody sent Miss E. another year's membership in the Equal Franchise Society and she is furious. Says it isn't a joke anymore "to be affiliated with that kind of women." I laughed and she got peeved. Poor dear!

I'm glad that you are to have your Saturdays free – I rather think that I will too later on.

Haven't had any chance to speak with Miss MacColl but will as soon as she gets back from church. Will tell you all about it Sunday. Ethel, dear, am I coming up at 3? May Garden is singing at Cooper Union Sunday night at 8 but I don't imagine that we would be able to get near it. *Was denkst du? Is das nicht recht, mein liebe Frau? Or non – ma chére femme –* you see I speak three languages and then I can speak pig latin and am learning *Yiddish!*

There are three boys looking over my shoulder while I write this and I can't say everything I want to – this letter should reach you tonight, my girl.

We will have so much to talk about Sunday that I think I had better come up in the morning – but I must go to church Easter Sunday – even if I have to stand up.

It seems ages since we were together – dearest – I have thought enough about you to fill a book. Be good dear till Sunday – all my love –

HARRY

*"Miss A" most likely refers to Miss Arms. She and Miss Ellis were settlement workers at Christodora House.

22.

[March 21, 1913]
Friday night

DEAREST:

You and I are going to have tea with Mrs. M. at 5 o'clock on Sunday afternoon at the Plaza! What do you think of that. Of course I'll tell you all about it when I can talk to you – and I thought perhaps I wouldn't be able to in the morning – so this is just to prepare you. So come up as planned at 3 – on Sunday – and if it's pleasant we can walk down.

Good-night dear – hope you're getting to bed early to-night. See you in the morning.
ETHEL

23.

[March 21, 1913]
Friday night

MY DARLING:

Have just finished your lovely letter – Ethel, my girl – if a man can love anybody – I love you. You mean more to me than any little words of mine can ever convey – I will show some day how I care. And can't it be next fall – even that would be six months or more away. It seems so long but then there is a great deal to do in that time and including some money to earn – even a job yet to get but I'm not worrying about that. Perhaps I should.

*"Ch" was Hopkins's shorthand for Christodora House.

Had dinner with MacGuire but was back to Ch* – at 8. The usual howl went up – everybody calling me up etc. but I guess they will live.

It was so good to steal this afternoon for you – I hope you enjoyed it as much as I. Miss King is awfully nice – I like her immensely.

Mr. Mason is trying to say good bye to Miss Ellis in the office hall – why don't they get married?

The more I think about it – the more I think Miss MacColl ought to know – better for all of us but especially for you. Can you break the news gently so the Settlement won't stop.

I am going to live with Lewis this summer and next fall until –? We're going to rent a 3 room apartment $21 per. on 35th St. Lew's got the furniture so we will hit it off fine. You can visit us or (me) there.

I am going to mail you this – the first thing Sat. a. m. – do come down for dinner sweetheart.

Good night little girl – I'm sleepy – darling
Your own
HARRY

24.

[postmarked March 21,1913]
Friday night

SWEETHEART:

I just had to talk to you this afternoon and it was so nice to have an excuse! You see I *had* said that I should be off on Saturday afternoon and I didn't know whether you were planning to see me or not. Even if I have to stay I don't believe it would be later than 3:30 or 4 o'clock. We could *look* at Victrolas, perhaps.

My sis won't be any different to you on Saturday from any *other* time. She has suspected nearly all that there is to know for some time. I don't believe she or Mr. K. will discuss it with you at all. My kid bro.'s letter *will* be an interesting document after he gets mine. I shall let you see it if I think best – dearest – I might have to write him several letters before he writes a letter fit for you to see. But I have every reason to think that he will understand – and if you really want to see it I will show you whatever he writes. But I haven't written my letter yet and I must get to it. Your letter this morning was so dear! It was such a nice send-off when I left this morning. What I meant over the telephone was that I don't want you to worry about making a point of telling C. I. I'm crazy to have her know – but I know it won't be easy for you to tell her – so that's why I said wait until she gives you an opening – and she will – because she's crazy to know herself – I'm thinking if I was down there I'd tell her. She's got to give us her blessing! If you tell her – say I said so – and I'll say a lot more if she'll give me audience.

So, I mustn't read "Damaged Goods." All right – I won't. But you'll have to tell me *why* I must not.

You can't get off Monday night can you – Besides if we are to see "The Sunshine Girl" on Tuesday – and by the way – you didn't tell me whether or no – and April 17th is the MacDowell concert at Carnegie Hall – and have you still your brother's ticket?

Yes, we're going to have plenty of good books – and you can buy most of them – even if we have to do without desserts. But I can see that won't be popular with you – I'll have to think of something else. But won't it be great – Harry Boy – planning for it all. All right Harry – we're the same age from now on – but please tell me – am I 22 or 26? Better let me know by return mail for I shall have to hold off all inquiries until I hear.

Sweetheart Good-night

I must get to work. Perhaps I'll see you tomorrow. If not, then *early* on Sunday. And what are we going to do on Sunday? Has Spring come? We could call on Mrs. Boyd in the afternoon. I can't go in the Easter Parade because I'm not ready.

Rec'd my first check from W.P. U. for a *full* week, to-day.

Now for my bro. letter!

Good-night – again – dearest –

ETHEL

25.

[date uncertain]

Written in Gross's hand.

DEAREST:

Go to Fifth Avenue Building tomorrow and get their Long Island Booklet.

Also to B'way corner 28th Street and get D. L. and W RR book.

That's all.

26.

[postmarked March 24, 1913]

ETHEL DEAR:

Just a note as I am frightfully busy but I must talk to you a little. You were so sweet and dear yesterday – Ethel – and the more I see of you the surer I am that everything is going to be ideal with us. I can hardly picture myself as a dutiful "hubby" and I'm not so sure that I always will "obey" and I know you won't!

C.I. wanted to know where I was last night – this at the breakfast table – I told her I went to a dance but she didn't believe it. I haven't talked to her yet to-day.

Am going over to Astoria's tomorrow afternoon to see some friends of mine – none eligible! Will be at Martha W. at 5:00 sharp.

Do you know I got home from your house in 25 minutes last night. 17 minutes on the subway! Read the first act of the "Playboy."

Do you realize Miss Innocence that you actually kissed me last night? Now don't get peeved dear.

Wrote a long letter home this morning but am not going to say anything about us till summer. Why worry them longer than necessary?

Now Ethel we must begin to figure all our expenses out tomorrow –

Have you read about the tornadoes out West. They are too close to home to be comfortable.

Good-bye – sweetheart – till tonight

HARRY

27.

[March 26, 1913]
Wednesday morning

GOOD-MORNING, SWEETHEART:

Hope you reached home all right and that you're not too tired this morning. Let me know by telephone if you are sending anyone I mean an office boy – over here to see me. So that I won't apply elsewhere.

My love to you –

ETHEL

28.

[March 26, 1913]
Wednesday aft.

DEAREST:

Have been "*sick*" two hours today – just came downstairs to find more letters than I've had in a week – three! First your dear little note. I didn't recognize your writing and my first thought was that someone was taking advantage of me – then a long letter from mother, which wouldn't interest you and lastly a friend of mine at Harvard writes that he will spend two days with me during the middle of April. He is an Irish Catholic so please don't fall in love with him – you won't – you know you can't play every instrument in the band!

I am wondering how you ever got up yesterday morning – your little head was *so* sleepy – and you did go to sleep, didn't you dear? I rolled in at 1:45 but managed to make breakfast in time.

Miss MacColl and Miss Austin have gone to camp for the night so the house is more or less vacant.

Now listen dear – would you *really* rather be married at city hall than at home by the Ethical Culture – you know I've been thinking about it and there is no reason why mother should know anything about me joining the Society. She certainly wouldn't come this far to see me married and I rather doubt if any of the rest of the family would either. My brother has just been in – we had a long talk about a good many things – you know Miss Harrington, his fiancée, etc., will probably be housekeeper at Christodora this summer and Lew is trying to get a job down here – they would have a big time but I rather fear for the work. I am not worrying at all about him – dear – he must like it.*

Geo. is waiting to mail this so must close – dearest – Ethel dear – you are the dearest and sweetest of girls that ever lived –
I love you
HARRY

Lewis Hopkins married Bessie Harrington December 25, 1914 in Grinnell, Iowa. Grinnell Professor John D. Stoops officiated at the ceremony.

29.

[March 27, 1913]
Thursday morning

MY DEAREST:

Your dear sweet letter came this morning and I love every word of it. I did so want to have a talk with you last night – Goldie stayed all night and I couldn't slip away – Even for a minute – to write. It rained so hard she couldn't go home.

I thought about you such a lot yesterday – Sweetheart – and last night. I don't think you could have rested very long yesterday morning – you called me so early. I am sure one of those boys would have been all right.

I want to write so many things – dear – but I don't dare take the time here at the office this morning.

Much work awaits me. Your bro. seems to have changed his mind about C. H. Thought you said he never would work down there. Circumstances alter cases!

I would be interested in your mother's letter – and you needn't worry about your Harvard friend.

Remember – that to-night – if C.I.M. – converses with me to-night – I might tell her. So be prepared. I promise not to do it at the dinner table! I expect to be down to dinner – but I may have to go home for dinner – If I am coming – I shall telephone the management.

Good-bye – dearest – until to-night

I love you.

ETHEL

30.

[March 28, 1913]

HELLO DEAREST

Knight was a Christodora settlement worker.

Am over here lunching with Knight.*

Hope you're not too tired to-day.

Will write you at length to-night if I can.

Busy as busy at the office today.

You were so dear and sweet last night – about so many things.

This is to-night – I wrote the above at intervals through the day. But I couldn't finish it sufficiently to send it. I must stop trying to write these busy days during the day. It takes my mind off work too much.

Sweetheart – I've been thinking about you such a lot to-day. Some things you say – some things you said last night – mean so much to me – more than you can ever know because nearly always I don't say anything in response. But I wish to record right here and now – that you're *such* a dear and I love you.

Am going to write to C.I.M. to say that what we talked about last night is a secret until we tell her otherwise. She simply must keep it quiet. Such a time as you would have! And it isn't necessary.

Wrote to Kansas City – and also sent a telegram to find out if my brother is safe and sound. Ben in Colo. – I know he is – but am worried about my other brother Ed – although I have every reason to think he is far enough West to be safe.

Wonder what C.I. has said to you to-day. Be sure and *write* me or remember to tell me all that she does say because it would be fun to hear her comments. The way she took the whole thing leaves nothing to be desired, does it?

I've been figuring and I enclose the result of my calculations. No – I don't believe I shall – You figure it out and submit to me a statement of the amount you need a year for clothes. I have mine all ready to submit. And according to my figures – providing the income is $200 a month – we ought to be able to save $50 a month. Do you think we ought to save more than that?

I have figured and figured and figured – and now I know everything I can and can't do – and as it's 10:30 – and I'm sleepy– I guess I'll stop.

Dearest – it's going to be great.

Good night

ETHEL

31.

[March 28, 1913]
Friday p.m.

DEAREST ETHEL:

I might as well have spent the night at your house for all the sleep I got – 5 hours! But it was worth it – that is some consolation.

Have been up to 42nd St. Hospital with another boy today – tuberculosis of the knee and doctor offered very little encouragement for the poor kid. Just returned from a foolish half hour trying to teach a foolish kid to count to six! He seemed to be able to count backwards but not forward.

Called up Lucy Haslau at the A.I.C.P. this morning but she was going to be busy today so I am going to her house for *breakfast* Sunday morning at 10. I am wondering if I can't manage to graft a dinner too – get my Sunday board free. The trouble is I have to pay for it [at] C. H. just the same.

What are we going to do Sunday dear? Isn't there a Jersey ferry up above 110th St. somewhere? If it wouldn't take too long – and the flowers are beginning to come out.

The things Miss MacColl said about you keep ringing in my ears – I know they are all true – you are the ideal combination of idealistic common sense – I love you and your ideas (that is nearly all of them).

Ethel, you have no idea how happy I am in the thought of working through life with the woman I love – more than an equal – to share all the troubles and always have that solid assurance there is one who really understands and cares. I have thought about bigger and better things since you came into my life – I feel the thrill now of knowing that I won't have to live a lie with you but can shape my own life – influenced already beyond words by the dearest of girls. We will have a great many troubles dear but they will only draw us closer together. I can't give all the reasons why I love you Ethel – no one can tell why they love a person – I do know that if you went out of my life now, it would make a big difference and that selfishly I would [be] happier with you than with anyone in the world.

The bell is ringing. Good bye sweetheart – Oh Ethel I do love you and will work – oh so hard to make you happy.

Darling, till Sunday

HARRY

32.

[March 31, 1913]
Monday

DEAREST:

I have had another talk with Miss MacColl! She made a definite offer for me to stay at Christodora which I refused – then she told be that I could live at Christodora till I got married if I wished, to spend certain evenings a week at the Settlement, which of course I accepted but of course there is nothing binding about it. And then – she said she was serious that I keep up some kind of connection with the house so that we – you and I – might be together here occasionally – so that everybody might know that she favored our marriage. She evidently thinks we need moral support to carry us through the "storm" as she calls it. She said "Of course there will be a great deal of silly gossip after you announce your engagement" – what about that! She also said – "I suppose that you will be getting married in six or eight months" and I assured her that that was the idea – and more – she asked if she couldn't tell somebody in strict confidence, one who was not connected with the clubs and I said *yes* – Ethel dear – you see I have no fear for my own life – please don't be too hard on me – sweetheart. But she was perfectly lovely and assured me that she would go through thick and thin with us – which isn't at all necessary as we are perfectly able to take care of ourselves yet I am glad she is on our side, as it were.

And listen dear – I am to change my free day from Tuesday to Thursday – is that all right with you? It doesn't go into effect till next week.

Yesterday was a perfect day Ethel dear – and that book – I wandered around in heaven with Stormfield all night. As might be expected I forgot to take that other book.

Will see you at the M.W. at 5:30 – darling.

Good bye dear.

HARRY

Have you heard from your brother?

33.

[March 31, 1913]
Monday night

MY DEAREST:

I hope you reached home all right last night and that you weren't *too* tired this morning. Yesterday was such a wonderful day – with you all to myself! Wonder if you enjoyed it [as] much as I did? Each time you are dearer and dearer to me – and each time I learn more and more about your own dear *self*.

You're so unselfish and sweet and *big* about everything.

And then you're such fun besides.

But whenever I try to write down or say any of the things I think and feel about you – the result is most unsatisfactory. I don't come anywhere near it.

Written on Equal Franchise Society letterhead.

So don't expect me to. I wish we could live in the country – Harry – the bushes in our back yard on 29th Street are beginning to sprout – and it makes me want to! I know – dearest – that we can't just yet.

To-day was a busy day – but for the *big* first time my work was finished when I closed my desk to-night. So far – I have always had some thing left over. And I left at 5:30 too. In time I hope to get things running smoothly and systematically.

Hope you'll get to bed early to-night.

Shall meet you – Martha Washington – 5:30 tomorrow night. Better ask your brother if he would like to come to the concert on the 17th of April.

Good night sweetheart. I love you so – to-night and I'm so happy. Until tomorrow –

ETHEL

Am writing C.I.M. not to talk. This stationery is a relic of the past. Don't mind it. E.

34.

[April 2, 1913]
Wednesday

DEAREST:

I can't get over yesterday – it was too good to be true! But six hours is not enough sleep for a perfectly healthy girl who is giving the best years of her young life for the sole purpose of jogging elbows with men, respectable and otherwise, at the voting booth. That was quite an effort Ethel and am wondering if it got over. But really we must get back to union hours or there might be a lockout.

I tried to read that book on the subway but didn't seem to grasp the atmosphere – will try again. By the way, there is a good story in McClures this month about a Jew's struggle in America.

Got a card from my sister and she has gone to Ohio to do relief work and may come to N. Y.! Wouldn't that be exciting? I think I will tell her all about it if she does come.

I rather think that meeting is called off for next Sunday night – will know definitely tomorrow. The family have all migrated to Northover today.

Why were you so nice last night, dear? – I have to laugh at your guilty conscience (prompted by Miss K.) about me going home with you.

And those figures, I am going to put them in here.

Rent – $30
Nourishment – $42.50
Light – 2.00
Clothing – 25.00
Carfare – 6.00 ?
Lunches – 15.00
Papers and mag. – 1.00
Insurance – 2.00
Manicure – 2.00
Amusement – 10.00
Incidentals – 20.00
Total – 155.50*

*$155.50 converts to approximately $2,700 in today's dollars.

Now if we can't live on that – we had better stop. It would cost a few dollars more to have a maid. Incidentals include everything I can't think of. I trust this meets with your *approval!*

Good bye – Ethel girl – till Saturday – sweetheart –
HARRY

35.

[April 2, 1913]
Wednesday night, after dinner

DEAREST:

It's nice to get into this room all alone and think about you. You're such a dear sweet boy. That's what I think about you to-night.

Wonder what C. I. M. said to you today.

No letter has come from my brother yet. It's almost a week since we had a letter. Perhaps I'll get one tomorrow.

Such a busy day at the office to-day! But *so* interesting. I like my work better all the time. Interviewed

Charles B. Stover was a Lower East Side activist and reformer who worked with the University Settlement and was Parks Commissioner from 1910–1914.

Stover's* secretary this morning. He was so suave and polite – I'd like to know what he was really thinking and what they mean to do about it. One thing – they'll make it as hard as possible. But enough of sad thoughts. – Let's start and write to each other about Saturday. If we could only make it on time – and I guess you can't – we could see Wm Collins – matinee. But it begins at 2:15 and then you'd have to rush right back.

Ask Miss MacColl for me if I can come to Children's Hour Sunday night. Will you? Ask her if *you* can bring me down. Say it's one of your "uptown" friends. And tell me what she says. & then while you're at your men's meeting – I can go and visit with my Aunt on 13th Street and you can meet me there – Or do you think I'd better let you alone to go to bed early on Sunday night? We can talk about this on Saturday if I see you. Am I going to? I suppose I do keep you up late nights and you'll get all tired out and it'll be my fault. Dearest – you must retire *early early* every night I don't see you and then I won't mind so much.

Saw Knight to-day. Said she called after us last night. Wanted to invite us to go back and spend the night after visit to the night court. You see she was still thinking of the way poor Ada's little brother had to go 'way uptown and down again late on a cold dark night. It was nice of her – but she couldn't make us hear.

Good night sweetheart – I love you so – and you were so perfect last night. There are no obstacles – Harry – you and I can just make everything happen. Be good. Much love –
ETHEL

36.

[April 3, 1913]
Thursday

HELLO DEAREST:

This is to be my only recreation today as I have been in the office since morning and am due for the evening. Slept right through breakfast this morning even though

I did get to bed at 11.15 last night – I was that tired. But I did stay up reading the "Idylls of the Gass" – a fascinating tale – but I was hoping Schimmelé would start a free synagogue or something like that but of course that isn't the idea the author tries to get across. I think she sized the situation up very fairly – we can talk about it later.

You speak of Miss King calling "us" back – I can't see exactly where I would fit in – and say, Ethel dear, please spell my sister's name with an "h" – she is very fussy about it. – Lew said he would be glad to go to the MacDowell chorus – I know you are disappointed.

Now about Saturday – I am afraid Collier is out of the question as we couldn't get up there much before three, dear – I wish I had something better to suggest – perhaps by tomorrow – but my mind is in its normal state today so you mustn't expect much.

Now what did you think of my figuring – I left out one or two little things but I think they can be covered by incidentals.

Am afraid your brother has a "mad on" – and isn't going to be led around as gentle as you had expected – but he will be home before long and perhaps we can have it out.

Ethel girl – I would give up everything for you – I love you more than everything in this world but I don't want it to be hard for you – dear.

Good bye sweetheart

HARRY

37.

[April 3, 1913]
Thursday night

MY DEAREST:

This is only a good-night note 'cause me is so sleepy! To-day was one of those hectic days. Had such a nice letter from my kid brother *in answer to mine*. It is just dear. You can see most of it when you come up. All of it if you must. Now I shall have to write again and tell him some definite things. Does it make you shiver?

Good night sweetheart. Hope I have a letter from you to-night.

Am not going to enclose my figures. They will wait until I see you.

So many questions I want to ask!

Much love to you from your own

ETHEL

38.

MY DARLING ETHEL:

You did get one ahead of me yesterday – your [drawn diamond shape] came smiling in about nine o'clock – they had to page the house for me – for I was on the top floor having a lovely row with Miss A. in which, I being a gentleman, came out second best. It was an awful stew and stirred the house to its very foundations – of course all the hens cackled together and I lost. So you will excuse the brevity of my answer won't you dear – I kicked myself for sending your note back – have you saved it?

And your brother's letter – may I see it all? I might as well hear it sooner or later.

Am getting dreadfully nervous over those rejuvenated figures or yours. What have you discovered anyway?

Will you call me up, dear tomorrow morning so that we can arrange to meet Saturday? If it is nice like today it would be a shame to stay inside – and I *do* like to walk. We could ride uptown on the bus and walk in the park. If it rains – we might go to Keith's or get wet.

I have filed an application with the A.I.C.P. – haven't been able to see Kingsbury* so don't know just what chances there are. I am going to try to get in with the Sage foundation† but they are desperately poor just now.

Now Ethel dear you mustn't work so hard – and why have any hectic days whatever those may be? It sounds like you were becoming militant – I can see Miss K. stewing over Miss Pankhurst.‡ I bet that she won't be in jail 10 days – they were so foolish to lock her up.

*John A. Kingsbury served as General Director of the AICP and later Mayor John Purroy Mitchel's Commissioner of Public Charities. He and Hopkins became longtime friends.

†Founded in 1907, the Russell Sage Foundation supported many charitable organizations.

‡Sylvia Pankhurst (1882–1960) was a radical and a militant suffragette who campaigned for women's rights in England and the United States.

Miss Mills called up this morning – said she saw us at the cubist exhibition – she knew now why I never came to see her. She was real peeved and I must go down and see her.

Ethel – I feel so sure everything is alright – all those queer feelings that I had at first are gone now for I'm sure you overlook all my faults and religion – which isn't easy – dear.

I had a long argument with Miss Ellis on woman's place in this world – I fear that I shocked her – but – dearest – we'll make it so ideal – that they will be converted to our way of thinking. I asked Miss Ellis if she would like to live like Dr. Reynold's wife and she said – no!

You know – the telephone rang and I forgot what I was going to say.

I must get to work – so good bye Ethel – sweetheart. With all my love

HARRY

Miss MacColl called you up and I wanted to listen but I didn't dare.

39.

[April 4, 1913]
Friday night

DEAREST HARRY:

I am very much impressed by your figures – the more I look at them. Except how you manage lunches $10.00 a month for 2 – I can't see – Less than a dollar a week a piece – It can't be done – but I have a new plan – that will make our living expenses about $140 a month – including every one of your items – and leave $10.00 for incidentals. I do not cut down on clothes or amusements – or food or anything – and under my plan we shall have more comfort. See if you can find out what I have done – Puzzle. It's quite hard to guess.

Am I to see you Saturday P.M.? Do let me know. C.I. M. has asked me to dinner and for the evening – but I'm not going to Loyalty* dance – if I come I shall do

Written on Equal Franchise Society letterhead.

*Christodora House sponsored the Loyalty Club for girls ages ten to fourteen, and the organization held dances at the settlement.

time book, or anything else. She said "come down in the afternoon if you are off" – but I shall tell her I can't come down very early – only just in time for dinner. I haven't yet bought [Gross crossed out "my"] our Victrola and I plan to do that tomorrow – need one or 2 other things.

The debate by Mrs. Blatch versus an anti[†] – is tomorrow afternoon – at the City Club.

Had a terrific day. Friday nearly always is.

Your letter sounded as if you were tired and pensive. Were you? Must glance through Idylls of the Gass to refresh my mind. Glad you enjoyed it.

Sorry I committed the unpardonable sin about the spelling of your sister's name. She must never know! Promise me.

Good night dear – until tomorrow. Call me up at the office and let me know what time you will meet me, because I need to know. Will tell you why when I see you.

And in the meantime – during your spare time figure what you think it will cost to buy the additional things that we need for the house. You know what they are. Don't forget the kitchen. I'll be doing that too. Now I must trim a hat – call on Goldie whose father is not well to-night, and do 5 or 6 other things before bedtime. The days aren't half long enough.

Are you happy, dear? It's the luckiest thing in the world that my work takes almost every scrap of wits I have – or – well I won't say what. At least I won't write it. Your five words came this morning via the Diamond Express.[‡] Hasty but to the point and just in time for me to accept C.I.M. invite gracefully.

Your letter this morning was nice – must get up my party for the MacDowell concert. Glad, yes glad, your brother can come.

Good-night sweetheart –

[shorthand symbol]

Love,

ETHEL

P.S. Don't you wish you knew shorthand.

[†] *"Anti" refers to a person who was opposed to woman suffrage.*

[‡] *The diamond symbol and "Diamond Express" were most likely some letter delivery system, possibly by a messenger, either a friend or a service.*

40.

April 7 [1913]

DEAREST:

I know you will think I'm foolish – writing to you – when I only just saw you to-day – I don't expect to get a letter from you in the morning – but I just wanted to talk to you a little.

Do you think we chose our records too hastily? Wish you could be here to hear them with me – the first time they play. Guess I'm sentimental again – and you'll say so.

Had a most exciting afternoon when I got back. Mr. M* – called up – wanted me to come see him for a few minutes on a matter "which concerned me."

Well it's a long story – but it came out all right. I'll tell you about it when I see you. But I was at my wit's end to know what to do there for a while.

Saw Mrs. M. this evening. A little more excitement.

And so – before anything more happens – I shall go to bed!

Sister spent the afternoon pricing table linens for me.

Sweetheart – we're going to be so happy – do you know it dear? I love you to-night – *so so.*

Good-night dearest. Be good – and write me a letter soon – Tomorrow night will seem all wrong without you.
Love from
Your own
ETHEL

"Mr. M." probably refers to Mr. Clarence Mackay, husband of Gross's previous employer, Katherine Mackay (Mrs. M).

41.

[April 8, 1913]
Monday night

DEAREST:

I really intended writing this last night but I was too sleepy so here I am at noon. Woke up this morning with a miserable cold, which Miss Forsythe* says I must have caught Sunday afternoon – I walked up to 42nd St. and back trying to lose it but it still hangs on.

Written on Christodora House letterhead.

Miss Winifred Forsythe worked at Christodora's Northover Camp from 1913 to 1937.

You know I've been thinking about that last record and the more I think the more I fear it won't do at your house! It may be religious – I'm not sure – if it is we'll take it back. Now don't get peeved Ethel dear because I didn't do it on purpose.

About Thursday – I've got tickets for "Geisha" – would it be alright if I didn't meet you till a quarter to six? I think that I will go up to the opening ball game of the Giants in the afternoon.

Your letter was perched conspicuously at the breakfast table this morning – you have no idea how it cheered me up.

I'd love to go [to] the suffrage meeting *if you will let me buy the tickets.*

Am anxious to hear about your affair with Mr. Mackay – it must have been exciting – *but I don't like the outfit.*

The job at the A.I.C.P. is still up in the air – there is no opening there at the present but there is every indication that there will be one very shortly.

Listen – I left a nail kit in your bath room Sunday if you haven't already found it – keep it till Thursday.

Ethel, I am never – never going to stay so far into the morning at your house again. Why don't you send me home?

But I love to be with you and long for the time when we can always be together. The electrician is waiting for me so good bye – my darling.

Your
HARRY

42.

[April 10, 1913]
Thursday 5:30

DEAREST ETHEL:

I'm in no mood to write letters – got a rotten case of tonsillitis and feel like the devil generally but a good night's sleep will put me in good shape I think – why did you ever learn to kiss me dear? I couldn't have possibly caught it from anyone else. I imagine you are saying the same thing about me.

Have been up to the Intercollegial Bureau – I know Miss Wyndblau who has charge of the social work there, very well. She wanted to pack me off to Boston and Philadelphia but for several reasons "I couldn't possibly leave N.Y." She would see what she could do – she worked for my sister at the School of Phil.* And I know will help me as much as possible.

I wish [I] might have come up tonight (Wed.) but I must take it easy – what did your sister have to say about the Victrola? – does she know that we are buying it together?

Did you ever read "The Promised Land" by Mary Antin – I started it today.

Ethel dear – I feel dizzy – wish you were with me now – because Oh I love you.

Good bye till tomorrow.

HARRY

*Adah Hopkins worked at the New York School of Philanthropy in 1912.

43.

[postmarked April 11, 1913]
Friday night

MY DEAREST:

It was so hard not to call you up early early this morning to find out if you reached home all right last night and if your cold was any worse. I was so worried about you. I felt so fine I wanted to be sure you did. Slept like a top all night and was ready to 'conquer worlds' this morning!

Last night with you – was so wonderful – dear. Each time you are with me – Harry – you grow dearer and dearer – So perhaps it's just as well we are going to have five months. Perhaps by that time I shall appreciate what a wonderful boy it is I'm going to have for a life companion.

Hanna came. She's gone now so I will stop and ask her to mail this.

Can't get an appointment with the dentist's tomorrow. If you get a chance to call me tomorrow before I call you – will you do it. I may not be able to.

Good-night dearest –

ETHEL

44.

Written on
Christodora House
letterhead.

DEAREST:

It must have done me good to be with you yesterday dear for I feel fine today even though I did have an abbreviated sleep last night. (Right here is where you came in on the telephone – your voice sounded better so I guess that you didn't catch anything from me – I was just going to call you up) – I'm awfully proud of our "baby" and don't think that is an impractical investment at all. We will get no end of enjoyment out of it.

This morning "Doc" and I waxed the "gym" floor – real work – got off from the office long enough this p.m. to go up to the A.I.C.P. – will tell you all about that Saturday. There is a play and a dance here tonight so I will no doubt be up till the wee hours – I will think of you sleeping in your little bed – covered with my sweater.

I have to laugh at your sister seeing us last night. Should we worry? And you know dear I like your sister immensely – wish it were reciprocal – and Kohn is alright and we are going to have some very good times together – that is providing they will accept me into the *fold*. I'm going to say something to your sister before long – see what she really thinks – and your brother will be home before long so the excitement will soon be over.

Now dear we mustn't have any more colds unless we invent a *sanitary* kiss.

I am glad we didn't go to the show last night – for I really think Ben and Fannie enjoyed it more than we would have. – and you were so nice and natural – my girl and I love you more for being with you – sweetheart.

Your

HARRY

45.

[date uncertain]
Monday night

MY SWEETHEART:

I've got your red carnations right near me where I can look at them every minute and I love each one of them. But you were a naughty boy to get them – and *when* did you do it? Do you know, dear, that I love red carnations – *particularly*? They're so bright and sweet and fragrant. Please consider yourself kissed – the best way I know how – Harry, you're such a dear sweet boy – and I love you so.

But I have a lot of things to tell you – *news.* Your friend, Mrs. M. – sent *us* 2 tickets – second row orchestra – for "Within the Law" for *tomorrow night.* I tried to get you on the telephone to see what you thought I should do about it – whether you would think it worth while to come in from camp for – or not – but you had already left for your train and then I suddenly thought that I would try to exchange them for some night next week. So to-night I rode down to the Tyson office on 59th Street where they were bought and tomorrow at one I shall know whether or not they have been able to resell them – because they never take anything back or refund the money. If they won't do it – I shall take them back to the theater at noon and exchange them for seats farther back – for next week. Perhaps I'll call you up on the telephone if I can't exchange them – to see if there's any chance of your coming in for it tomorrow night. If you have any suggestion different from this – to make – call me up at the office before 12 – 9880 Madison. I saw "Within the Law" but I don't mind seeing it again and I know you would enjoy it more than anything. Or would you rather I exchange them for tickets for the "Beggar Student" or the "Geisha" or anything else. I can do that too – I think – but I'd like to see "Within the Law" again – so if you would – we'll do that. Write and tell me what you think.

It was *so* nice to see you to-day – and the more I think about the A.I.C.P.'s offer – the more I think it is wise to accept it. All these thing that are happening make our

plans more real and more possible – and therefore it makes me sing when I think of it –! Everything that we have planned is possible – dear – and I love you so to-night. Now do get a good rest. I send you a very special lot of love and a very tender kiss. Good-night –
ETHEL
P.S. Miss King is coming to the concert on Thursday.
PS. #2 Don't work too hard and write to me.
PS. #3 I began to get lonesome at 4 o'clock to-day and to-night it seems as if you'd been gone a week!
This is a very long letter.
E.

46.

[April 14, 1913]
Monday night
Northover Camp

MY DARLING:

Ethel – why didn't you come along with me – I have the big club house all to myself and a big roaring grate fire is crackling in front of me – and I'm all alone dear and kind of lonesome – and listen – there are two perfectly good beds in my room – come out tomorrow. I want to be with you all the time my girl – last visit was a long session but you were so big and fine – I'm making up the sleep tonight – 9 o'clock for me.

I called up Miss Ingram and I am to look her up as soon as I get back from camp. Am glad that is settled although something might come up even yet. If you want my brother to go after Miss King – write him at 200 E. 27th or let me know about it.

It is frightfully muddy out here and I may not be able to work in the garden but I am going to stay out for a rest anyway.

Rats – the youngsters have all come in and are lounging on the piano and they drive all the nice things out of my mind for "In the Blue Ridge Mts. Of Virginia" – "Watching and Waiting" etc. Oo – she plays like h___. It's wicked. I must bounce them.

My eyes won't stay open dear and I must close even though I would like to talk on to you all night. I guess it is lucky you aren't here tonight for I never would make up that sleep – you are more perfect than ever to me dear – and tonight I am thinking about you all the time – sweetheart –

I've got to take this down to William so that it will be mailed the first thing in the morning – and I'm tired anyway – Ethel – good night – with a kiss for I love you dear.

HARRY

47.

[April 15, 1913]

DEAREST:

Your dear sweet letter came to-night – and it was so good to get! I'm so glad you had a real rest last night for you needed it. And I think you need a few nights more like it – for you mustn't get run down and all tired out – But then – I'm responsible when you do – but I'm really going to help you not to – from now on.

I wonder if you received my letter? I hope you did – for there are two things in it I want you to know. The carnations look as fresh and pretty to-night as ever. We have been having them on the table.

I have reserved two seats for The Beggar Student for next Thursday night – (next week). All right? Have you seen the Mikado?

Must show you the note Mrs. M sent me. Had another letter from my kid bro. – but nothing special in it. Might write to him to-night. Guess I'll go to the concert tomorrow night.

I don't believe it will be necessary for your bro. to call for Miss King. I've sent her a ticket. She won't expect it – and besides – he doesn't know her. If I have time I'll find out how she feels about it tomorrow and if she really would like it better etc. – I'll let you know.

I wonder if you're home to-night? The big grate fire in the club house in B.B.* sounded very attractive – until

* *"B.B." refers to Bound Brook, New Jersey, the location of Northover Camp run by Christodora House.*

the girls came in and banged on the piano. Met Marion Reich on the subway last night. Said she was going to camp for a week to rest up.

Good night dear – I think I won't do any of the things I planned to do to-night – just go to bed.

Wonder if you'll start your work tomorrow. I'll think about you, sweetheart – Hope no one else will get hold of my letter to you yesterday and open it by any chance. Not that anyone is apt to – only – I hope you've rec'd it. Good-night,

ETHEL

48.

[April 18, 1913]
Friday morning 9:30

MY DEAREST:

Please go to bed early to-night. Can't you just say you're all in and go to bed right after dinner? Or just get the night off and go to your brother's and get to bed there – early. I'm worried about you, sweetheart.

ETHEL

49.

In bed
April 18, 1913

MY DEAREST:

Your voice sounded so tired to-night – and so sort of sad. Whatever happened to you last night – dear? Wish you had told me because I am wondering all sorts of things.

Don't be worried about me, dear. There's not anything wrong with me anywhere – except the reason I have had that ache in my head is because of my cold. The doctor said that it was sort of catarrh and he said that that space on my forehead that ached was a little inflamed and needed a little treatment, that's all. I don't even need to be in bed. But I am getting rested at the same time. I'll tell you what that [undecipherable] did to me when you come tomorrow. We expect him almost any moment.

And dearest – if you stay away like you said you would over the phone – I just won't get well – I'll get very very sick – so you'd had better come up! Wish you would get caught up with sleep, somehow – somewhere Harry boy – I wonder what happened to you last night. It's all my fault whatever it was. Wish I had [undecipherable] you [undecipherable] here. Now do take care of yourself sweetheart. I love you and am worried about you. I shall look for you in the morning.

Good night from your,

ETHEL

Please tell Miss MacColl I'm laid up and can't be down tomorrow night. I told her I would call so be sure to tell her. E.

50.

[April 18, 1913]
Friday night

MY DARLING:

Oh Ethel girl – I'm so sorry that you're sick, dear – and it's all my fault for staying so long last night – it was wicked and I feel terribly guilty. I *am* so worried about you Ethel but if I don't do better than I did last night – I will be no better than your sister with her quinine. But you were so wonderful last night – and I love you more than all the world – like I ought to – sweetheart. So please get well dear – I won't bother you anymore and keep you back – that is I won't see you any oftener than I *have* to. Dear – I am thinking about you all the time – and will tonight and tomorrow – hope I can see you Sat. but something might come up – oh no it won't, for I *must* see you *Sat.* – Ethel. You know you look so pretty in bed – please don't get mad at me –

I am wondering what the doctor said to you or is saying to you about now.

Written on Christodora House letterhead.

Ethel it is getting late and I must stop – make up for last night – *4:10* – oo!
Good night dear – till Sat. morning.
With a kiss for the girl I love
Your Own
HARRY

51.

[postmarked April 21, 1913]
Monday

DEAREST ETHEL:

I'm all alone in the office and the big house is so empty – residents have gone to camp and all the familiar faces have entered the matzos marathon. Lew has been down a good share of the evening – we have had a good visit. He had a funny time with Miss K – I will tell you all about it later – I wanted to hear your voice, dear so telephoned here – strange that you were writing to me at the same time –

I'm awfully glad that you are well and strong again Ethel – I won't be bad anymore darling and keep you up so late. I fear I haven't made up all that night yet but am going to get a good start tonight. I have got to [take] Casey down to court in the morning – he is charged with disorderly conduct – a ridiculous affair, and I know he will get off. He was crying like a baby when I saw him this afternoon.

The boys are coming in from the feast – 10:05 – and I am going to bed. They can celebrate the holiday in the park.

You must stop working so late – dear – I see that we have got to get married so I can take care of you.

You were so dear last night girl – the time went too fast. I loved when you were sick dear even though you were bad when I first came up.

My eyes are getting heavy – dear – good by my love – sweetheart –
Your Own
HARRY

52.

[postmarked April 21, 1913]
Monday night

Good-night sweetheart. I'm sleepy too. Hope you'll get to bed very very early. And listen dear – don't try to get off for Wednesday at all. I can fix it about the tickets so that we can use them on Thursday. And this is where your telephone call came. It was awfully hard to hear you.

Whatever did Miss King do to your brother! I must go and see her. I want your bro. to come up soon – but not next Sunday.

Good-night dear. I get so I want to hear your voice of-tener and oftener. It was nice to have you call me up – and remember to *keep Thursday* for the Mikado.
All – my – love – ETHEL

53.

[postmarked April 22, 1913]
Tuesday night

MY DARLING:

I wasn't going to do a thing tonight but go to bed but I feel like writing a long letter to you dear – because this noon wasn't very nice and I wanted it to be. Ethel girl – I know just how you feel when you are "moody" – but dear you wouldn't be that way if it wasn't for me. I guess I never did do the little things in life that make people happy but Ethel I want to – and I did feel so badly today because I hurt you when I was really bubbling over with love for you dear and wanted to take you in my arms and smother your pretty little face with kisses. Will you forgive me – sweetheart – for being bad today? I know you weren't happy – I wish we were married now – tonight – so that we wouldn't have to write these things but you could sit on my lap in the big chair (we're going to have a big chair aren't we?) and talk everything out. I've thought about you a long, long time today Ethel – everything is perfect

Written on Christodora House letterhead.

and ideal but one thing – that is the waiting – you will insist on breaking into my letters with telephone calls – but I feel better now dear, you are so sweet. You will show me your brother's letter won't you? I want to know just how he feels because you know I will see him before long anyway and we will have it all out then – I don't expect him to be wildly hilarious or kill the fatted calf or even say he is *glad* – for I know he isn't and there is every reason why he shouldn't be – but you know it won't do him any good not to be nice and he could make it awfully uncomfortable – but I am sure he will be nice about it so why worry? I know too that he is interested in you so vitally and loves you so dearly that no matter what he says – I know it will be because he is interested in your future happiness so consequently won't be peeved at any attitude he might take. And your other brother – have you written him yet? Ethel dear – I love you so that I don't see how they can object. Every interest I have, is centered on you – everything that I do is done for you dear and we will be happy no matter if the whole world objects – and tonight I am lonesome for you and wish you were here – close – sweetheart.

I won't say anymore little things that will make you "moody" Ethel – dear – you always know I love you more than anything else – don't you? And that when your feelings are hurt – that it hurts me too for I am a part of you if such a thing is possible – good night Ethel dear – I love you tonight more than ever.

HARRY

54.

[April 22, 1913]
Tuesday night

DEAREST BOY:

Your headache dates straight back to me – and I'm so sorry, dear. I do hope you'll get a good night's rest and feel just fine in the morning.

It is now 11 P.M. – So this won't be a long good-night. Goldie took it upon herself to give me a long lecture on ways and means to-night and I'm trying to get my breath back. Don't worry about my bro. letter. It's a very dear letter and I could not expect him to say anything different from what he did say. I have much to talk to you about, dear. – when I see you.

Good night –

Sweetheart –

I'm sorry I was so sort of moody this noon – just when you didn't feel well. Where can we go on Sunday to just talk things over? Wish I could write more – good-night and a very special lot of love from

ETHEL

55.

[April 23, 1913]
Wednesday, after dinner

MY DEAREST:

I called you up today because all the long day – while I was taking dictation – giving out work – and ordering people around generally – and very very busy – I was wondering how you were and if you stayed away from work or not – and so – before I started for home – I found out and that's how you happened to get a call at 5:30.

And speaking of telephone calls – I just had one – and whom d'ya suppose it was from? Very hard to guess.

Sweetheart – your letter this morning was such a wonderful letter and oh, it made me so happy to get. You said in it just the things I longed to hear you say – dearest – and I just love every word of it. Is it bad to want you to say those things to me? For then I was – oh very very bad yesterday – for I wanted it *so* much. That's what made me so moody I guess. You're so wonderful to me – Harry boy – that I ought never to have any doubts – and I suppose I ought not to have been hurt at what you said – but oh, dear – I love you so – and I care so much when I don't see you – that I just couldn't bear to have you say it – just then.

Tomorrow night at this time I shall be with you – on the way to the theatre. Then I shall tell you much that

I'm not going to try to write. Another letter came from Ben to-night – to my sister and me this time. He'd be all ready to say "God bless you my children" if it weren't for the money – that troubles him. He'll probably be home in 2 or 3 weeks – and I'll do whatever you want about showing you his letters.

Good-night – my sweetheart – I love you so to-night – and wish you were right here so I could tell you so and make sure you understand everything. And you're tired out – Harry – and I want to take care of you and I ought to.

With a very warm good-night kiss – I am
Your
ETHEL

56.

[April 25, 1913]
Friday night

MY DEAREST:

There is such a racket that I know I can never write the kind of letter I want to tonight dear –

Have talked to you twice over the phone since I started this. And your brother is coming in the morning! You must be that excited!

More telephone – one of the fellows who lives with Lew just called up saying he had been taken to Bellevue tonight – indo-poisoning, whatever that may be – so I have more to worry about. I am afraid he is pretty sick and will go see him the first thing in the morning.

Of all the times that I have wanted to be with you – I never wanted you so much as this minute – I feel like h* in more ways than one. I guess last night's dissipation, together with thinking about the Canadian job and the excitement of your brother's appearance on the scene and now to hear that my brother is laid up in the hospital is too much for my young life to digest all at once.

Ethel girl – I simply can't write a decent letter tonight.

*"h" is shorthand for "hell", which neither Hopkins nor Gross would spell out until after they were married.

Sweetheart – you don't know how much I need you – I'm here all alone now – 11 p.m. – thinking about you and *us* – you won't let anyone come between will you dear? I don't know why I say that because I know you won't but I am tired tonight. Will call you up in the morning after I've seen my brother?

You had better meet Ben.

Good night – little girl – this is a bad letter – please please forgive me – my darling – *all my love.*

Your

HARRY

57.

[April 25, 1913]
Friday night

Good-night Sweetheart: I'm writing to you because I think you sounded sort of worried and tired over the telephone to-night.

I love you dear – oh so much to-night – nothing can keep us apart – You're so funny about Canada – and the other night I felt just as you do about wanting to think about it – and be sure – before we turn it down.

Good night – dearest. I'm trying to clear things up so as to make room for my bro. I've spread out so while he was away.

When I think of the hour you must have reached home last night – I feel very wicked. But dearest – it was so good to be with you and I wouldn't have one minute of it cut short when I think of that.

Be good now – dear – I shall think of you a lot until Sunday morning. And dearest – do please lock yourself in your room Saturday afternoon and take a *good rest.* I'd feel so much better if I thought you were doing that. Please do – sweetheart.

Much much love from

Your own

ETHEL

P.S. Remember 10:30 Sun. morning.

58.

**Gross's office was the
WPU at 13 West
42nd Street.*

[†]*Gross was referring to
a suffrage parade.*

DEAREST BOY:

Tomorrow night at this time I shall be with you. An-other terrific day at the office* to-day – am going to be good and go to bed early to-night. Hope you are – too.

Sweetheart – I'm afraid I was an awful bore last night. Whatever made me so weary – I don't know. You're so dear – though –whether I'm tired or not – I like to have you near me either way – after the parade[†] I promise not to be tired any more. And dearest – you mustn't work too hard either. Had a talk with Ben after you left last night. Quite lengthy – but to no account. Perhaps though we understand each other better – I don't know.

I am looking forward to tomorrow night. I hope I won't be too late getting down. It's so hard to leave the office before 6 o'clock these days.

Good-night dear. I've thought about you and – us – such a lot to-day – and the more I think about it – the better it seems – and the fact that others – can't see it as we do – only makes me surer – I feel very sure to-night that we are going to be oh, so happy – and that our life as we plan it is going to be wonderfully fine – Isn't it dear – I send you much love to-night and a good-night kiss which I should like to deliver in person instead of the postman – just now –

ETHEL

How is your brother, I wonder?

59.

**One of Hopkins's
responsibilities for the
AICP was to act as a
"friendly visitor,"
going directly to the
homes of impoverished
immigrant families to
ascertain their needs.*

I am going to steal bits between times to write you, Ethel, dear – have called up twice today but the line was busy both times so I gave it up – worked hard today – made twenty visits among the Italians.*

Just saw Miss C.I. – she wanted to know if you were coming to dinner tomorrow – we seem to still be on her list for she threw out a few lovely remarks about you. Incidentally, hoped that we would pack up and go to Canada.

There is a big parade poster staring me in the face! An organizer is coming down tomorrow with pledges. I fear that the harvest will not be very abundant.

Went to see my brother this morning but he had picked up his bed and walked – he is laid up at home.

There are 57 varieties of people hovering around this desk and I simply can't write the things that are on my mind. Was coming home on the car tonight and the conductor told me that I couldn't smoke in the car. I told him I wasn't smoking. He says "Well you have a pipe in your mouth" and I says – "Yes, I have feet in my shoes but I'm not walking." That is neither original or funny –

Frank S. has been down tonight – as serious as ever.

You know, little girl, when I work every night and you work so hard all day – we are [in] better shape to go to bed than anything else when we get together on those few rare occasions. I have been miserable company for weeks.

Is Ben militant? I feel terribly worried about him for he can make it decidedly uncomfortable for himself as well as the rest of us. But I know he cares for you, Ethel, and don't blame him at all for being more or less peeved at your running off with a poor devil like me. But he will have to get over it dear.

Can you come down early tomorrow dear – I'm going back with you.

Good night Ethel – sweetheart – with a kiss from
Your
HARRY

60.

[May 1, 1913]
Thursday night

HELLO DEAREST:

Hope you reached home all right last night. Every minute with you was so good. Hope you're not too tired to-day.

Had a long letter from big bro.* this A.M. He congratulates me – among other things – Poor thing has troubles of his own just now. Will tell you about it. It was lonesome today without a telephone call, but both our wires were going just all day long. Will sort of expect to hear from you tomorrow – sometime.

Am not going to try to go to Metropolitan House meeting tomorrow night. Good-night – sweetheart. Am writing this standing up – have to sort out all winter clothes and pack them in a trunk to-night. So I must get to work. I love you dear – to-night – more than ever – Several very nice kisses from
Your own –
ETHEL

61.

[May 6, 1913]
Tuesday eve.

DEAREST:

The shock was so great for poor Miss MacColl that she has taken to her bed today – thoroughly discouraged and disheartened in her first attempt to bind us forever in that spiritual bond of hers. She evidently wasn't informed that you had raised *horns* instead of *wings*.

Ethel girl – I am awfully glad that you told her just what you thought for now we are working for one definite end. It is very evident that you never would have been happy in Canada and that is all that matters.

I love you so dearly tonight Ethel – you are the most wonderful girl that ever lived and I do appreciate you dear. Your voice sounded very nice over the telephone a few minutes ago – sweetheart and I wanted to be with you. Did you buy a new suit?

This has been a racking long day, whatever that means, and I came home early to make up some two hours of lost repose. I feel very good at this minute, dear, thanks to your telephone.

About tomorrow – it may be frightfully hot which would make it more or less close in a Bowery opera house – why suffocate when there is so much fresh air!

Oh by the way I have got to go to Sea Breeze tomorrow afternoon which may mean that I will not be in till rather late but I will phone you about that.

Good night dearest – you are my ideal, sweetheart and oh – I love you Ethel.

All my love

Your

HARRY

62.

[May 6, 1913]
Tuesday

MY DEAREST:

I'm worried about you and the way you are working – and about how tired you are. Do please take a rest next week – make arrangements to just lay off both jobs and go off somewhere. And sweetheart – if you want to go to bed right after dinner tomorrow night – just tell me over the telephone tomorrow – and I will understand.

I've been thinking about you the whole day and it worries be because I think I may have helped you get away earlier the nights you have been with me – and sweetheart – I'm sorry.

And last night when you were so tired I made you talk and say things you didn't want to say. I'm bad – dearest – Please forgive me. And tell me that you *are* going away next week – you could go to that place you know about and Miss K. knows about – you know – for social workers. I tried to get you on the telephone to-night – but I couldn't. They said you were not in. I wanted to know how you were.

I love you dear – and I don't want you to get all tired out.

Written on Equal Franchise Society letterhead.

I shall expect to hear from you tomorrow.
Much love – from
Your
ETHEL
P.S. I am enclosing also herewith a kiss.

63.

[postmarked May 8, 1913]
Thurs. May 7

Written on
Christodora House
letterhead.

DEAREST:

This has been a long day – and I have tramped all over this city.

Last night was too short Ethel – girl – don't you honestly think that we were about a half hour too good? And Sunday is ages off.

Miss C.I. wanted to know if the Canada affair was all off. She said that she didn't know you took that attitude toward *religion*! Poor dear – had a *very* – *very* long face and evidently fears that the wrath of God is upon us. She also wanted to know the attitude of your family toward "us" etc. –

I stopped in to see Miss Mills at the Sea and Land today – she is funny as ever.

I don't know what is the matter with me Ethel but I am getting so I need a couple of nights sleep every week too – I'm going to make this all up darling when we get married – that is if we ever get the dishes washed – and the bread set – and the fireless cooker cooking – and the baby sent to bed (where is that baby going to sleep anyway Ethel – he probably will never sleep at night though) – should I worry?

Good night dear – I will call you up in the morning. Sleep is my middle name tonight.
Your
HARRY

64.

[May 1913]
Thursday

ETHEL DEAR:

Oh but my legs are tired tonight – it has been walk – walk all day and they expect me to be nice down here tonight! – Had two very funny experiences today which makes up for it all however.

Lewis was down tonight – a little too worse for wear – he evidently made a "catch" at the hospital for he is taking one of the nurses to "Arizona" tomorrow night. It's a shame the way he falls for a nurse's uniform.

Listen dear – I talked to Mr. Washburn tonight about a place to spend Sunday. He says he goes over to the palisades nearly every Sunday with his wife to spend the day – across 125th St. ferry and on the car up into the woods – real wild woods and loads of flowers. Shall we go over Sunday morning?

Haven't seen Miss Carsten yet – but will in a few minutes. I don't think she can take us to Canada.

I got in at 2 *this morning* and nearly went to sleep at the lecture this morning at the A. I. C. P. This house is going to be closed early tonight.

But I don't care – you were so dear last night Ethel and everything seemed so sure and does now. And wasn't the water nice? When are we going up the river together? (not Sing Sing)

Miss Carsten is coming down stairs and I must close – sweetheart – I hope you sleep a long, long, time tonight in your little white bed, which I feel isn't big enough for *two*.

I had a sad accident today which won't do to write.

And Ethel – I love you dear more than I ever can tell – good night – my darling.

HARRY

Written on Christodora House letterhead.

65.

MY DEAREST:

It was *so* good to see you at noon to-day and to be with you. I love you dear – more and more each day – Your letter this morning was especially dear – and I read it and read it.

Good-night sweetheart – call me up in the morning.
I got my raise.
Much love from your
ETHEL

66.

Written on Christodora House letterhead.

Wasn't it good to be together today dearest – just a little while? It made the work a lot easier this afternoon. But you looked awfully tired sweetheart – and I don't like it – perhaps we had better go way off – alone to-morrow afternoon so that you can rest. You know dear – we mustn't get sick – either of us for it will simply mean waiting longer and that will be *very* hard. Sept. is far enough away.*

*Gross and Hopkins had originally planned to marry in September.

I think about you all the time dear – you are perfectly ideal and I am so proud that you could care for me Ethel. We simply can't help being wonderfully happy – if I do my part and don't get peeved or crabbed too often – I guess you know already that I'm real nice only very seldom.

Bedlam is turned loose in here tonight – this is the last place on earth to write a letter to you –

I haven't written a letter home in over a month and certainly haven't received any – I suppose they think I am rapidly drifting away from the fold. But you know how much time I have.

And Sunday in the country! All day *together*!

Good night Ethel girl I love you – oh so much tonight.

Your

HARRY

67.

[postmarked May 12, 1913]
Monday
En Route to Albany 10:15 A.M.

DEAREST BOY:

It was such a nice surprise this morning on this train – to open my bag to find out by accident – as I was putting other papers into my bag last night – your pictures got folded in with them – so that when I opened up my list for the reporters in order to revise it here on the train – there was you inside the papers! So I revised my lists first – then tore off the rest of the paper – so that I could write this note to you – for you see – if it wasn't for these lists – and your picture – I don't suppose I ever would have thought of it – though I might.

Everybody I talked to on Saturday who thought they couldn't possibly get away – but would try – is on this train this morning. They simply could not resist coming. I have been sitting next to Mrs. Florence Kelley* until just a little while ago when Mrs. B.† came through to talk to her. That's another reason why I couldn't have written this note – if I had stayed sitting there. Mrs. Higgenson – the lady who is always worrying about my health and happiness – dear old soul – is here with us also – and she asked me if I went up to the country yesterday as I told her I should. I said yes – I did – and then I told her what a pretty place Alpine was. When she asked me – "I suppose a whole party of you went up – boys & girls – I said "yes" just as if it wasn't a lie – and then I added – for no reason at all – just because I'm wicked down at the core – somewhere – "but there were more girls than boys" and then I went on glibly – "Boys

*Florence Kelley was a prominent social reformer associated with Jane Addams and Hull House.

†"Mrs. B" is Harriot Stanton Blatch.

are so nice to have along because they can build a fire and then they have such good ideas" – and then I told her how one boy thought of putting the grape juice bottles in a cool brook to cool. Of course that was another Sunday – to be sure – but I was so keen to entertain the dear lady with as much of a description as possible – that I used *all* the material I had. Besides this is such a long ride! And she enjoyed it – Harry – She said – no wonder I had red cheeks to-day (I was probably blushing or warm after my efforts – but here – again – I lie – it isn't such an effort as that for me to manufacture these fabrications. –) And she went on to say how much more fit I should be for work this week etc. etc. – until I almost believed it! You see how I can lie – Harry – and I feel much better now that I have told you.

I suppose that you are dodging tenements this morning. Wish you were here. Just when I thought I had this seat to myself – a man sat down next to me with a "Between the Acts" cigarette lighted. Wonder if he thinks this is a smoker. Of all weeds to smoke – B.T.A. is the limit. I hope you don't like them because really – Harry – they're awful. If they only didn't smell so.

The scenery is really very lovely all along here – with the Hudson on one side – with its Palisades – and springs & brooks & falls & woodsy spots on the other side. Also swamps – but even they look picturesque at the rate this train is going – and you can judge that from this writing.

I know everything that's in the 'Times' this morning. Read it from cover to cover. I haven't read it so thoroughly for months and now I have decided to take another paper. It certainly is the limit without publishing 2 column articles about what Mrs. Arthur M. Dodge[‡] thinks about what women ought to wear who believe in suffrage. She used to talk about what frumps we all were. She also said all suffragists were flat chested – once. Now – she turned out to see the parade[§] and as she couldn't evidently – go on saying that because too many other people were watching it the same day – as well as the grandstand – she uses the other argument – We must have looked awfully nice. "She appeared garbed in a manner which would have aroused resentment among any set of ladies & gentlemen." Also –

[‡]*Mrs. Arthur M. Dodge was then the president of the National Association Opposed to Woman Suffrage.*

[§]*The parade Gross referred to was a large suffrage parade. Approximately 10,000 participants marched down Fifth Avenue on May 4, 1913 including members of the Equal Franchise Society and the Woman's Political Union.*

"The costumes worn by women in the parade . . .
showed that they relied on their sex in their appeal" . . .
I didn't think we looked as nice as that, – but of course
I couldn't be in the parade and see it too.

Mrs. B. just leaned over to talk to me. Wonder what
she thought I was writing. I must go back to Mrs. Kelley.
Only another half hour left.

Good-bye – when are we going to take a long train
trip together? Of course, I've spent most of my time
with you this trip – but that doesn't count. I'd make
you pull the windows up & pull it down again – just to
see if you could do it – and I'd make you put my coat
on the shelf & take it down again just to show everyone on the train that you were looking after me like a
lady across from me is doing with a long-suffering
male. He isn't as tall as you are – though—but he's
long-suffering. But I must stop this nonsense – and
stop thinking about *males* at once. That is not what my
expenses are being paid for. Good-bye – dear – see
you tomorrow?

ETHEL

68.

[postmarked May 14, 1913]
Wed. – 6 P.M.

MY DARLING:

I am alone in my room talking to you Ethel and away
from all the riff-raff which usually goes with my letters.
Miss C.I. is as distant as the North Pole – should I
worry? You know this is the first time I ever really felt
good about losing a job – I have learned to like the boys
very, very much and hate to think of giving them up altogether but as far as the residential sections of this
plant – I feel sure that this spiritual food would be more
palatable with me far away. I have fully decided that if
this house in on the side of the Lord, I am going to
straightway apply below. But still they are dear, innocent
people and will never hurt anybody especially themselves intentionally.

*Written on
Christodora House
letterhead.*

And Ethel dearest I wish we were married now – tonight – wouldn't it be great to be together every time we got home from work – But we *will* be in Sept. and there is lots to be done between now and then so why be *disturbed?* I won't be any more dear for I know you didn't like it. – But darling I will be ideally happy with you and we – together – will live out our own natural life to the limit. The whole thing is perfectly wonderful – sweetheart and I know we will make a go of it.

Are you working too hard Ethel? – *Please* don't. I am going way down on Cherry St. tonight to make a visit – will try to get back alive.

You were darling last night Ethel and I, such a pill to be *disturbed.*

I must get away now Ethel – I love you a lot tonight dear and wish we were *close* – very close. All my love is for you – Ethel

Good Night

Your

HARRY

69.

[May 14, 1913]
Wednesday

MY SWEETHEART:

It was so good to hear your voice – I've been lonely for it all day – especially as I knew I wasn't going to see you to-night. I love you – dear – good night –

And a very tender kiss from

Your own

ETHEL

70.

[May 19, 1913]
Monday

SWEETHEART:

Just a line for I have a lot to do tonight. Say – Ethel, what in heaven's name did I catch from you last night – one side of my face has taken on the proportions of the full moon and I've looked like hell all day – it is receding now and I trust will presentable tomorrow.

Did Miss Arms ask you to secure a suffrage speaker for you? Please get a good looking one – Mrs. Laidlaw?*

Dearest, You know I don't like to miss a day seeing you anymore! – you are perfect but I mustn't go on – only why that awful sigh last night? – it bothers me.

Will I see you tomorrow! I will call up in the morning.

Good night Ethel – my girl – a kiss from

Your

HARRY

P.S. *I ate too much desert for dinner.* I know very well where my stomach is located now. Good bye.

Written on Christodora House letterhead.

*Mrs. Laidlaw was then the first vice chairman of the New York State Woman Suffrage Party.

71.

[May 19, 1913]
Monday night

MY DEAREST:

I hope you are getting to bed early early to-night. My hair has been scoured and rubbed and brushed – and now I'm going to turn in.

Sweetheart – I wish your family at home knew about us. I find myself wishing that every once in so often. Somehow – sometimes – it doesn't seem right to go ahead and make plans when they don't. But it's true I only think about it sometimes.

There is a sale of linens at Alturaus's I think I'll investigate tomorrow.

And Harry – you must plan a time when your brother can and will come up here. Because I really would like to get acquainted. And what evening this week or next are we going down to Knights? Or don't you want to?

Hope you didn't have to trot around too much to-day. Thought about you lots – sweetheart – and if I hadn't had so much to do every minute – I believe you would have had a letter from me every hour – instead – I sent a wireless about every few minutes – did you get it?

I love you dear – and I don't feel half good enough for you.

Good-night – sweetheart –

All my love –

ETHEL

72.

[May 21, 1913]
Wednesday

Written on
Christodora House
letterhead.

SWEETHEART:

Am too tired to work tonight so it is early to bed for me. Funny about getting locked out!

Ethel darling I feel terribly blue about this last trouble – sorry for Ben and the rest – that's all. But I suppose we shouldn't expect to have everything come our way and I know it will blow over after we are married.

You are so close and so much a part of me, dear, that I simply can't comprehend the attitude even though they may object – but Ethel please don't stir up any unnecessary trouble for it will simply put the peace pipe that much farther off.

I can't talk to you long tonight dear because I want to straighten up the bank acc't and perhaps write a letter home – I may break it to them gently.

I will call up in the morning. Good night dear.

Your

HARRY

73.

[postmarked May 21, 1913]
at the office, Wednesday

DEAREST SWEETHEART:

I'm so sorry you had such a time last night. That was too terrible!

I hope you'll get to bed *early* to-night and not work too late.

When you called up – the office was full of people and I couldn't talk. Tried to get you afterward because I wanted to see you this noon if you weren't too busy. Will call a family conference to-night. Am I to see you tomorrow night?

Good-bye – dear – hope all goes well with you – much much love –

ETHEL

74.

[May 22, 1913]
Wednesday night

GOOD-NIGHT SWEETHEART:

The house is full of boys playing cards with Ben – 5 of them. Just got home after doing a few errands in the neighborhood.

That awful telephone operator switched me on to Miss Haslaw – who insisted on knowing what my name was – asked me until I had to tell her. Did she tell you about it?

You probably won't like my calling you up down there.

Am awful sleepy—Hope you stopped working long ere this and that you are going to get a good night's rest. If you work late to-night you simply must go to bed tomorrow night right after dinner.

I shall wait for your call tomorrow morning.

I've been troubled about you to-day, dear.

But in reality – Harry – I think everyone in this house is ready and waiting to break the ice. No one's comfortable –

As you said last night – it will take time for certain things to wear off – and we have to go through it.

But, oh, I love you dear – and everything is going to come out right – we exaggerate my bro's attitude and he exaggerates ours – let's just take it for granted that all is well – and act accordingly. I know I haven't been– and I've put ideas into your head. Good-night dearest – don't work too hard –

My love to you –

ETHEL

75.

May 26, 1913
Monday night

Written on
Christodora House
letterhead.

DEAREST:

Miss MacColl has asked me to stay in the office tonight as I am back at the old stand – but very, very tired and am going to get off to bed early if possible. Miss Lennon says that she is not going to use her bungalow – will you do the rest? – or have you lost your enthusiasm? and the suffrage meeting was a sad mistake – only the club turned out – I told Miss Ellis that they didn't want to have a good meeting and she got peeved – now this is all the news.

Dearest – we had a wonderful time yesterday didn't we. The sail home was great! And Ethel girl I love you so right now only I'm not worth anything you might give back – and darling I am worried tonight – things are too one sided dear – you have everything and I have nothing not even a good job – I will call you up Tues. morning – no more tonight.

Good night dearest – with all my love

Your

HARRY

76.

June 12, 1913
Tuesday night

MY DEAREST:

It's bed time and I'm all ready to turn in. I've had a girl caller this evening. She's engaged and these engaged girls are such bores!

Hope you're getting to bed early to-night – dear – you looked tired last night.

The whole family is assembled in this room so I can't say all I want to say.

Did brother enjoy last night, I wonder?

Saw Knight to-day. She did.

Good-night sweetheart – I love you dear to-night and wish you weren't so far away! Wonder if you're thinking about me like I am about you to-night?

All my love to you dear –

ETHEL

77.

[postmarked June 23, 1913]
Monday night

SWEETHEART:

I have been thinking about you all day and must write you all about it tonight. You won't mind will you dear even though we have been so very, very close the last two days. And Ethel – this is your *birthday* – you great, big darling – I am going to kiss you twenty-seven (no more) times when I come up tonight. Please be awfully happy today dear – I want you to be – you know I will make up this year very shortly and don't feel terribly bad. But I suppose that you have got to a place now where you have become so used to having birthdays that they don't create more than a little mild excitement with you – but Ethel dear – I do wish you a most happy birthday but next time you may be sure that you will be wished it with a very tender kiss on

Written on Christodora House letterhead.

your sweet little lips the *first thing in the morning*. Birthdays are funny things – and twenty-seven – *oo*! Please stop for four years.

Miss MacColl came back tonight looking very much refreshed and evidently decidedly happy. She is leaving for camp tomorrow – and is to be at the home only one day a week throughout the summer.

I heard from mother today and I am afraid that she is far from well. She doesn't seem to write with the same optimistic confidence and is evidently badly broken down nervously. Rome has gone to Minneapolis and Emery is working in Wisconsin.

You know sweetheart that I seem to know you better after being so close and feel somehow that we were much more a part of each other than ever before. To love you Ethel – and better still to know that you care for me – makes everything that I do, even the little common places, much easier than before. I guess it is because we are working with this very definite goal always in mind that makes us so happy. And Ethel we are going to be married this fall – Good night sweetheart. I love you darling – oh so much tonight.

Your
HARRY

78.

[postmarked June 23, 1913]
Monday night

Good-night
Sweetheart
Much
Love
ETHEL

79.

[postmarked July 3, 1913]
Wednesday night

DEAREST:

I'm worried about you because of the way you must be working these hot hot days. You looked tired last night – I've been thinking about you a lot to-day – I tried to talk to you but you weren't home – you must have worked awfully late.

Good-night – sweetheart – Do let me hear from you tomorrow so that I'll know you're all right. Latest news is they've found something at Far Rock* – desirable in every way – except what I think about it and that doesn't seem to matter. It's ½ of a house – 5 rooms – tomorrow Beni goes out to see it. Don't work too hard and do take care of yourself – all my love to you.
ETHEL

*"Far Rock" is Far Rockaway, a beach town on Long Island where Ethel's sister, Fanny, and brother-in-law, Benjamin Kohn, regularly rented a house for the summer.

80.

[July 14, 1913]
Monday

DEAREST:

Just finished talking to you over the phone and want to tell you darling how much I love you right now. Wish I could come up and cheer you up tonight for I know how much you care for Ben and how hard it must be to have him away.

I know that I have been miserable company the last few days which certainly doesn't tend to make you any happier. You are a big, wonderful girl and I feel terribly small and selfish when I think of all the things you have to go through with, without a word. Ethel, darling, I love you – oh so much – and want you to know that I am always thinking of you.

Worked hard today and have one visit to make tonight.

Written on Christodora House letterhead.

No word from Adah today but it is probably coming.

Lew borrowed $16 from me tonight is evidently going on a regular bat. Wouldn't tell me where he was going.

Must get ready for dinner now. Good bye, sweetheart, I'll be thinking about you till I see you again – With a very hard kiss on your sweet little lips –

Your

HARRY

81.

July 17, 1913
on the boat,
Thursday night, 6 P.M.

MY DEAREST:

We havc just started and I am sitting at the back end of the boat with my back to everybody – armed with "Women and Labor' and the "Sun" – but before I tackle either I want to talk to you a little. Your letter of yesterday was oh, so dear – I don't suppose you like that adjective applied to anything of yours – but it just was. So you'll have to put up with it.

I'm glad that Mrs. M. didn't fill up all the pages of her letter to me.

But to proceed:

Has Adah written you yet? You never said anything about it over the phone to-day.

Dearest – I don't think you're miserable company – when you feel blue or worried about anything – I want you *always* to tell me right off so I can know about what you're thinking and so I can share it with you. I'm always going to tell you when I'm worried – and I want you to do the same. Please promise me you will.

The old fiddles are scratching again in their merry way. Mr. Gelhouse – the general owner and manager etc. is on so everybody is doing their darndest to show him what a fine boat this is.

Sweetheart – you don't know what you mean to me and how nothing seems to matter just so long as I have you.

I've been very happy all day – and I've thought about you lots. Last night was so nice – I slept like a rock until 7:15. Good-bye – sweetheart until tomorrow when you call me up. Had a letter from Ben to-day. Enclosed herewith is a kiss.

ETHEL

82.

[postmarked July 30, 1913]
on the boat, Tuesday

DEAREST:

I was lonesome to-day after you called up. – so I thought I'd write and tell you.

When I was out at noon – in the scorching hot sun I thought about how you had to do it all day. Wish you didn't dear – and I'm glad you don't have to do any more night work.

Hope you turned in early last night and got a good rest. I did. Just fine.

A hectic day at the office to-day – So will all the rest of the days this week be.

Will tell Fannie that Lou* is surely coming over Sunday. Do you think he'll think it is stupid out there?

I hope you remembered what you wanted to tell me last night and forgot.

Hope you'll get a good rest to-night – and that it will be cool in the city so you can. Mrs. De Forest† has returned . . . We're supposed to move to 42nd St. Thursday and Friday. Mercy! Good-night dear – I miss you. –

ETHEL

*Lewis Hopkins was called "Lew" by his family. Gross sometimes misspelled it as "Lou."

†Mrs. De Forest is Nora Blatch De Forest, Harriot Stanton Blatch's daughter. She also worked for the Women's Political Union.

83.

[postmarked August 13, 1913]
Tuesday

Written on The Equal
Franchise Society
letterhead.

DEAREST BOY:

Please forgive me for being so bad last night. I was mostly tired and for the rest – I was just peevish I guess – I can't think of the word that just describes it but I guess I needed to be spanked more than anything. You're the dearest and best boy in the world – dear – and I love you.

Hope you and your sis had a good evening together – You really haven't seen her at all. Won't she mind your going away tomorrow night? Wish I could stay in town again – but I can't.

Home all alone to-night and writing letters to my heart's content to everybody. Good-night dear. Wish I was good enough for you but I'm going to be better and better all the time. See if I don't. Sweetheart –

ETHEL

84.

Aug. 18

To my dear boy with best wishes for a very happy birthday and much love from
ETHEL

85.

[August 19, 1913]
Tuesday

Written on
Christodora House
letterhead.

SWEETHEART:

I would have written you last night but I was sick as the devil then and don't feel any too well now. Something I ate evidently acted wrong – tried to go to work this morning but had to come home and go to bed where I have been up till now – 6 P.M.

The books came – you little sweetheart – why did you do it. I kiss you 84 times. They were exactly what I wanted and I tried to read "Travels with a d – " last night but my head went round.

Adah is putting on a show here tonight but I can't say that she is very enthusiastic. Thursday night a friend of Lew's is going to take all three of us to Conn. in his motor. Adah will stay and the rest of us come back in the morning.

The work is going pretty fair but I haven't been there long enough to know whether I am going to like it or not.

Don't know just when I will get out to K—, Friday anyway – it is a long time to be away Ethel dear and I wish I could get out sooner but Adah only comes once a year. Lew is leaving Aug. 29 so it won't be long till I am the only representative.

My mind isn't working very well so good bye Ethel for tonight – I love you oh so much and if you were close I know that I would be well.

All my love
HARRY

86.

[August 20, 1913]
Wednesday

DEAREST HARRY:

I sort of expected a letter this morning – but it didn't come – but I know how short the evenings are and how busy you must be these last few nights with your sister Adah in town. And I guess it means that Adah is not coming out here before she goes. She said if she could plan it she would arrange it with you.

I'm having a lovely lazy time* – Have been in for a swim this morning – It was high tide and the water was very very rough for some reason. Yesterday afternoon we went off to the woods and it was lovely – only we took the carriage and that was a nuisance.

*Gross was writing from Far Rockaway.

It has been very cool out here ever since I reached here on Monday night. I'm trying to get rid of my cold – but I guess it has to take its course.

Hope you're not working too hard, dear – And I hope it's just as cool in the city. Wonder how your new work is going. And I also wonder if you received the books by now. You were bad – sweetheart – not to tell me about your birthday instead of "stringing" me like you did – but we had the day together anyhow – and it was nice – and you were so dear – I think Adah was peeved because we didn't make it out on Sunday – and she had a right to be after she planned it. I'm sorry I didn't see more of her while she was here and that I did not get to know her a little bit.

I think I'll wait and give you my bank book when you come instead of sending it to you in order to make that deposit for me.

Good-bye dear – I hope you're coming out soon – I began to miss you as soon as I got here on Monday – All my love –

ETHEL

PS. Sweetheart: – I'm here at the Post-Office – and your letter has just come – I'm sorry dear – that you've been ill in bed – *so* sorry – wish I was there to take care of you! Hope the ill effects were not from Sunday – but you're tired out dear – and you don't have half enough rest. That's a fine treat Thursday night – I shall think about you – and I hope you'll all have a dandy time. Will look for you on Friday – but if you don't feel just tip-top – don't come until Saturday – wish you could come Friday night and stay in Sat. morning!! Do try to manage it. Much love to you dear from

ETHEL

87.

[August 21, 1913]
Thursday morning

DEAREST:

Just a line before going to work – your good letter came Ethel a few minutes ago.

I can't possible get off Sat. morning dear and don't you think it would be foolish to come out Friday night to come right back again? But darling I can't stay away any longer so expect me on Friday! Am feeling infinitely better but am still a little unstable on my pins (meaning feet). Went with Adah to "Believe Me, Xantiff" last night, an impossible farce but very funny. John Barrymore plays the leading part you know.

Must stop now – sweetheart.

Your

HARRY

88.

[August 21, 1913]
Thursday

DEAREST BOY:

Suddenly – right out of the clear sky – I found myself with 2 children on my hands. Fannie decided to go to the city this morning – without warning – on the 7 o'clock boat – so was up to me to get up and play nurse and mother. And now – 3 o'clock – Baby is sitting on a blanket on the floor – after having been bathed – fed 4 times napped twice and walked and driven around the village in state in her perambulator! Albert* has had 1 spanking – one nap and several scoldings besides 2 meals and an apple. Looks like as if I was going to have peace for a minute. So I shall try to write.

*Albert was the son of Gross's brother Ed.

I hope you could read the few words I inked in to my letter of yesterday at the post-office. After having received yours. Hope you really and truly are well by now – and that you've been having a few good night's rests since last I saw you. You mustn't get too tired out because it's so much harder to work well. I had a letter from Miss Brown yesterday asking me about some things. I should think it was almost time for you to start on your trip. This is a lovely day for it and you ought to have a nice ride. I miss you dear – all the time and I'm looking forward to tomorrow night. I hope you are coming on the 4:30 boat – and that you can stay in Saturday morning and until Monday morning. That would give you a lovely rest. I hope you can. –

I'm writing under difficulties – two kiddies are getting into trouble every minute and I have to keep getting up and straightening them out. We have company on the front porch on the floor with baby and such goings on you never saw. Never again will I stay home and be nurse here. Next time Fannie feels a call I'm going too. Hope you have written to me because I'm anxious to know how you are. It seems a long time until tomorrow and I can't even be sure you are coming then. Hope you surely are.

All my love to you dear – and excuse this awful letter. I'm lonesome.

ETHEL

89.

[August 24, 1913]
Monday night

DEAREST:

Went to the doctor this A.M. and evidently I have been eating something I shouldn't have for he gave me some terrible medicine to take. I feel rotten just at present and if I don't feel better tomorrow then I do now – I don't expect to be out to your beloved city. Stayed in bed most of the afternoon and got to work in time to say good bye to all the force.

Last night was wonderful Ethel dear – wish I could be with you again tonight – of course if I feel better I will be out tomorrow but don't count on it.

Good night sweetheart – I love you
Your
HARRY

90.

DEAREST:

Ask Lou if he would like to come out some evening with you – so that I can see him before he goes. He's probably full up for every night this week – but this is in case he isn't.

It's such a wonderful day – wish you could have stayed out all day.

I hope you feel better to-day and I'm anxious to know what the doctor said. You're the dearest boy in the world and I love you.

Don't work too hard and come out soon.

All my love –

ETHEL

91.

[postmarked August 29, 1913]

DEAREST HARRY:

Enclosed is a ticket which a man has just sold me at a great reduction because he can't use it. I hope it will get to you on time to use tomorrow. I've written Lou a letter. Perhaps I'll enclose it in this – if I find at the P.O. that it won't get through on time to send regular postage.

I waited until the boat pulled out this morning – but I couldn't find you. Wherever did you go?

Now I must get this off and get at my sewing. Don't work too hard and I'll expect you on the 1:30 tomorrow. Wish you'd call up Goldie – 3950 Cortland – and find out if she's coming out on Sunday. Tell her I'm counting on it. Will you?

Much love to you dear – and remember the book you're going to bring sweetheart.

ETHEL

Friday morning

P.S. Sent you a telegram to-day to buy Lou Eyes – for me – Please give him enclosed letter with it before he goes –

ETHEL

92.

Sept. 15 [1913]

DEAREST BOY:

Wish we could look at some of those apartments adv. in the Sunday Times! I'm going to cut some out and if we can't get to them sooner – let's do it. Sat. afternoon next. Can you? I showed Mrs. B. – Mrs. M's letter to-day and she took it as a matter of course. Dearest – the more I think about it – the more I think we ought to *Gross was discussing* make it by Nov. 1st if possible.* Have written to Ben to-*their wedding date.* day to find out when he's coming home.

But of course we'll do whatever seems wisest.

I love you to-night – dear – and I'm getting tired of seeing you only sometimes – for an hour – and then at the end of a long day when you as well as I ought to be in bed and asleep – and that is where I ought to be right now – by the way – good-night dear – It was so nice last night – to be with you – found one of your letters in an unexpected place to-night – that is what made me write particularly.

That is one of the reasons – sweetheart –

ETHEL

93.

[September 18, 1913]
Thursday night

SWEETHEART –
I love you.
Good-night
ETHEL

94.

[September 22, 1913]
Monday night

DEAREST BOY:

Fannie says she sees no reason why we can't use my bedroom set. She says that no one buys double beds in an apartment any more – that they use 3/4 beds like mine and that we could fix up and paint my dresser and chairs and use them to good advantage. So I think we'd better do it – for the first year anyhow – and perhaps after that get a nice set. It would be such a saving and the more I think about it the more unnecessary it seems to me to get a new set. What do you think? It's just as we'll not to have too much on credit – don't' you think – and next year well surely have enough to get it outright.*

Saw another auctioneer to-day – Anderson Galleries. They are more than anxious to put the things on sale – want me to send them right down – say they are sure of selling them. Have an appointment with 5th Ave. A.R. man tomorrow – I'll see what he says about buying it outright.

The man is acting strangely about my library table. I think he's going to charge me storage on it. Have written to-day to Stromeyer asking him to let me know or rather give me his advice about my velour portiers and whether he can make my carpets into rugs.

Dearie: – I think we can make it by the 15th or 20th. There isn't much more to do. When we go up about the lease on Wed – we can find out whether their paperer has a shop downtown where we can go and select out paper – then on Saturday we can do that and also select furniture. Then there will only be the dishes and the silver –

What do you think?

Saw Knight. You know I think she's awfully nice. – thought so especially to-day – for even though she's almost a fanatic about some things – she has the keenest mind and she's very fair. We had a long discussion to-day. I also heard Beatrice Forbes Robertson[†] lecture

*Gross was referring to the preparation of their apartment together once they were married.

†Beatrice Forbes Robinson was a Shakespearean actor and a suffragist.

for a little while to-day at the E.F. Society on expression. Must tell you about her – but not on paper.

Good night dear – I love you – and I'm very happy – Your
ETHEL

95.

[October 5, 1913]
Monday night

MY DEAREST BOY:

I like to think of you – 'way out there amid all that pretty foliage and good clear air and plenty of SKY – but I miss you – strange to say – hope you've had a good day – and that to-night you'll have a good rest. Didn't go to the dressmaker's to-night. Didn't feel like it so I came straight home only to find that Fannie had not yet returned from Montclair. I tried during the day to get her because I wanted to send home for my bank-book – but she did not get home until nearly eight o'clock. She was able – finally – to get Rose a good girl and I hope all will be well for a while.

Sweetheart – I'm very happy dear – and I'm not worried about anything – the more I think about it – the more I know everything is going to be just wonderful. –

Mrs. Blodgett was most encouraging this morning and very very helpful. She said if we could get a "Mrs. Sillion" kind of woman – she would not need to come before four or five o'clock – that in that time she could get dinner and straighten the apartment and be through by eight o'clock – and that $2.00 and her dinners and carfare – would be ample pay – per week! I wonder if we could!

Miss Brown came back to-day – Much excited over what we're about to do. Spoke to Fannie about the wording on the announcements. She thinks as long as there's no reception – it isn't important whether she announces it or not. So we can have our own wording – the furniture is gone – and I'm glad of it. The enclosed picture came via one of the reporters to-day. Don't kiss the wrong girl. I got my hat to-night – and I like it. Hope you will.

Good night – dearest – oh – I love you so – dear – and I wish you were right up close to me now – 15 more days – to-night it seems long – except when I think of all there is to do. – Be good – and get a good rest. Will write again tomorrow.

All my love to you dear –

ETHEL

Sweetheart – called up Miss Ellis and gave her message about club and laundry. E.

96.

[October 1913]
Saturday night

DEAREST:

I can't help writing you a letter to-night – Even though I'm going to see you before this letter reaches – but I can settle down to what I have to do – better – if I talk to you a minute first.

You are such a large part of my every thought and I love – and miss you so when I don't see you – how do you suppose I ever got into such a state?

But I've waited for you for oh, so long – Harry – that now that I have found you – well – I suppose I'm trying to make up for all the time lost!

Just as I finished writing this it began to thunder and then came lightening and buckets and buckets of rain – Do you suppose that the Powers-that-Be are displeased at my frankness – with you.

But rain and thunder and lightening never did scare me – and to-night it sounds as if someone was wildly rejoicing about something – somewhere –

Two married ladies brought their husbands here to play cards with my brother-in-law to-night and they are chatting with my sister in one room while the men play cards in another – and such a stupid time those poor dear ladies have! Every time I go into that room I get sleepy. And as they are much happier without me I have come into this little room to do some writing – and some reading – while I think about you.

But I mustn't make it thunder any more.

I hope you enjoy the concert tomorrow. While you listen to sweet music – I shall be listening – probably – to some wild radical speeches – which – however – might be softened by the presence of that little new baby.

Good night dearest – I wish I had gotten your letter this morning! You looked so funny when I said what I did about a letter – yesterday noon – that I wondered what you thought.

Until tomorrow night –

ETHEL

97.

Monday night

DEAREST BOY:

Your letter has just come – as I was about to start for Hanna's – but I must talk to you first. It's such a dear sweet letter – and I've read it twice already.

But dearest – you mustn't think about that "inventory." It's all such ancient history and I can't bear to have you connect it in any way – with us. – I shouldn't have gone over it so carefully – for after all – it really doesn't matter. I only hope you didn't feel as badly about each one as I felt about the *one* you told me about.

Sweetheart – you have no cause to be jealous – because I am yours so absolutely now – nothing else counts – so, please consider yourself kissed – and stop thinking about it at once. I command you!

There never was anyone like you and there never could be again – you know that – don't you dear? I was just wicked last night to say anything about it al all.

10 p.m.

I have returned from Hanna's. Had a nice visit. And I'm going to finish this so I can mail it in the morning.

I'm going to get tickets for "The Sunshine Girls" to-morrow or the next day – for next Tuesday evening. All right?

I'd hate to have your evenings tied up so awfully much this summer. Besides, if you are going to work hard all day you ought to have your evenings to "recre-ate." I realize dear, what a saving it would be – but there's no reason why you should work you head off – besides I think it would tie up every spare minute you had – but we'll see what C.I.M. will report about it – and you'll know best what to do.

I can imagine the tenor of the conversation at the breakfast table this morning. Poor you. Wait till I see Miss MacColl again. She won't make any more remarks after that. It was nearly 11 o'clock when I left last night. You ought to see the floral offering which I received – it was fearfully and wonderfully wired. And I was much touched. They are dear girls.

On Friday night I am to be home all alone – my sister and bro-in-law are out for the evening. So I think I shall take that opportunity to write a long epistle to my kid brother. I'll tell him everything and then when Sissie comes home I'll perhaps let her read the letter or just tell her what I said in it. I don't dread it at all. I rather look forward to doing it.

Good-night – sweetheart – had an awfully busy and interesting day. I really like it very much. Underwood called me up about another "excellent opening" today – I'm going to stay where I am.

Now please forget the "roll call" at Goufaroni's – I do understand how it made you feel and I don't think it's because you're "not big enough."

It's only because you're so *human* – and that's one of the reasons why I – love – you –so –

Good-night –

ETHEL

98.

New York, October 17, 1913

Written on Women's Political Union letterhead.

DEAREST:

I gave Fannie a blank check today, from my check book to fill out and pay for the furniture when it comes. I telephoned to the Supt. and asked him to let Fannie in when she arrives. I also telephoned to Manges and told them that there would be no one to pay for the furniture unless they delivered it before 1:30 o'clock. They said they would.

Why can't we get your brown suit on our way home from City Hall on Monday. You could wear your blue suit down and so will I.

I made two deposits which ought to go down in the stub: Salary $25 and check for old B.R. furn. $25.00.

Am rushed to death. Will have to work tomorrow morning here at the office. Call me up.

These are notes that I thought you ought to know about.

All my love

ETHEL

Chapter Two

Marriage: World War I and Civilian Relief, 1915–1918

AFTER GROSS AND HOPKINS MARRIED in 1913, the couple lived for four years in New York City. Hopkins worked first for the AICP as a friendly visitor and then as head of the newly established Bureau of Child Welfare (BCW) as administrator of the Widows' Pension Program. Hopkins was ineligible for military service because of poor eyesight and so, sought alternative ways to serve his country. In early 1918, He became assistant director of the Gulf Division of the American Red Cross's Civilian Relief, and the family moved to New Orleans. The bulk of these letters occur during the summer of 1918 when Gross took their four-year-old son, David, to Far Rockaway Beach to avoid the heat of New Orleans. At that point, the family had only been in New Orleans for a few months, living in a short-term rental. Gross and David stayed with Fannie and Benjamin Kohn, her sister and brother-in-law, who regularly rented a beach house in Far Rockaway.

99.

[August 25, 1915]

DEAR ETHEL:

Am enclosing letter from the Goulds. What do you think?

Hastily,

HARRY

The letter from the Goulds addressed the possibility that Hopkins and Gross might rent a vacation house in Great Barrington, Massachusetts.

100.

[postmarked August 25, 1915]
Tuesday

DEAREST:

I have just heard from Mother and it seems that our plans must be upset somewhat. I am enclosing her letter. I rather think we had better give up the trip to the Berkshires and perhaps I could come out to the camp* and stay an extra week after which perhaps Mother would be gone† and we could spend the rest of the time at home. This would be very inexpensive and I am confident that I would get a good rest. I am planning to come out to camp Thursday night – will you ask Miss Ann to have the car meet the 4:32 train leaving about that time from N.Y.? Would come out tomorrow but there is to be a Grinnell group‡ at the settlement on Wed. night and I am very anxious to meet them. Mr. and Mrs. Young§ are coming over also.

I slept like a log for ten hours last night and expect to duplicate that feat tonight. I walked to the train in a little more than 35 minutes Monday morning, but was rather tired.

Everything seems natural on the East Side – the barber – the tailor – the bootblack all welcomed me with open arms!

It is decidedly lonesome without you and David – will surely come Thursday.

Good bye till then.

Much love,

HARRY

Written on AICP letterhead. Hopkins was working at the AICP as a district visitor doing field work on the West Side.

*Gross and David were staying at Northover Camp.

†Hopkins's mother, Anna Pickett Hopkins, was visiting from Grinnell, Iowa.

‡The Grinnell group came from Grinnell College, Hopkins's alma mater.

§Harvey Young, a classmate of Hopkins's at Grinnell College, was awaiting ordination as a Methodist minister.

101.

[postmarked Aug.23, 1915]
Monday

DEAREST:

I have managed to get outside a good meal and as soon as this letter is finished am going to bed. Fanny called up saying she was mailing some of the babie's dresses to you today – she evidently had a good vacation.

Of course I would have to forget something. This time it was my glasses. Can you send them on?

I phoned Mr. Dunham asking him to send the mail to the office and later had the address changed to Northover.

Miss Hoag tells me Mrs. Carson has been out to camp today.* Did you see her? I missed the Stennis [by] a few minutes.

I've been thinking very much about you and Jerry.† Hope everything is well.

Good night dear. Kiss Jerry for me and if you are real good and apologize – why I'll give you one too.

HARRY

*Hoag and Carson were settlement workers. Sarah Carson was the co-founder of Christodora House and may be the person Hopkins was referring to.

†Gross and Hopkins named their first son Jerome David and, for a time, called him Jerry. However, because Hopkins's family disliked the name, they began calling him David.

102.

[probably 1918]
Sunday morning

Hopkins to Gross at Northover Camp.

DEAREST:

Now after you have seen me and we have talked it all over – you are getting this foolish letter – but I had to talk to you a little.

Just got back from a long walk with Bruce and David – way back through the woods – Oh how I wish you were here with me – everything is so lovely.

This week end has been a sad mistake but you know all about that now.

103.

July 11, 1918

MY DEAR:

Ben wires that your address is 306 Grandview Avenue, which does not correspond with the "138" that Ed gave me – I am addressing this note to both places.*

I have a reservation on the three o'clock train Friday afternoon, but there is a possibility that I will change it to Friday night as the conference is to be extended through the afternoon. It has been a great meeting and I find myself tied up to a tremendous job, the details I will tell you about later. I assume you have received my several telegrams as none have been returned.

If I go up in the afternoon train Friday, I will stay with Adah and Mother Friday night – try to get my work done Saturday morning. Do you think you could arrange a theater party with Adah for Saturday night or possibly afternoon. I could go out to Far Rock – early Sunday morning and remain till Monday. I must leave Friday afternoon or evening.
Hastily but with much love,
HARRY
It has been perfect weather.

Written on Hotel Powhaten, Washington, D.C., letterhead.

*Gross and David were in Far Rockaway staying with her sister and brother-in-law, Fanny and Benjamin Kohn.

104.

[July 16, 1918]
Tuesday

MY DEAR:

Have just come home from an afternoon tea party given by Mrs. Freed. Met some of my second cousins there that you have never seen. I find that they expected to be invited down here to meet you on Sunday as did a host of others. See what you missed. Sometime though, I should like to have you see them because they are my father's first cousins and they look just like him I am told.*

*Gross's father, Bencion Gross, died in Hungary just before the family migrated to the United States. There is evidence that he had written to his relatives in America but there are no references to their names in the letters or Gross's oral history.

I did not take David on the beach today because he has signs of a cold. Aside from that he's as fine as a top and happy as the day is long. He asked me today whether Daddie was big enough to go on the train all by himself.

It has been wonderfully cool and comfortable out here all day. I am thinking about you in Washington and wondering if you are worn out. You must get in just lots of sleep when you get back. I hope you have telegraphed Lorena to meet you at 7721[†] and at what time. I wrote her that if she did not hear from you to call you up at your office Thursday morning.

Be sure you write me as soon as you get home just how things are.

I am reading "Changing Winds" and enjoying it very much. I am also making a luncheon set for your table while David plays in the sand.

Goodnight dear –

Much love to you –

David say – "Tell Daddie love to him" when I asked him if he had a message for you.

ETHEL

[†] *7721 refers to an address on Sycamore Street, the boarding house run by Thornton where Hopkins stayed in New Orleans. Lorena (spelled sometimes "Lorina") was the housekeeper there.*

105.

July 16, 1918
Washington, D.C.

MY DEAREST:

I have just returned breathlessly from the ticket office where I calmly left my ticket after purchasing this morning. Fortunately, I found it.

Washington apparently remembered today that it is a Southern City for it is hotter than blazes and everyone is in a bad humor.

Persons* is having some difficulty with the War Council and gives me to understand that his relations are very strained. I have spent the day loafing around Persons' office and have done little or nothing to earn my salt. Persons has written Carroll about the Directorship and about my salary increase as well.

Written on The Raleigh, Washington, D.C. letterhead.

*Frank Persons was the American Red Cross (ARC) Director General and Leigh Carroll was manager of the ARC's Gulf Division. They were Hopkins's superiors when he worked for the Gulf Division in New Orleans during World War I. Persons hired

The big offensive seems to be on and we may look for some casualty lists that compare with England's soon. Fortunately, the Americans seem to have stopped them.

I will write or wire as soon as I reach N.O.

Much love and a big kiss for you and David – do rest your little self. Am feeling fine today.

HARRY

Hopkins as Assistant Director of the Bureau of Civilian Relief. Emmet White served at Director until he was drafted into the army in July 1918, when Hopkins was appointed to that position.

106.

[July 18, 1918]
306 Grandview Ave.
Thursday

MY DEAREST BOY:

Your letter from Washington came today and I tell you it was good to get it. You were lucky to find your ticket after leaving it. They say a kind providence watches over babies – so now you know what you are.

We had a hot day on the 16th too – but I never know it's hot in this house – it's only when I get out and walk in the sun. We have a stiff breeze blowing here all the time since I came. I'd wear my sweater all the time only they all make fun of me.

The news in the paper is very thrilling tonight. There is no doubt the casualty lists will be large after this. But it is thrilling to have the American boys make such a splendid showing.

Hanna was here today. We took her for a ride – Jeannette* driving. I wish you could have gone while you were here – but Ed didn't dare to take his car out after his experience the night before. He was only fined $2.00 next day because it was only the first offence.

*Jeanette is Ed (Edward) Gross's wife and Albert's mother.

A letter from Mrs. Prest came today asking me to bring David and stay with her from Thursday to Monday next week – but as the Saturday that comes in there is Eleanor's birthday and as I promised to entertain about 25 children on that day – I asked her if we could come another time. I am perfectly happy staying here. The days seem very full with a swim in the ocean every morning. David's cheeks grow pinker each day – and his cold seems much better tonight. I wrote and asked Mother to come out and spend the day with me tomorrow. Jeanette and Helen are going to East Orange – for Friday and Saturday.

I think I have told you all the news. Your telegram came today telling of your arrival in N.O. I am anxious to hear about Lorena – and how you are managing. I bought a wedding present for Adah today – or part of one. It's a very beautifully embroidered linen center piece – big enough to cover the top of a table. It cost $4.50. Is that all right or is this a bad time to do it. It's really quite nice and a bargain. I shall give it to Adah from us both for her chest.[†] Perhaps if she ever gets to keeping house we can add something else. I should like to cash one of the checks you left for me for about $25.00. I'm supposed to give that to Ben[‡] in payment of our debt – and he, in turn gives it to Fannie as part of my "entertainment" here. Ed shares the other half. I should worry. I'm not supposed to know about it. Is it all right to cash it for that? And as I spent about $1.00 at the drug store and $4.50 on Adah and a little more in incidentals, I shall probably draw $5.00 extra for cash.

It is past 10:30 and David has just only gone to sleep. He has a nose cold and found it hard to breathe I guess – but I have greased him up with camphorated oil outside and castor oil inside and an enema besides – so I guess that will hold him for a while and we'll call it a day and I'm going to bed.

Good-night – dear – the breeze is coming in this window so strong that I have to move. Would you like some of it in a can?

Much love and a big kiss,

ETHEL

David says he wants you to make him a man next time you write "if you know how."

†Adah, Hopkins's older sister, married Frank Aime in 1917

‡Ben (Benjamin) Gross was in the diamond business in NYC with his brother Ed.

107.

[July 19,1918]

My Dear:

Your letter telling me of David's cold – which I hope to heaven isn't whooping cough – arrived this morning at our city home.

Written on ARC letterhead.

Lorina was fully entrenched in Mrs. Thornton's house with no thought of leaving – said she did not receive your letter etc. I haven't disturbed her other than to get the key to the house. I am going to get all my meals down town and will get along alright with a maid!

New Orleans is hot as blazes and you can thank your lucky stars you are not here although it is a bit lonesome. There is a great deal of work to do. Carroll has officially appointed me Director at $300 a month.* Our neighbors on both sides are away and there is little sign of life on Sycamore Street.

A salary of $300 a month in 1918 would be comparable to $3,400 a month in 2000.

My trip home was quite uneventful – the day in Washington was pleasant and aside from an evil half hour of hunting my ticket to N.O which in my nonchalant way – I left on the counter and walked!

Persons is in a very serious row with some officials at headquarters and may resign. Worse luck for me if he does.

The war situation looks good – we may expect some big casualties in the near future. Tonight I am going to the theater with Leppert and tomorrow will be the day for the big sleep. Have offered Harvey Young a job.

Cash the check for all you need. I have just deposited $245 – as soon as my book is balanced I will let you know how much money we have and consequently how long you can live.

Much love and a big kiss for you both.

Harry

108.

MY DEAREST:

*Garrett P. Wyckoff was chair of the Economics Department and professor of sociology at Grinnell College. He left Grinnell to work for Hopkins at the ARC training institute.

With Wyckoff* getting started and two new field people arriving – I have neglected my letter writing dreadfully – but that is no excuse. Your good letters have come regularly and tonight I received the last telling about Mother's visit. I am delighted that you are having a good time my dear – but don't forget to come home – How about Aug. 15 – it may be hot as blazes here then. If it wasn't for the weather you would have to come back right away!

Have about decided to take Leppert on – Carroll is willing and I need him. Am sleeping hours every night although the bed is not particularly comfortable without you! Lorena telephoned that she is coming up tomorrow to clean up. I haven't paid her anything and won't until you get back.

The big battle seems to be over – Germany's plans for this summer have gone badly astray. Did you read Wilson's statement about lynchings, etc. – it doesn't sit very well down here. I'd give a farm to see David – give him a big kiss for me. I have [a] letter from Lew which I

†Hopkins's brothers, Lewis and John Emery, were both in the military.

must answer – won't you write Emery?†
Much love my darling – and a kiss
HARRY

109.

Written on ARC letterhead.

MY DEAREST:

I have just completed my first bachelor week end with very little luck! Saturday night I went to the movies and had prepared for a long sleep Sunday A.M. when at 7 sharp the carpenter began to lay flooring just next door! Owens took me out to Camp Masters and I had lunch at the St. Charles as a guest of Miss Alling, who by the way had just gone to Hattiesburg, Miss.

Miss Gober sailed in this morning and she and I had a rather stormy meeting at which I didn't come off second best. I frankly confess that I enjoyed rubbing it in which I certainly did. The lady will leave for home in a few days. The men in the field are getting on fine especially Perring and Lyon.

I have received all of your letters – you certainly are doing yourself proud. I am glad to hear that David is better as I was afraid he was getting whooping cough. Your visit seems to be turning out better than anticipated and I want you to stay as long as necessary.

Today I met the only Kate Gordon and she has asked me to come up her house tonight to talk over t.b. work.

I have no other news of great interest so will say "au revoir" – "bon nuit ma cherie."

Do cash the check for whatever you need only be sure and let me know how much. We have $300 in the bank – so go the limit!

Much love and a big kiss

HARRY

110.

[*July 29, 1918*]

MY DEAREST:

Another busy day – in fact two have passed – and no letter to you. I received your good letter this morning written from Prests – you must have had a delightful time. How I'd like to have been with you! But, my dear, it is hot as blazes down here – no place for the baby and I really wish you would keep him there for the summer – if you can be happy. As for me, I do nothing but eat – work and sleep – chiefly the latter. Am really getting on fine – *so don't worry about me not being comfortable – I'm alright.* I get a good breakfast at Childs every morning and always finish the day with a real dinner.

The work is going splendidly and I am looking forward to an interesting fall and winter.

Written on ARC letterhead.

We must have another house but I think I will keep it until Sept. anyway. Everyone tells me that you're plain crazy to come back here in the middle of August, so you better put it off. Now don't think I don't want you for I do – I love you tonight my dearest very, very much and wish you were here. We're gong to have a dandy winter and for David's sake I believe you had better make the summer of it. Stop worrying about me getting too gay – Miss Alling – age 50 – has been my only company – and she paid for my dinner on that trip!

I hope the baby keeps well – and you also my dearest – love to Fanny and the rest and big kiss for you and David.

HARRY

Be sure and remember me to everyone you see and tell them I *especially* wanted to be remember to them. You know how to do it!

111.

[July 31, 1918]
Wednesday

MY DEAREST:

I am going to the movies tonight with Charlie White – [undecipherable] dissipates me! What? Last night I was in bed at nine and slept straight through until seven, so you see I am catching up on my sleep nicely. Have had no letter from you today, but will probably find one at home tonight. I forgot to endorse my check yesterday so am sending it today.

I drank a quart of milk and am going to try to put on four or five pounds while you are away. Mrs. Eustis' little boy has come down with malaria – mosquitoes have been after him – it is rather prevalent and is fearfully hot today.

I expect to go out on the road about the fifteenth to be gone about ten days so don't come back then – that is unless you are very uncomfortable. I am preparing tonight for my conference of Home Service agents at the Grunewald* tomorrow.

*The Grunewald Hotel was located near the French Quarter.

Nothing very exciting has happened. I read a Grinnell paper today telling about the cows – pigs, etc. – also a letter from Adah telling me that she has seen nothing of you since my visit. Do call on her? Has Mother gone back yet? Is Ed still peevish and how are the girls treating you.

How I'd like to jump in the water with you, but nothing doing! I am going to rent for another month. I'd like to be with [you] tonight but we'll have a long winter and a happy time soon.

With all my love and a big kiss,

HARRY

112.

July 30 [1918]

MY DEAREST ETHEL:

I just finished a good dinner at the Lodo next to the Lafayette and have come back to the office for a minute to write this letter and then I'm off home and to bed. I slept hours last night – like a lamb and was consequently in good humor today.

Written on ARC letterhead.

By the way before I forget it – where are those pictures of David. I want to get them. If I can I will send them on to you dear.

Harvey writes that he is very interested in our Home Service* and is thinking seriously of coming in. He says Booker is in the army and that Bill Tuttle is going into the YMCA work in the fall. Blanche has not been very well and I imagine that my letter didn't help the situation any. Why don't you write her?

Hopkins was ineligible for the draft because of poor vision in one eye.

I put a budget for my work today of $29,000 for six months – about $5,000 a month excluding the A.F.O.s in the camp. Carroll took it with good grace.

Mrs. Owens is leaving tomorrow for the north. Owens is going with her to visit the naval yards in Norfolk and Charleston.

I am enclosing the blank checks – use all the money you want – also a card from the draft board. I think I'm ok there.

The big battle seems to have let up and apparently they are preparing to settle down for some weeks and then begin the last offensive of the year. Our losses must be very heavy. By the way, do write Francis a note – I did a few days ago.

I love you very much my sweetheart and send you a big hug and a kiss. As for David, he better learn some classical music. But kiss him for me any way.

Your boy

HARRY

113.

[August 1, 1918]
August 2, 1918
Far Rock, Thursday evening

DEAREST BOY:

I was so glad to get your letter today because I was getting very homesick. If you want us to stay here longer, you had better write oftener. David asks about you more and more, it seems to me each day. He said today "lets write Daddie a good old letter and tell him to come here because we are so lonesome." I told him that his Daddy was at home and that we had to go to him when the time came. He is very happy here and out of doors every minute except meal times. He is eating very well and drinking grade *A* milk so he so he ought to gain in weight. The weather is delightfully cool and I wish I could bottle some of this breeze and send it to you. If only you were here and we had our own house, it would be perfect.

In your letter today, you say that you want us to stay as long as the hot weather last in N.O. I won't make any promises – if we stay until the end of August, will that be long enough? That is 29 more days!

I'm not worried about you getting too *gay* – what I am worried about is your *health*. Do say specifically how your are and how you stand the hot weather. Whether you are going on the road and when. Have you made connection with the laundry for your shirts and your palm beaches and what do you do about the rest of your washing. Can Lorena get you someone who will give you one day a week to clean the house and do the washing or have you found a better plan? How do you get your wash ties laundered?

I am looking forward to next fall and winter and I think it's going to be fine. I want to get back however in time to find a suitable place to live. I am glad the work is going so well but I felt sure it would. Is there any more about Mr. Persons and the War Council?

I hope you have sent me a check, I'm broke.

Mother says Emery is in the big fight now. She saw that his division (The New England) was taking a very prominent part (in the Sunday Times).

What do you think of Landsdowne's* letter today. I agree with him that to talk peace terms now would seem less as if we were weakening than if we did it at a time when we were not making gains at the front. It will bring forth some interesting comment.

Lord Landsdowne was a British statesman who had proposed a negotiated peace with the Germans.

I love you dear tonight – very hard and I want to come home – much. But I'll try to be good. Much, much love to you – and several big kisses –

ETHEL

David and I are going to spend the day with Mother next Thursday. Had dinner at Hanna's the other night and she is coming here to lunch next Tuesday.

114.

[August 2, 1918]
Friday

MY DEAREST:

I didn't write you yesterday – did I? My conference lasted all day and part of the evening and not until now have I had a minute in the past two days. The conference went fine and everyone is fairly happy.

Written on ARC letterhead.

Tonight one of the new Home Service men, who has three boys in the army – took the editor of the Times Picayune and me to a stag dinner – $1.50 a plate – and everything in the world to eat. But my mail tonight is piled high and I hate to think of what the morning will bring forth.

I read your nice little note – my dear – in bed last night and am so glad you are having such a nice time – Fanny is a dear – I know she is largely responsible.

I am getting another Grinnell man – Prof. Stoops*– I think I will use him for after care of crippled soldiers. The work is going great – I am anxious to tell you all about it.

*Dr. John D. Stoops was Hopkins's professor of philosophy at Grinnell College.

Our young hero next door was awake at eleven o'-clock last night and up at seven this morning! Some boy!

Be sure and let me know if David shows any sign of whooping cough. How I would like to see the little dear.

Please don't worry about me – I am well – in good spirits – getting plenty of sleep – eating well – and behaving myself. Am going to Montgomery Tuesday and Birmingham Wednesday and to [undecipherable] Thursday and home on Friday.

I love you very much my sweetheart – and give you a big long kiss!

HARRY

115.

[August 3, 1918]
Saturday

Written on ARC letterhead.

MY DEAREST GIRL:

Peck* is coming in this afternoon from Camp Shelly to go over a pamphlet with me that we are getting out for drafted men. We are having dinner with Leppert tonight and will probably work for awhile afterwards.

*John Frederick Peck taught Hopkins European history at Grinnell College.

I got David's picture – it is much admired by everyone – but were we not to get several small ones as well? Shall I send it on to you?

Unless you have worn out your stay – I wouldn't come back on the 15th for two reasons – one is that it is hot as blazes and the other is that I will be away for several days about that time. While I want you at home – I think it would be better for the baby if you stay until Sept. 1.

All is lovely here – I seem to be thriving on restaurant cooking – it is expensive however if one is to get a decent meal. I deposited $155 today so do your worst.

I have a dandy picture today of the Director of Civilian Relief which I am going to frame and take care of.

I get my washing done at the laundry and have changed my sheets several times – think of it! My palm beaches are in perpetual motion – and I spend a good deal of time keeping them clean, but have managed pretty well. I met the Hunters last night – they're all well and happy.

Do be good – have a good rest and remember I love you very very much and have no intention of letting you go again. Kiss David for me and take one or even two for yourself.

As Ever,
HARRY

116.

[August 3, 1918]
Saturday night

SWEETHEART:*

It is very late – but I just want to say good-night and that I love you very, very much. Your letter yesterday in which the blank check was not enclosed came – and then today came your second letter and card from the Draft Board and signed check. I am delighted that all seems well at the D.B. and I am much obliged for the check.

Will write more tomorrow. Good-night dearest – and all my love –
ETHEL

*Gross wrote this letter in two installments, on Saturday night and Sunday night and then mailed them together.

[August 4, 1918]
Sunday night

DEAREST:

This has been pretty much like all other Sundays. The maid left last week so we all pitch in and no one of us has to do very much. This morning a swim – then dinner – dishes, and nap and then some time with Ben and then supper – tucking David in bed – and a letter to you. Last night Ed took us all in the car to Long Beach and it was a lovely ride and the night before we went to the movies and saw Wm S. Hart and Edith Story. I was told that I resembled the latter celebrity – but I see it not. The days just seem to fly by – but I get oh, so homesick when night comes and sometimes it just seems as if I couldn't wait any longer.

I note what you say about Mrs. Eustis's little boy having malaria. That's too bad – and I suppose I ought to be glad to be here with David. But it's hard to have you so far away. I can't believe that it's hot in N.O. We are having such delightfully cool weather here – day in and day out. In fact, seems like early spring more than summer.

You will want to know the result of the x-ray on my teeth. They found that the tooth that has the gold cap on it, did not have two of the canals filled in properly after the nerve was killed. That, in itself, would be enough to give me sciatica – but in addition to that, they found I had an impacted wisdom tooth – you remember I had one left that had not come through. They advise me to have it right out by Hasbrouck. They say that any disorder in the mouth will cause or aggravate sciatica and if I don't have that wisdom tooth out, they predict all sorts of ills. I shall consult Hasbrouck and show him the plate and see what he says. If that will end my sciatica and improve my general condition, I shall be more than glad to go through with it and come back to you strong and cheerful. Fannie will go in with me and then when that's done, I'll have the gold cap taken off my tooth and they plan to thoroughly clean out those canals and fill them and then put the gold cap back. That dentist I went to uptown did not do his job well at all and if I did not fear more slipshod work, I should go back to him and ask him to make good. The plates plainly show where the canals were not filled. What would you advise? This new dentist down here – who has a very good reputation and who took the x-rays, wants $20 to fix up that one tooth with the gold cap on it. So you see I am going to run up quite a bill before I get through. Hasbrouck will probably charge

$5 for the extractions and $2 or $3 for each dressing and there may be three of four dressings. But if I can get rid of my sciatica that way and perhaps avoid further trouble – it will be worth-while, won't it?

Now don't worry about me and I shall let you know what Dr. Hasbrouck decides. He may decide not to touch that wisdom tooth at present. But however it turns out, I think it will take about two weeks to have the work done and then I shall take another week to get well rested up after it and then after that I think we shall have to come home, David and I. Fannie's apartment is vacant now – so I can stay there overnight whenever necessary. And I can feel sure that David is well taken care of. He looks browner and better every day. His cold is completely gone – just a little bit of a play cough once in a while when he wants his sweet cough medicine. Ed gave Albert and David a box kite and they spent the day flying it and you never knew such excitement.

Everybody loves David and he has a host of friends. The other night Jeanette *slapped* Albert in the *face* in David's presence. David was furious. He spoke right up as spunky as you please and said, "People don't spank children on the face but on the bottom." He is devoted to Albert and Albert to him. I was glad he said what he did.

Everything is going beautifully here. We have lots of fun getting the work done up and going down to the beach – and going out for rides – and we are all the best of friends.

I have not seen Adah because I haven't gone in to New York after my return from Great Falls. One reason I haven't gone in is because I was broke and another because I wanted to stay close to home until David's cold had entirely disappeared. And I am very glad I did because he responded to treatment so nicely and has gotten safely over it. (Mother said it was no use asking Adah to come out here because she wouldn't.) For I must confess to you now, that while he coughed I could never feel that it wasn't the whooping cough, in spite of what the doctor said. We have much to be thankful for. It will be so wonderful to be together again – all three of us. Now please do as much traveling while I am gone as you can – so we will have you with us when we get back. I note you are going away for 10 days on the 15th. Do take good care of yourself and while you are in N.O. can't you find a nice boarding house for breakfast and dinner? Wouldn't it be better than the restaurants?

How is Mrs. White getting along? I note that Mr. White is called Field Organizer and Mrs. Eustis "Bureau of Communications" or something.

Ben continues to be very happy in his work and will probably get another raise.

Goodnight dear – and a great deal of love – and a big kiss from your devoted

ETHEL

P.S. When I cash the blank check it will be for $25.00 so that I will have cash to pay the dentists. Is that all right? Let me know what to say to Bache.

117.

[August 7, 1918]
Wednesday

MY DEAREST BOY:

We are having a really hot spell and it makes me think of New Orleans. Yesterday we spent the day on the beach and took our lunch with us and had a glorious time and today David's nose is peeling! He went in the water by himself and "dived" – (in water about 3 inches deep) and had a beautiful time and did not want to come out. We reached home about 4 – had an early supper and went to Long Beach with Jeanette in the automobile, first calling for Hanna and Lillie (her bungalow pardner). Their husbands stayed home and washed the dishes, as all good husbands should, and they and Jeanette, Helen and I started off. We had a glorious ride – and, incline your ear – we stopped off at Castles-by-the-Sea in Long Beach and had some lemonade and watched them dance. The dance floor and the dancers at Spanish Fort had nothing on these society folk. It was a perfect scream to watch some of them. Among the dancers on the floor was Frances White and a gay young officer – all for 75 cents a drink of lemonade! We also each received a fan as souvenirs which I shall preserve to show you. So you see we had a large evening. Although yesterday was a scorcher – it was cool as could be driving.

Are you being careful, dear, to keep out of the hot sun these days – Fannie was almost overcome by the heat when she reached home yesterday after attending a fancy luncheon party. And you must be sure and tell me *just* how you are in *each* letter. I am glad you seem to be thriving on restaurant food and fare. When you go away, be sure and tell me where to write – and if to the office – will it be opened if I mark "Personal" on it? I am relieved that you are making connections with the laundry – but you have not told me whether Lorena ever came to you to clean after she called up.

You're not doing a thing to the Faculty of G.C. They'll be calling a halt on you soon. Isn't Prof Stoops a short man with a mustache? I didn't know that your Bureau would actually organize for the after care of crippled soldiers. In fact I didn't know that it was coming under Home Service. That seems like such a large piece of work in itself and a most interesting one. You must be getting your work fixed up in fine style. I wish I weren't so far away from it all.

I was going to N.Y. to spend the day with mother and Adah tomorrow and take David – but Mother called up today to say it was very hot and she advised me to wait until it was cooler. I am going to try to have them both out for the day soon. It's hard to arrange things like that out here now. The maid left a week ago and no chance of getting another.

I want to tell you how things stand with my teeth. I made an appointment with McBride in N.Y. (who is taking all of Hasbrouck's patients while the latter is away on vacation) and went in to see him last Monday. He would not attempt to take out my wisdom tooth. Said he preferred I should wait until Hasbrouck's return Sept. first. The only other man in town who can do an impacted tooth is a specialist named Schaumberg – but his charges make him prohibitive. I am told he never removes an impacted tooth for less than $500.00. Did you ever hear of such a thing? So I don't know what to do now – if I wait until Sept. first to have it done by Hasbrouck – the dressings would take at least 2 weeks – and I don't want to stay away from you so long. I shall see my dentist again and see what other advice he has to offer. Hasbrouck's charges for an impacted tooth rarely come over $25 and often they come under that. Schaumberg, they say, wants a limited practice and prefers to do millionaire's impacted teeth only. He is like Craigers who will not deliver a baby for less than $1000.00.

I am, however, going to let the dentist begin work on my gold-cap tooth. It's a $20 job – worse luck – and if we don't become bankrupt it won't be my fault. The x-ray of my mouth was $10.00. Because of all this, I drew that blank check, you sent me, for $50.00 and I shall keep track of my expenses. Let me know if I am going too fast. And do you think I ought to wait for Hasbrouck to have that impacted tooth out? I shall try while I am waiting to hear from you, to find another man who can do it, before then.

I must stop now and make an apple tapioca for dinner. I am feeling great and weighed 111 lbs. yesterday on a reliable scale, so you see I have gained. David weighed 32 – only – but he looks and feels great and now that his cold has left him, I am sure he will gain.

As for his pictures – we are entitled to two large ones and four (4) smaller ones. I paid for that many and you have the receipt. I had to pay in advance because they said it was a special offer – a "coupon" they called it. Be sure you get all these photographs. And if you can send me one for Fannie and for Mother. (of the smaller ones).

Yes, as I said in my last letter, David's cough is gone it was not whooping cough at all – just croup. I am so relieved.

Ever so much love to you dearheart – I do want you so sometimes – it hurts – but I know we must stay here while it's so hot – but we won't ever go away again – so don't get too used to a bachelor's existence.

A great big kiss –

ETHEL

118.

Western Union Telegram
Aug 7, 1918
New Orleans, La.
Mrs. Harry L. Hopkins
306 Grandview Ave., Far Rock
Leave this morning for Lake Charles. Tornado. Will wire later
HARRY

119.

Western Union Telegram
Aug 9, 1918
New Orleans, La.
306 Grandview Ave., Far Rock
Conditions in Lake Charles bad one. Thousands homeless. Am in charge of all relief work. Leaving for Lake Charles tonight to be gone for four or five days. Telegraphing communication uncertain. Am feeling fine. No time to write much.
Love
HARRY

Located in southwest Louisiana near the Texas border, Lake Charles was hit by a hurricane on August 6, 1918. Damage was extensive with 2,600 homes destroyed and $10 million worth of property damage. There were 34 fatalities, including two soldiers killed at Gerstner Field, an aviation training camp 15 miles southwest of Lake Charles.

120.

Western Union Telegram
[date uncertain]
New Orleans, La.
Mrs. Harry L. Hopkins
306 Grandview Ave., Far Rock
Everything going fine but weather hot as blazes. Harvey Young may come with us. Am going to hire Leppert.
Much Love
HARRY

121.

Western Union Telegram
August 10, 1918
New Orleans, La.
Mrs. Harry L. Hopkins
306 Grandview Ave., Far Rock
You can wire or write me care Majestic Hotel Lake Charles through Wednesday next week. Am leaving for Lake Charles tonight.
HARRY

122.

[August 10, 1918]
Saturday night

*Gross wrote this letter in two installments, on Saturday night and Sunday night and then mailed them together.

DEAREST:*
I love you so much tonight and I want you so. I hope you are missing us a little bit tonight too.
How wonderful to be able to go to Lake Charles and help to straighten things out. I told David all about it and he was much impressed.
Good-night sweetheart.
All my love –
ETHEL

[August 11, 1918]
Sunday night

MY DEAREST:
Although I wrote the above – in the dark – last night – before I went to bed I did not mail it because I wanted to write more today – but it just seemed impossible to get to it until now – and now it is very late. I have just come home after seeing "DeLuxe Anne" with Norma Talmage at the movies – It's the first time I've been in two weeks.
The thing I want to say most is – that I think I can surely be home by Sept. 1st. I consulted another dentist and if I have to have that impacted tooth out at all – I think I have found a man who can be relied on and who can do it at once. This new dentist I consulted (who is

an acquaintance of Fawn's) says that if the tooth isn't bothering me to let it alone for the present – so I may do that. But in either case, I can get through and be home about the first of Sept.

I am so homesick for you tonight and oh, so proud of what you are doing at Lake Charles. So you had a disaster after all. I wish I were with you – helping you.

I hope you are taking care of your precious self. Adah called me up tonight. All seems well there, but she is getting a bit weary of her job – she gets so little co-operation. She and Mother may come and spend the day with me next week. They had two letters from Emery last week. They were dated "on the banks of the Marne" and were written a month ago. Evidently Em is in the thick of it now.

It was so good to get your nice letter and your telegrams. Keep them up if you can't write.

We are both well and having just a good time and a lazy time so don't worry about us. Ben has been formally appointed First Assistant Inspector. He is very pleased. Good-night my dearest. I do love you so and don't see how I can stay away much longer. Write soon. Ever your

ETHEL

123.

[August 12, 1918]
Monday night

SWEETHEART:

I received some clippings today from your office telling about Lake Charles – and I felt prouder than ever of what you are doing. It must be a great satisfaction of bring so much comfort. I wish I were with you.

This is just to say good-night and that we are both well and happy – David and me.

The dentist began work on the tooth that had the cap on it today. I have to decide whether to go back to wait for Dr. Hasbrouck to return from his vacation or whether to go back to N.O. without having it out and going to a Dr. Kells there who is an expert on impacted teeth, I am told. What would you advise? My own dentist seems to think I ought to have it out – but will not consent to my going to anyone short of an expert.

Every one of my letters contain some dental news – I'm afraid it's not very interesting reading. I'll be glad when the work I need to have done is finished. But I want to tell you, most of all, that I love you very much tonight, dear – and want to be back home with you again. All my love,

ETHEL

P.S. David has had another hair bob. He looks very cunning and grown up also very brown. You ought to hear him tell about the Lake Charles tornado. He doesn't omit a detail. He sends his Daddy a big kiss.

124.

Western Union Telegram
Lake Charles, La.
Aug 12, 1918
Mrs. Harry L. Hopkins
306 Grandview Ave., Far Rock
Everything going nicely. Rained today and some suffering here. 500 tents up today. Will be here several days. Wire me night letter.
Much love
HARRY

125.

Western Union Telegram
Reading Pa.
Aug 15, 1918
Mrs. Harry L. Hopkins
306 Grandview Ave., Far Rock
Watch positively correct gentlemen's size. Harry will be very pleased
ED

126.

Aug. 14 [1918]

MY DEAREST BOY:

It's to wish you a happy birthday and many happy returns of Aug. 17th – that I write for this night. I wish I were where I could waken you with a kiss and tell you so myself on that day – It'll be a long, long time before I go away from home again! But I think it's been good for me to get away and to realize what a wonderful thing it is to be at home – with the family – our own little family – intact. Twenty-eight years is very old – but you haven't let the grass grow under your feet and you have filled each day of the past year in a very worth-while manner. I think the next year to come will bring wonderful experiences for you – and for us both – because I can't help feeling that whatever comes to you comes to me too. I have thought of all sorts of ways that I can improve on my role of wife and mother. I only hope I don't forget them before I get back! And speaking of getting back – I find that Dr. Hasbrouck who is to take out that tooth of mine won't be back until the middle of September. So I don't think I shall wait for him. The tooth is not bothering me in the least and it's only because they think it may aggravate sciatic condition and also cause other things that I am advised to have it out. The tooth that I am having re-filled and capped now is supposed to have caused sciatica, so we shall see.

So – what do you think about my coming home September first? After we are all settled in a new house I can go to Dr. Kells who is an expert on impacted teeth in N.O. and have him take it out. If I wait for Hasbrouck to come back, it will be October before I am through with dressings and the dentist here is not willing that I go to anyone else in N.Y. – except Dr. Schaumberg who is just frightfully expensive. So I want you to write and tell me if you think Sept. 1st is a good time for me to come home.

I am sending you your birthday gift this week under separate cover. I am afraid it won't reach you in time because it wasn't right. But it's coming and I saved the money that it cost long ago and it didn't come out of

Handwritten heading:
306 Grandview Ave.
Far Rock

the house either! I hope you will like it. I want you to let me know as soon as you receive it.

I made a fruit cake for the beach party Mother, Adah, David, and I are going to have on Friday. I hope it's a nice day and, vain hope, that you were to be among those present.

These hot days we have been taking our lunch on the beach in our bathing suits only reaching home in time for supper and it's been fine. Hanna spent the afternoon with me yesterday.

The rest of the family have all retired and I mustn't keep this light going any longer because it draws mosquitoes.

But I send you all my love tonight – and consider yourself kissed on the morning of August 17th. David and I shall celebrate the day here.

Ever your devoted,

ETHEL

P.S. I sent you a night letter to Hotel Majestic, Lake Chas. last night and also a letter that ought to have reached you there yesterday or today.

E.

127.

[date uncertain]
Thursday

DEAREST HARRY:

Enclosed is a statement showing where the money goes and how even though I am being entertained here, I can't seem to keep from buying some things. Next week the dentist will be through with my tooth and I will have to pay him $20 and I only have $11.00 to do it with. You see, I was in debt about $10.00 before I cashed your blank check for $50.00 that you sent me – and that is why it went so fast. I took Albert and Eleanor to the movies the other night – and here they are 28¢ a head – whether a child or no. And I have taken Albert several times. That $28.75 is made up of such incidentals and ice-cream cones for the children and the other things mentioned on the slip. I suppose I ought to have $25.00 more – in order to pay the dentist and have some money on hand. If fixing this tooth will stop my sciatica – $20.00 will be cheap – will it not? I think, however, that while this man out here is high priced, he is very expert and it saves going into the city each time. But if I have any more work done, I shall try to get Goddard to do it or else wait until I get back to N. O. This man says that when he finished this tooth, there is $20.00 worth more work to be done in my mouth – but I think Goddard would be more reasonable and if not I shall wait until I get back home. This is all exclusive of the impacted wisdom tooth that has to be taken out.

I can see I shall have to go to work – or put David to work – or something.

I am wondering what you think about the Russian situation now.

The Times yesterday said the suffragists were undemocratic because they wanted a Federal Amendment – It called us all sorts of nasty names for not being willing to submit the question to the people – by states – If it happened to be something they believed in and advocated themselves, they wouldn't have any scruples about dealing with a small body of men who are supposed to be representatives of the people.

I see this morning that McAdoo is demanding an 80% tax on war profits. I wonder if your friend – the Dir. of Military R. will still be able to give his full time without salary? I shall have to save this clipping for Ben & Ed because they declared to me last Sunday, that there were no war profiteers. That people who had government contracts could not make any money on them, etc.

I am sending you a watch for your birthday under separate cover. It has orders to tick many happy hours during the coming year for you – and for many years – for you mustn't lose it on the Pullman or anywhere else for at *least 5 years* – because I am sure it will take me as long as that to save up money for another. It also carries much love – *all* my love – and a big birthday kiss. When I get home I shall have the date engraved on it.
Ever your
ETHEL

128.

MY DEAREST:

I don't know whether to be worried about you or not to-night – I sent you a night letter – I haven't heard from you since last Tuesday and I don't know whether you returned from Lake Charles or how you are. I hope I shall have a good letter from you tomorrow. No matter how good a time I am having – or how well things are going, if I don't hear from you – it makes me depressed and homesick. I don't expect long letters when you are busy – a wire or even a postal keeps me satisfied that you are well – but I want some word from you.

Mother, Adah and I & David just had a wonderful day together last Friday. I put up a picnic lunch and we spent the whole day down on the beach. We didn't leave there until 6:30 and we didn't want to go then. We ate so much all afternoon that we didn't want any supper & so Mother and Adah took the 7:19 train home. It was a lovely day and we *went in* the water morning and afternoon. David spends most of his time flying kites that Albert makes for him – and he did that day. Uncle Frank sent him a lovely little handkerchief with little children printed all over it and David said that he would never blow his nose in it. He told Adah that. He also greeted them with "Gee, you ought to see me swim!" He dives in the shallow water and kicks his feet and makes an awful splash and I have hard work getting him out of the water. He gained one pound in about ten days and now weighs 33 lbs. I weigh *113*. What do you think of that? I was ill about ten days ago.

We all went down to the beach this morning and played ball out on the sand-bar – Ed, Ben, Jeanette, Albert, David and I. Then we went in and had a dandy swim. The weather here is cool, almost too cool some days for swimming – but it's delightful.

Now about coming home. The 31st is on Saturday (I think). Labor Day is the following Monday. Now, shall I start home the 28 of August and be at home for that week-end & Labor Day or shall I wait until after Labor

Day and start home on the 3rd of Sept.? As I have written you before, when this dentist finishes this one tooth, I shall not have any more work done – but get ready to come home. Find out whether Dr. Kells (dentist) is still in N. O. (I hope he hasn't gone to France). I can have the rest of the work done after I reach N.O. You haven't written me your advice in this matter and so I am planning to do what seems best to me.

It seems to me too, that unless you have found another house, that we had better keep that bungalow for another month so that we will have a place to come back to and so we can leisurely find another house. Perhaps you can make an arrangement to pay for it week by week in Sept. and then we could stay as long as we needed to. Otherwise you would have to pack and you wouldn't know what things are ours in the kitchen and what things were not and it would take so much of your time and so much trouble.

Now please sit down and write me a long letter and answer all my questions. If it seems best to you not to keep the bungalow through Sept. and if you think I ought to get home in time to find a house and move out by Sept. 1st, let me know at once.

It seems to me, however, that unless it is unbearably hot, it would be better to stay through Sept. and let me do the packing after I get back. Of course if you have found a nice house or can secure one before I get back – do take it.

You did not tell me what to do about Mr. Bache, so I wrote and told him that we preferred not to have a credit and asked him to settle our account at once. I have not heard from him yet. But there's hardly time since I sent it for an answer.

I hope you have sent me another check so I can pay the dentist. How are our finances anyway?

I know you have been very busy in the past two weeks – and I don't mean to be impatient – but when you get time do write me a good long letter and if you haven't time just send me a wire and tell me so.

If there is any good reason why I should stay here for a week or two in September, I think I could probably arrange to stay. Tell me if you have to be away in Sept. and also whether you are to have a vacation.

David and I get very homesick to be back home again – and while we are having a lovely time here – I do want to get back. We won't mind a little hot weather in Sept. after all this delightful weather here.

So do write to me dear – at once – and remember I love you very much and I don't like to be away so long. David seems dearer each day – just full of new utterances and newer tricks and games and I want his daddy to see him. Everybody loves him – that sees him – but I promise you I won't have him spoiled.

Good-night dear – all my love – and a big warm kiss –
ETHEL

129.

New Orleans
[August 15, 1918]

Written on ARC
letterhead.

MY DEAREST:

This is the first time I have had a minute to write a note and this must be very short because a Red Cross dinner takes place at the Grumwald in about two minutes.

The situation in Lake Charles is rapidly clearing up and I hope to be away from there for good on Sunday.

I will be in town for a few days and then off for a short trip – I don't' think you should try to get down here before Labor Day – the weather is fierce and the little house is quite uncomfortable – fortunately I am there very little and will be in the next few days.

We will have a lot to talk about when I see you my dearest – the South is alright except the weather which is bum.

Mr. Owens sprained his ankle is naturally in very ill humor.

Much love and a big kiss
HARRY

130.

Western Union Telegram
Aug. 19, 1918
306 Grandview Ave
New Orleans, La.
Mrs. Harry L. Hopkins
Just returned from Lake Charles. Probably be here for next week. Have not been home so have no way of knowing whether or not watch received. Am going to Birmingham next week. Will probably be away for some time.
HARRY

131.

[postmarked August 21, 1918]
Tuesday night

DEAREST BOY:

Your telegram came last night and I was much relieved to get it. It sounded as if you were a bit impatient at me for worrying over you again – but the weather, I knew, must have been hot down there and I knew you were working specially hard – and I wanted to know that you were all right.

You say you are "going away for some time." That sounds rather vague. I hope you have written me a letter which tells me more fully about your plans.

I received your letter mailed last Thursday and I was right glad to get it. It was a dear letter – if you did write it hurriedly. I know I mustn't expect too much of you in the way of letters – but you must acknowledge that I've been pretty good about that, and I can't help wanting long letters often even if I don't get them.

Someone once said that women who love their men *just a little* get along much better then those who love them a lot – because instead of spending so much time fretting – they go blithely on and are fretted over instead. But I'm glad I love you a lot – and I'm going to keep right on doing it – even though I know that you can't possible miss me as I miss you. Now please *don't* be cross at me and please don't think I don't understand just how busy and anxious you have been about your work in the past two weeks. I am so proud of what you are doing – and I was so glad of your telegrams when you couldn't write.

It is now near midnight and everyone is asleep – but I am writing this because I want to say good-night to you and because I love you –
ETHEL
P.S. David sends his Daddy a big kiss. He is very well.

132.

[August 21, 1918]
Wednesday

GOOD-NIGHT DEAREST:

I've spent most of the day sewing underclothes (new) for David. They are going to be very nice. Mother sent me some letters from Emery which I shall send on to you as soon as I answer E.'s letter to me.

I love you dear, and I want you to take good care of yourself.

No letter came from you today but I hope to receive one tomorrow. I sent the watch c/o Am. Red Cross P.O. Bldg and am rather anxious to know if you have received it. Ed says you must take it in to a jewelers to have it regulated. He didn't have time to have it done before sending it. It was through Ed that I got it.

It would do your heart good to see David's antics in the water. He goes in everyday and has such a good time. He said he had a letter from you today and then he began to read it to me thus "Dear Mother & David: When are you coming back to N.O.? I fixed the soldiers all up and am back home again. Wish I could come and see you at Aunt Fannie's house." He said all of this just so. He insists that it was the soldiers you had to fix up in Lake Charles. He threw a stone at Eleanor the other day and he came up to where I sat (after she began to howl) with "Will you punish me if I tell you the truff?" And then he told me and then I told him he had better stay on the porch for the rest of the morning – he said "it was too hot in the sun anyway." He's a handful – I can tell you – but very cunning – and pretty good most of the time. I shall stay here until after Labor Day – but are you going to lease or rent the house for the month of September?

All my love to you to-night –

ETHEL

133.

[August 22, 1918]

MY DEAREST:

Your good letter came to day together with your admonition that I must do better or you'll pick up and come home! My dear you have no idea in what a maelstrom I have been in for two weeks in and out of Lake Charles and I don't seem to be through as yet. Believe me, I have had my fill of disasters! The ladies of the town and I clash continuously and the men are little better while little Harry has his hands full keeping his temper. But the people are housed and no one is suffering for lack of food so I am not worrying.

I have made three trips in all to Lake Charles and am anticipating a fourth this Sunday and the mosquitoes there are 100% efficient! They bite in most unconventional places and are quite as ferocious as the fiercest Hun! Hundreds of [undecipherable] have been given out at $2 a piece.

My own work* is growing quite rapidly and I am planning to put in another worker– a girl from Cincinnati – We handle about 300 letters a day! I hired a new steno today, age 50 so don't worry.

Owens is much better and I had a long talk with him yesterday. Amongst other things he says he thinks it very unwise for you and the baby to come down until at least Sept. 15 – please don't get mad – if you had a little of this weather you would heartily agree. It's fierce! And no relief in sight. Let us know what you think. Personally I

Written on Lafayette Hotel, New Orleans letterhead.

*Hopkins established training institutes for ARC relief staff and was opening one in Shreveport, Louisiana.

am alright – eating well and sleeping a-plenty. I didn't see our home in two weeks and tonight am sleeping at this hotel across from the post office.

The watch arrived and is a beauty for which I give you a big kiss on the spot. I'm buying a chain forthwith. Everybody around the office says I have some little wife.

Before I say anything more, here is my check for [blank line]. Our account is in fairly good shape – I think about $330 so go ahead. I think I should get all the dentist work done in N.Y. – your dentist wasn't in at 5 this evening but will call up tomorrow.

I think you did just right about Bache – I hope he comes across.

I'd give a farm to see David but it won't be long – I'm going away about Sept. 1 for a few days – the institute opens at Shreveport on the 9th so I'll be there then.

Use your own judgment about coming home but I wouldn't come till the middle of Sept. if I were you – the weather really would be almost unbearable and I believe David would suffer. Let me know.

Mrs. Thornton wants us to take her house with her – it's up to you to decide. Miss Villere's house will be free Aug. 1 and I know we can stay where we are until Sept. 15 at least.

Much love and a big kiss my sweetheart.

Your Boy

HARRY

134.

Western Union Telegram

[August 23, 1918]

New Orleans, La.

Mrs. Harry L. Hopkins

306 Grandview Ave., Far Rock

Watch received. It is dandy. Long letter sent last night. Letter from Emery indicates that he is in the thick of fight.

Much love

HARRY

135.

Western Union Telegram
New Orleans, La.
Aug. 24 [1918]
Mrs. Harry L. Hopkins
306 Grandview Ave., Far Rock
Just returned from Lake Charles. Everything going well
there. Weather hot and you had better not come for a
while. Am anxious to see you but am going to be out of
town until after the 12th.
Much love
HARRY

136.

Western Union Telegram
New Orleans, La.
Aug 31, 1918
Mrs. Harry L. Hopkins
306 Grandview Ave., Far Rock
Ahrens wants house Sept. 1 and I am moving our things
out and storing them at Villeries. I will board there un-
til you come. Will try to get in new house before Oct 1
if possible.
Much love
HARRY

137.

Western Union Telegram
New Orleans, La
Sept 7, 1918
Mrs. Harry L. Hopkins
306 Grandview Ave. Far Rock
Am in Lake Charles for weekend and going to Shreveport Tuesday. Putting on ten new Home Service men.
Nothing new about the house.
Much love
HARRY

.

138.

[August 26, 1918]
Sunday night

MY DEAREST:
Every time you tell me I mustn't come home for two weeks later than planned, it has the effect of making me feel terribly homesick (did you ever see a pen act up as this one is doing to-night?) [*she changes to a pencil*] I suppose it must be very hot. Ben said he saw somewhere that the temperature was 110 in N.O. I can't ever find it in the Times. I'll try to be good and stay until Sept. 15th – but to-night it seems a long time to wait to see you.

The weather here is perfectly delightful. We use a blanket and a comforter on our bed every night – David and me – otherwise we are cold. Adah and a Miss Roberts came down last Friday and we had a lovely day picnicking on the beach. David stayed with us all day. We did not leave the beach until 6:30. Adah met Mrs. Sonnechson – do you remember who she is – her name now is different, she has taken her maiden name since her divorce – and she had a barefoot Russian singer with her (a man) whom she introduced as her friend. They both spouted like red hot radicals and I sat with my mouth open and went back to the pavilion for more in the evening. We all watched the moon come up and Adah left on a 10:08 train for N.Y. They had supper on the beach. Adah says she is coming *alone* next Friday and we are to have a good visit. I shall bring her back here for supper.

Did Mrs. Thornton call you up and ask you to take part of her house and is she to be in the other part and are there kitchen privileges or a boarding proposition? I *am* interested in Villere's house. If it is what you think we want and if there is any danger of it being rented before I get back, why don't you take it.

I am glad you like the watch and I hope you have had it regulated at a jewelers. I have sent you several letters to 7721 Sycamore St. Do go and get them.

I am glad to learn that you are "eating well and sleeping aplenty." Do you still use the fan? Where do you expect to go for "a few days rest." I wish I were going too – and David, but you'll probably get a better rest without us – because if I ever get to you I certainly am going to make you talk. Your letters are so few and far between and they tell so little. If you would only set a certain time aside everyday to write to me, it wouldn't be so hard to stay away. I would punish you by writing as seldom as you do – but I couldn't do that without punishing myself – because I get much comfort in pouring out my heart to you – and I like to do it every night after everyone is asleep.

Many thanks for check. I shall draw it for $50.00 (don't faint). But after I pay the dentist $20 I want to have some money in case I have to have my other teeth done – and I want to go in to town to say goodbye to Mother next Thursday and I shall see Goddard at the same time. And then I shall have to give Fannie some money each week because I cannot expect Ben to pay my board any longer. Ed is paying part & Ben the other half. Ed will probable keep doing it while he is here – but he may go back to his apartment any day. It seems to take $10.00 a week to feed David & me – so I want to have some money on hand.

Fannie says I should stay all of Sept – she says I can't stay too long to please her. But you must be sure to tell me you miss me very much and write to me often if you want me to stay longer. I'm homesick.

Good-night my sweetheart. I'm never going away from you again.

Write soon – all my love – and a big kiss –

ETHEL

David sends his Daddy a good hug – and a nice dry kiss. He's as well and as happy as he can be – and the joy of the household.

139.

[August 25, 1918]

MY DEAREST GIRL:

I've received all your good letters even the one written in pencil which was extremely discourteous of you! Think of writing your husband in pencil! Before we go further, editorially speaking – let me take you to the Palace and there cast your eye on the movie screen and see your own protector caring for the poor sufferers of Lake Charles. It was too terrible – my manly figure stood forth – every line of it, even the life line if you know what I mean and the lovely features of my face cast its radiant light over the sufferers – and the audience – well one woman says –"I wouldn't mind the storm, but think of having to be assisted by that" – at any rate my ambition is realized and I think I shall move to other fields for conquest. It's an ill wind etc!

Now to business my dear – Miss Villere* wants us to take her house next door – four big rooms, sleeping porch, large and screened – fine yard and 15 minutes from town – I am going to go all through it this p.m. – They will be free there on Oct. 1 – and I think we might possibly stay in Ahrens until the first. It sounds good and I will probably wire you tonight. It's heated by stove in hall which is taken care of by a porter and has two dandy fireplaces.

We are going ahead with big plans here for winter and I am very anxious to tell all about them. Prof. W. is giving two institutes beginning Sept. 9 and Oct. 9 respectively. Leppert is out in the field and I have in mind making Mrs. Eustis assistant director – she has given me great service. More coming. I want you very badly, but it won't be long at any rate and why come here now to boil in that terrible house of ours. I am going to Meridian and Jackson, Miss. I think, next week. Our conference at Alexandria is off, but will be held about Sept. 5, probably here. I must be in Shreveport the 9th and 10th and in Alexandria and Baton Rouge the 11th and 12th of Sept., after that I'll be home for awhile, so why not come along about that time.

I have letters from all the family this week and must try to answer some of them today. The watch, my sweetheart, is a perfect beauty and I am delighted with it. I'll kiss you later. Do take care of that young heir of ours – the water is very deep, you know.

This is all for the time – my dearest – a big kiss for you both.

HARRY

*Gross and Hopkins spelled the name "Villeres" in a variety of ways in the correspondence.

140.

Western Union Telegram
August 26, 1918
Mrs. Harry L. Hopkins
306 Grand View Ave.
Far Rockaway, N.Y.
Miss Villere's house available five rooms. Two bedrooms dining room kitchen screened porch an sitting room very well furnished. She provides heat electricity and janitor [indecipherable]. She asks sixty dollars a month. Available October first. She must know immediately whether or not we will take it. By all means best house I have seen in New Orleans and think it very desirable to take it. Wire me at office. Also write office in future.
HARRY
Charge American Red Cross
Gulf Division

141.

[August 27, 1918]

MY DEAREST ETHEL:

I hope you received my wire today about the house at Villares – the place is exquisite – clean – bright and airy – two lovely bedrooms – a peach of a dining room but a rather small though very well appointed kitchen and closet – nice bath – screened porch – sitting room – mahogany furniture and generally a perfect place to live in. I want to rent it and have everything ready when you come here. She pays for electricity – coal but not gas – 60 a month. Why not take it?

This is written as I am rushing to a H. S. meeting — but I love you my darling very, very much, tonight especially –

Many kisses and all my love.
HARRY

142.

Wednesday
August 28, 1918

DEAREST BOY:

I feel satisfied to-night that I have a very nice husband for I have just finished reading your very nice letter *of Aug. 25* which I found on my return from a day in N.Y. with Mother and Adah.

At last you are in the movies – I shall haunt all the shows here in town until I see the famous picture. The fates are cruel – that I should have missed such a treat. What was the name of the current weekly that published it?

I am glad you like the watch and I hope you have had it regulated at a watch maker. I am trying to get you a chain through Ed so if you have not already bought one – don't. If so you will have 2.

I have had a lovely day with Mother and Adah. I went to lunch with the latter and to the theater to see Holbrook Blinn & Blanche Bates in "Getting Together." It was a highly entertaining performance – through part of which I wept. Only Mother went with me because Adah had to go back to the office – but it was Adah's treat. I afterward took Mother to dinner at a French restaurant and reached home at about 9:20 – to find David peacefully asleep and looking fatter than ever.

I am much thrilled about Miss Villere's house although I had hoped we wouldn't have to pay quite so much. But if it's comfortable and if you think we can't do any better – I hope you took it. It will be fine to be so near your office – and I hope we can find some kiddies for David to play with.

Tell me – do you think I should ship our fireless-cooker? It is here and would be so useful. I could freight it.

Is there a good complete kitchen with a gas range – and necessary pots and pans?

Now I am coming home Sept. 15th and I won't stay here any longer – although I am having a lovely time. I had a long talk with Mr. Bache and he showed me on paper how we owed him $61 interest and $10.41 water tax & $5 for something else – and also how the total amount of our payments amounted to $75.00. And he added "you pay me what you owe me and I will return what you paid me." He said if we had sold our lots he would have given us our $75 as commission and would still if we could sell two others – and he still insists that he will credit us for $75 against any future purchase of lots in Great Kills.* He's a very slick business man and I take my hat off to him. Don't scold me.

*Great Kills is a town in Staten Island.

Good-night my darling – I dare to use pencil again – but I tell you my fountain pen is out of commission – and I sharpened my pencil this time. I am writing by a dimmed light.

Much love and a big kiss –

ETHEL

P.S. Mother leaves for Canada on Friday where she will stay for 1 week and then go on to Grinnell. Adah is much depressed because she hasn't heard from Frank in two weeks. Frank is now in France.

143.

[date uncertain]

MY DEAREST GIRL:

As soon as I received your wire, I called up Miss Villere and hired one house! It's a dandy and know you won't be disappointed. I should like to have it all fixed up before you return. I am that ambitious! Don't worry about my inability to move alone – it's the best thing I do. David, by the way, will have lots of room to play – can have a big sand pile and a yard to himself. Did I tell you there is a work house in the rear with tubs, etc. The furniture is much nicer than our own. I am really delighted with it – the expense is alright in view of free light and heat. The sitting room you know is downstairs. I could have got the four rooms upstairs for $55 but the room downstairs is a dandy and can be used for an extra bedroom. The maid can sleep there possibly – that will be the only difficult part.

It is unfortunate that Owens has a broken leg and not a sprained ankle so that he is in very ill humor and is cursing his bad luck. Two or three new men are coming in next week for camp work.

How is your dentist work coming – I do hope they leave some teeth in your dear little head.

I want you to send my mail to the office because I expect to be away for some time soon and want your letters forwarded. David's swimming antics are too interesting for words – how I'd like to be with him. Give him a big kiss for me.

Goodbye for tonight – my best love,

HARRY

144.

[September 1, 1918]

MY DEAREST ETHEL:

It has been at least three days since I have written, except my wire last night. Ahrens called me up and told me that he had a chance to rent the house and wanted to know if I would be willing to get out – as I am to be [away a great] deal – I told him yes – under any circumstances we had to move on the 15th – so I am going to tomorrow – pack up and move down to Villere's I hope. She hopes that the people in our house will get out in a few days and I would then move right in there. I will let you know about this as soon as I learn definitely. Our new house, by the way, is dear – I know you will like it.

I wrote a long letter to Emery yesterday and one to Lew – be sure and write Em and Frank too for that matter. Letters mean so much to them.

Am head over heels in work and see no let-up – but am really feeling fine and my friends say looking well. I can hardly wait to see you – this is your last vacation alone – make up your mind to that little sweetheart. I love you very much, Ethel dear and want you near me.

The weather is hoternell – the sweat rolls off in buckets – it's so wet that it saves me from taking a bath!

Written on ARC letterhead.

Your letter yesterday was a dandy – do be forgiving of my shortcomings in letter writing – I apologize. Don't lead too gay a life on the sea shore – Mon Dieu – no!

My best love to you and a big warm kiss for you and David, the dear.

Your Boy

HARRY

Did you get the candy? Here is a rusty story: The husband had put his hand on the door which was newly painted and the lady of the house sent for Jim Johnson to come over and paint it up.

Housewife to the painter: "Let me show you where my husband put his hand last night."

Painter to housewife: "No, thank you – I just came over to paint" –

Exit this way.

145.

[August 31, 1918]
Saturday evening

At the top of the letter, next to an ink blot:"my fountain pen again."

MY OWN DEAREST BOY:

In the first place I want to say thank-you for that lovely box of pralines. Everybody in the house is enjoying them including myself. It was very thoughtful of you to send them and I send you a sweet large kiss.

The best bit of news I have to write today is that I weighed David and he weighs 35 pounds. You remember we never could get him much past 32 [and a half]. He was 32 on the scale (Fairbanks) that I always use, when we came here, and that same scale balances 35 now. He should weigh for his age 33 [and three quarters]. Isn't that great? He is just wonderful in every way and I am anxious to have his daddy see him.

I received your letter today saying that you have engaged Miss Villere's house and I am very much excited about it. (I here abandon my fountain pen. It is impossible).

I can't tell from your letter whether you have the upstairs or downstairs apartment – you speak of the sitting
room being "downstairs." But I know I will be pleased
whatsoever.

Are there hot water facilities of any kind and is china
and glassware supplied? Are there enough beds and
one for David? I am just crazy to get home and to see it.
In view of the fact that gas is so high – don't you think
I should have the fireless cooker freighted? Have you
still that stove that was expressed to your office last February?

I am delighted that it is all so beautifully furnished –
and it will be splendid to be so near town. And to think
of having a sand pile for David. It all sounds fine and I
am so pleased. David insists on drawing you something
before he goes to bed. I asked him what he wanted to
say to you and he said " I am writing him a letter myself." Jeanette never goes to the village without bringing
something home to him and he has completely won
over everyone in the household. He got under the
shower of his own accord after his bath in the ocean today. He cautioned me not to run it fast and not to touch
him and when he was under awhile he said "Now run it
fast." Which I did. Now I must put him to bed. I told
David that there was a sand pile to our new house and
he said "I told Daddy to get me a lot of little boys to play
with in my letter." I enclose the letter. The man is
copied from a picture.

Now as to moving. Do you mean to move in before
Sept. 15th? If you are bound to do this you must know
that there is cutlery – steel knives and forks and a paring knife or two and an aluminum steamer that consists
of 1 large aluminum pan with handles – one medium
sized one and one small one; one set of five custard
cups – a holder for them and a large aluminum ring
and a cover. Those are the only pots that belong to me.
But there is also a potato masher (steel). Also all the
mason jars (glass). I think there is one pint jar and at
least thee quart jars. And all the tin boxes marked
"Sugar." Also all the spices and things. Not the jelly
glasses. The toaster belongs to us – also the electric
toaster that is on the top shelf is ours.

But I shall stop this zig-zag list and make you out a separate one on a sheet of paper. I predict that after you see it you will be very glad to have me come home in time to do the packing. I am afraid it's going to be kind of a nuisance for you to do it. Perhaps (if your heart is still set on doing this moving and if we need to get out before I get back) you could get Lorena to come & help you pack. I gave her instructions about how & what to pack and she knows my things in the kitchen. I think I shall write Mrs. Thornton asking her to lend Lorena if you should decide to pack without me. I think she would.

If you will look in the drawer of the sitting room for an envelope marked "Cards," you will there find a card of the Gallagher Express Co. I am not sure that the above is the name, but they moved us so nicely from Mrs. Thornton's as you know for something like $4.00 or $3.50. They were very prompt and seemed most reliable. It's the only card of a N.O. Express Co. in there so I think you cannot fail to find it. They may call themselves "Movers or Storage Warehouse."

I don't like to put all this work on to you – but if you are bound to do it I think you should have all this information.

The 15th of September falls on Sunday so I can do one of two things – either come home or rather leave here on Friday the 13th (horrors) reaching N.O. Sunday morning – or else leave here on Monday the 16th and reach N.O. on Wednesday morning. It would be nice to have Sunday to ourselves – If I come on a week day you would not be at home. Of course I could leave here on Thursday the 12th & reach N.O. on Saturday morning the 14th. I shall do whatever you say. If I arrive on Sunday perhaps we could arrange to have our dinner at Miss Villerie's on that day. I shall do whatever you say so sit right down and tell me.

Be sure and remind me that I have something interesting to tell you about Pres. Main* when I get back. Also some things that Mrs. Sonnechson said.

I had a letter from Mrs. Eustis today. Be sure and tell her I was delighted to get it. It was a scream.

*Dr. J.H.T. Main was acting president of Grinnell College from 1901 to 1903 and president from 1903–1928.

Among other things she said you just returned to the office after having "blowed Miss Dinwiddie & Miss Clifton to dinner." She goes on to say "that did prove somewhat of a tax on Mr. Hopkins. He came in pretty thoroughly tired, but I think he has pulled himself together & feels about all right now." That must have been *some* dinner. Of course that last sentence of hers might refer to the Lake Charles disaster that she refers to farther back. But I quote verbatim & in sequence.

I asked Mrs. Eustis to write and tell me how you seemed & looked. She wrote me a nice long letter in which she tells me all the good & bad points of the "new clerical help" physical as well as mental but mostly physical.

I note you say you will probably appoint her Asst. Director. Why not Assistant *to the* Director.

Adah couldn't come out today because some girl had arrived from out of town that she had to see. I hope to see her next week.

I won't have any more dental work done until you tell me how much more money I can spend.

As for that impacted tooth, I won't have it out unless I have another attack of sciatica. It may not be causing it at all and the clearing up of the roots of the tooth I have just had treated might be enough to take it away. I have two more fillings that should be fixed sometime, but I won't have it done now unless you say we can spare the money now. This dentist here at F. R. might charge $20.00 more to do it – besides the $30 already spent – and if I go in to Goddard the car fare is so much. I can wait until I get back to N. O.

This is a very lengthy epistle. You will have to take a day off to read it. I hope you have a long ride or something before you when you receive it.

I can't tell you how much I love you to-night. Just oceans – and it will be wonderful to be at home again.

Good-night my love and be good – and do all the things that I like you to do – and don't work too hard. A great big kiss from

ETHEL

List of our belongings at 7721 Sycamore St. as far as I can remember

<u>Kitchen</u>

1 aluminum pot with handles (large)

1 medium " " without "

1 small " " " "

1 set of 5 custard cups and ring in which they fit

1 large aluminum ring

1 " " cover.

3 large glass jars

1 pint " " (perhaps they are broken)

3 or 4 brown tin cans containing flour, sugar, etc. but all marked "sugar."

1 toaster for gas stove

1 electric toaster (on top shelf of kitchen closet).

(Be sure you get all the parts complete of the electric toaster).

1 potato masher (steel or iron)

about 3 steel knives and forks that match.

A large bread knife

" " carving " & fork (kitchen)

A can opener that matches above.

Another " "

1 small pointed paring knife

" " potato peeler.

Our set of ivory carving knife and fork in drawer of buffet in dining room.

1 set of straw mats for table

4 or 6 asbestos pads for table. (small, plate size)

All the linen in drawers of buffet and all the silver.

Copper cream pitcher and sugar bowl.

Teapot (that should be packed with care.)

Our pictures that are on the walls or standing on the mantles.

Any scarves that are on the dressers – buffet, etc.

Everything out of every drawer in each one of the dressers.

There isn't much in David's room – but in our room and in the Buffet.

Dish towels and aprons in the kitchen.

All our books that have been unpacked.

The typewriter and the empty typewriter case in the shed.

1 case of unopened books in shed.

1 case (but I am taking it for granted that Lorena emptied all the books out of the large case in the shed. Books and papers.

Stationary and stuff out of drawer in sitting room.

My ivory clock (which is probably in drawer of my dressing table).

1 clock in sitting room (leather case)

The above might also have been put in a drawer somewhere.

and

Books – Books –Books –

The cover off sitting room table.

1 small market basket.

Linen in bottom drawer of your chiffonier.[†]

[†]*At the bottom of the list of belongings: "walnut 228." There is a check mark next to the following entries: 1 electric toaster, a large bread knife, 1 small pointed paring knife, dish towels, the typewriter, 1 case of unopened books in shed, my ivory clock, 1 clock in sitting room, and the cover off sitting room table.*

146.

[August 28, 1918]

MY DEAREST ETHEL:

Your good letter came to the office today and my dear you know I miss you – so much so that you may be sure I'll never let you go again! But as long as you're away – make the most of it and escape the fierce weather here.

Out of the clear sky today Prof. Gannaway & Almy[*] dropped on the scene and we have had a delightful day – took a walk through French town and lunch in our French restaurant (price raised to 60¢) and Wyckoff took them on a bus ride this afternoon. We had dinner in Galatories, my treat, and a long reminiscence over our cigarettes and coffee. Both men may come with us.

Miss Dinwiddie sent me an unbound volume of her poems – a bit mushy but indicative of a free spirit. They are called "Blossom Time" – can you imagine it?

I broke the crystal on my watch so there is nothing for me to do but get it regulated. I doubt if ever [I] would have accomplished it without an accident!

Please stop talking about that baby – it makes me homesick – I am sure I shall not know my offspring. By

Written on ARC letterhead.

[*]*John W. Gannaway taught Hopkins political science at Grinnell College; Almy might be Frederick Almy of the Buffalo Charity Organization Society.*

the way, have you seen Florence King – I should love to see her baby.

The war is going great even without me.

Do have a good time my dear – we are going to have a delightful fall and winter together, so why worry about a few weeks – you couldn't see much of me anyway, if you came down now.

I love you a great deal tonight me dearest and give you a big hug and a long kiss.

HARRY

147.

Sept. 3rd [1918]
Tuesday night

GOOD-NIGHT DEAREST:

I am very sleepy and tired tonight after a long day in NY – I bought me a hat! What do you think of that. But I had a chance to get one wholesale – and it's very good value. My blue one is such a sight and my leghorn is too large to wear on the train home.

Your dear letter came tonight. So Miss Dinwiddie sent you a book. I'm glad she "blossomed" out with something. She seemed as dry as dust to me – the times I saw her – Did she indicate her free spirit by writing "verse libre" – or is she just generally free. She can stop picking on you or I'll show my free spirit when I get back. Who is Miss Clifton?

Thanks for the bulletin. I always read them right through. I am going to try to get hold of Florence King if I can before I go back. But how she will scold me:

I bought a copy of the Liberator today.

I went in to N.Y. on the car with Jeannette this morning and we left here at 7 am. So I am ready for bed now that it's after 10:30 pm. I hope you have written me whether I can start home on the 12th or 16th. If not wire me because I have to have enough time to make plans here. Only nine more days between now and the 12th. I also bought some black ties today that I can wear all winter. Your next letter won't be too soon for you to send me a check for my ticket home, will it? I hope we'll have enough money left.

Good-night my dearest – I'm glad the time for going home is drawing near – a great big kiss –from –
ETHEL

148.

[September 3, 1918]

MY DEAREST:

Again I have neglected you my dear – I am so sorry – I'm simply up to my neck in work. I believe I am safely moved at last. I'm some little packer – books – pajamas – pictures – clocks – all in one – you will give me H-E-L-L, but I am moved so why worry. Everything is stored in our front room at Villere's.

Our house is upstairs – with the living room downstairs – the bed room will be a good living room however and I doubt that we will use the rooms downstairs except for company. Now I don't know yet just when we can get in. I think you had better leave on the 16th because I will be away on the 14th when you would arrive. I think we can arrange to board at Villere's until the hour is ready. My dearest – I want you home the worst way – it's lonesome as the devil here and that boy of ours will have forgotten his daddy.

Spend all the money you need – we're going to have to start all over again anyhow – so why worry – do take care of yourself my dear and bring David back as well as you took him. I am delighted with his weight and his little messages.

I love you my dear very very much and want you so much. I need you badly but it will be soon. I am off for Lake Charles Friday for two days and am going to Shreveport Tuesday then to Birmingham and back home. I must go to Miss. after that.

My best love to you my dear,
HARRY

149.

[September 8, 1918]
Sunday afternoon

DEAREST HARRY:

Adah came out here yesterday afternoon and stayed until this morning and we had a good visit and a nice dinner last night. Fannie and Ben were away and Adah had their room. Helen and I and the children had the run of the house until today when Ed & Jeanette & Albert returned. Everybody is moving in to New York next week. Ed & his family move next Tuesday & Fannie the end of the week and so as next Monday is Fannie's holiday, I have decided to leave here next Sunday, a week from today and so reach New Orleans Tuesday morning September 17th. It isn't convenient for me to leave on the sixteenth and I will explain why when I see you. I would have to upset everybody else's plans if I did. I shall do this (leave next Sunday) provided your check comes in time for me to get my ticket and make my reservation before that date.

I wired you on Friday night asking you to send it also asking your advice about the date to leave here. A letter came from you the next morning, however suggesting that I do not leave before the 16th. If your check does not come in time for me to leave on Sunday the 15th – I shall have to wait over until the latter part of that next week – but if I can possibly start on the 15th I shall. I do not want to have to send my trunk to Fannie's apartment and I should have to do that if I stay after next week. I hope you have written me whether or not you think it worthwhile to ship our fireless cooker – and if you do not make out the check you send me – I hope you will tell me how much I may draw.

Is the weather warm in N.O.? If I can get a cloth suit here now – may I – or had I better wait until I return.

It is a cold, bleak, autumn day today and we have a fire in the grate. It has rained most of the day. I have just finished writing a long letter to Emery – and I am going to try to get one in to Frank too.

The enclosed letters are from Emery – as you will see – Return the ones that are not addressed to us to where they belong. On the little sheet of paper is a letter to you from your son. When I asked him what he wrote he said "It's a secret." He says there are O's and E's on it, and for you to find them. I asked him "what will your daddy do when he sees you." – and he said – after thinking a minute "He will hug me and kiss me" So you'd better get ready.

A week from to-night, if all goes well, I'll be on a train speeding towards you – it's been worth the separation – almost – to know how much you mean to me – and the joy of getting back. I believe I'll come next Sunday whether you will be in town or not! All my love to you dearest boy – only 10 more days! Sweetheart.

Ever your own,

ETHEL

P.S. Do you get all my wires, I wonder? Ben wants you to write to him very much. He says a letter would "help to make the week shorter" and each time I see him he asks me if I remembered to ask you to write to him. Do –

I wish I could get little gifts all around before I go back. Everyone has been so nice.

I paid the dentist bill – $20.00 – so that's settled – but so is the $50.00 you sent me – by the time I gave Fannie some and bought myself some shoes – and a few other necessary things – like underwear, etc. it was gone. I have tried very hard not to be extravagant – but everything is so high.

Good-night dear – and don't be cross at me –

E.

150.

[September 9, 1918]

MY DEAREST:

Your two letters came one after the other and my little dear you cannot get down here too soon to suit me. This bachelor life is hell and when I tell you some of my experiences you never will leave home again. You may be sure I will never let you. You women – damn

Written on ARC letterhead.

you – don't need to have men around but my dear I've had to bite my lip hard several times to keep from going astray! You little dear – I miss you so much and I know how much I love you – tis ever thus when ever away – you will say.

I am not living at Villeres – there is no room – nor at Owens and Mrs. Thornton and I are off each other. I'm not going to explain it all now but it's best that you didn't come – except that I want you and need you badly. We'll be broke but happy when you get back! Yours truly has been living in a hotel! Never again.

Am enclosing a clipping some family what! Ain't you proud kid? Poor old Em bumping into machine guns don't compare with me Oh no!

Have as good a time as your conscience and pocketbook will permit – remember I love you more than anything in the world – you and David.

A big kiss

HARRY

Am working *like hell*!

151.

[September 9, 1918]

MY DEAREST:

Am enclosing check – Use $100 if you need it – I will plan on that. Am sorry about Villere's. I thought there would be room but they told me today there was nothing doing.

If I don't get a wire from you today, will wire tomorrow.

I want you very much my sweetheart.

All my love

HARRY

152.

MY DEAREST ETHEL:

I'm taking some time out of the afternoon to write you a note because otherwise I should never get a word to you my dear. The lecture this morning was only fair and I feel a little disappointed but Wyckoff tells me it was alright so why worry. The class contains 18 good country women all more or less interested in Home Service.

Your telegram about coming to N.O. was received just before taking a train at Lake Charles hence the delay in answering – I will be away on the 14th which is the day you would arrive if you left on the 12th and there really would be no place for you to go – poor thing! I shall be in town on the 18th and will probably have some place to take you although I'm afraid it will not be to our new home. Miss Villere is very short of room. I will get a definite answer from her tomorrow and wire you. Could you possibly stay in N.Y. to the 28th and arrive here Oct. 1 if I can not make arrangements at Villere's? Bang! Here the fireworks!

My train leaves at 6:30 this evening but I am invited out to dinner at 5:30 with the Jones – they are the leading people in Shreveport and I think will kill the fatted calf! Here's hoping! Wyckoff and Miss Alling are going along.

You ask who Miss Clifton is – 46 years – a New York school teacher and friend of Miss Dinwiddie's – very much her style – please forgive me – she's terribly homely and I am partial to good looks.

I send you all my love – my sweetheart – and want to see you so much – a big kiss on both cheeks – and for David a spanking.

HARRY

153.

Western Union Telegram
New Orleans, La.
Sept. 9, 1918
Mrs. Harry L. Hopkins
306 Grandview Ave., Far Rock
Advisable not to leave until September sixteenth. Am
not sure that we can live at Villeres until October first.
Am leaving for Shreveport tonight. Will write you fully
today.
HARRY

154.

[September 15, 1918]
Sunday afternoon

The handwritten
return address, 549
W. 113th St., probably
refers to the Kohn's
home.

DEAR HARRY:

When I received your wire a week ago (in answer to
mine asking whether to come home on the 12th or
16th) in which you said "come back on the 16th because I will be away on the 14th", I began immediately
to make plans to leave. Fannie was coming to N.Y. for
her holiday on Saturday the 14th and so I decided to
come with her & leave on Sunday the 15th in order to
avoid being here on a holiday which is a fast day. The
reason I did not want to wait until after the holiday was
over – is because Fannie was having the apartment re-
painted and re-papered on Tues. and Wed. and was
planning after that to go to F.R. again for a week to pack
up the house there preparatory to coming in here for
the winter. You can see that with all this in hand that we
would be very much better out of the way – *So* I found
I had to send my trunk to the station on Friday in order
to have it checked on my train on Saturday as so many
people are going back to N.Y. and the express men
were very busy. I therefore packed my trunk and sent it
off Friday afternoon – and was all ready for my journey
home – (The neighbors streamed in all afternoon to

say good-bye to us) when your long message came telling me not to come until October 1st. It didn't seem possible to change then. It would have meant recalling my trunk – unpacking it all again – and following Fannie back and forth from Far Rock to N.Y. – at a time when I was absolutely in the way. Although Fannie would think it was blasphemy to acknowledge such a thing – even to herself. So I wired you that I could not change my plans – that I was leaving as soon as your check arrived. Then came your second message in which you still persisted that you would have to engage rooms at a hotel until Oct. 1 if we came – and from the general tone of which I could see we were not wanted at present. So after another wakeful night – I decided it would be better to stay here – even if it wasn't convenient – than to go back home when you didn't want me to come. I shall have my trunk sent up here from the Pa. Station tomorrow and then when Fannie goes back to Far Rockaway on Wednesday, I shall go with her for a week and on Friday the 28th I shall take the train at noon from N.Y. to Washington arriving in N.O. on Sunday morning the 30th of September.

I shouldn't have minded staying until the above date if I had planned for it – but I planned to go after your telegram said to come on the 16th & the whole family here made their plans accordingly – and it's awfully awkward to unpack the trunk – and to send it back and forth. You see after your telegrams on Saturday, the 8th, I did not hear a word from you until Sat. the 15th – and I thought it was alright to go ahead and do what you said to do.

Of course at this distance I could not see why we couldn't share your room at Villere's. If they object to children why did Mrs. White's little girl stay there. And if they object to David and me so much – why do they let us rent their house next door? Nor can I understand why we would not have been able to go to Mrs. Thornton's or Mrs. Todd's or to the other dozens of boarding houses in N.O. for ten days. Even to the one that the Owens stayed at.

But I'm sure you did your best and that there will be a very good reason why we couldn't do any of these things.

I know too that you are busy and haven't time to bother too much about these things.

But I'm sure you took care of the Guatemala refugees and the homeless at Lake Charles much better.

Please forgive me if this letter is discouraging – or if you don't like it – *I must get these things off my chest.*

Perhaps I'll feel better after I do. As it is now I feel no enthusiasm about staying here – and less about going back to N.O. – now.

I could hardly wait until today to start – but I could no more start back today knowing that you would be annoyed and displeased after I arrived, than I could take a trip to Alaska, where it's cold.

I'm thinking some of taking the boat trip if I can get someone to reassure me about the safety of it. That would consume a week and I would not have to recall my trunk. I would leave here on Wednesday & reach N.O. about the 25th or 26th. In my wire this morning I asked you about the feasibility of this plan.

Ben said this morning that if I was to start back a month from now – it would probably be two weeks too soon. One of his little jokes not relished by me right now.

Of course it will be much nicer to go directly to our own house – I don't deny that. But it was because my visit here ought logically to end now – and principally because I was terribly homesick to get back – that I wanted to come now. You know I never expected to stay as long as this. You keep saying you want us to come back – but every time I make an attempt to come you discourage it.

If only you would write oftener it wouldn't be so hard to stay away as I have said before.

I know that you will hate me for this letter – but it's the only kind I could possible write today. Perhaps tomorrow I'll feel quite better.

Your special delivery from Shreveport came to me on Saturday and I'm glad Miss Clifton is 46 and plain and I'm awfully glad I'm young and beautiful since you are partial, as you say to good looks!

I do love you dear – and I'll try to be good from now on –

David spent this morning on Riverside Drive with me and his Uncle Ben and Fannie took him down this afternoon so I could write this. You will say she is no friend of yours to give me an opportunity to write such a letter as this to you – but I sure am powerful mad – but I'll try to get over it. If I didn't know how hard a hotel bill would hit our balance in B. I would be on my way now with David – reading "High Adventure" by Norman Hall – a present from Adah "to be read on the train."

ETHEL

155.

[postmarked September 15, 1918]
Sunday night

SWEETHEART:

It's just a few hours since I wrote you – but I want to follow my last letter up by saying that I think I'm going to have a very happy time here in the next two weeks in spite of my reluctance about staying. I have made up my mind I'm going to have a happy time and I'd like to see anyone stop me! When I say "happy" I mean as happy as possible with you hundreds of miles away – so don't worry about my last letter or about David and me.

I am enclosing a letter from David. He says there are two birds in it and for you to find them. He says that you are his "Daddy and nobody else's" – "*So.*" He has a way of ending his statements with "So." I don't know where he got it. He asked me today what "captured" means – and the other day when I was reading aloud to Fannie he caught prenatal and he said "What does prenatal mean?" So I had to tell him.

I am looking forward to this winter – more than I ever have before – I know it is going to be a wonderful one for us all. Even if you are busy we will be near enough to the office for you to get home soon after your work is finished. And I am going to make an effort to be of some use – outside – if only a few hours a week.

I am bringing our small machine home in the trunk. It will be good for mending and making clothes for David and perhaps myself.

Good-night dear – I love you – and if you'll just be a little bit glad to see David and me when we get back I'll forgive you for everything you've done.

Be good – and take care of yourself.

All my love and a big kiss –

ETHEL

156.

[September 18, 1918]

DEAREST HARRY:

Enclosed I am sending you my trunk check. The congestion is so bad that I found it would take 3 days to have it shipped here & 3 days to have it shipped back to Pa. Station, so we are living in a suitcase and I shall buy my ticket when I go downtown in a little while, check my trunk, and slip the check into this letter so that you can claim it in N.O. and have it sent to our apartment if they will receive it there. I am doing this in order to save paying storage on it at Pa. Station.

Goddard is to fill a tooth for me today, and after I buy my ticket, etc., I shall take the train to Far Rockaway, where Fannie went earlier in the day with David. There we shall stay until Thursday, the 26th. On that date we shall come back to this apartment, above address, and stay here until I leave.

I should like to leave on Friday the 27th in order to get home on Sunday morning but if you don't want me to, I shall come on the 28th arriving on Monday morning. Answer about this as soon as you receive this.

I cashed the check for $150.00. I had debts to pay – for board – to Fannie – (I am paying in full for these two weeks @ $9 a week) and I had some back board to pay because Ben stopped paying mine 3 wks ago. Then I bought a hat and some stockings and gloves – I have the list of expenses to show you.

My ticket including sleeper is about $60.00 and I am allowing $20.00 for meals and extra cash on hand. And then I shall have to pay Goddard from $3 to $5.00. So the money goes.

Ed moved in to Montclair last week so I ceased to be his guest!

I must stop now in order to make the dentist. Write me to Far Rockaway where I shall be until Thursday the 26th.

Hastily – with much love

ETHEL

Saw Ann Boyd yesterday & Hilary. He & David had a great time together on roller skates! One pair between them. Off to F.R. now and it's pouring cats and dogs.

Dr. Goddard fixed me up fine – Gold inlay & cleaning – $4.00. Another dentist wanted $11.00 for the same job. Much love to you dear – Will write again soon

ETHEL

P.S. at Pa. Station

I had to buy my ticket today for a certain date so I bought it for Friday the 27th. So you will have to find some place to stay for two nights if we can't get into our house then. Can't we share your room at Villere's – even if we have to have meals out I'm not going to worry about it. It's up to you to house us after we arrive!

I checked my trunk through today and enclosed is the check. It ought to reach N.O. when this does.

Please look and see or as you remember if my umbrella is there with our trunk. Then write and tell me. There is one here that might be mine. Did I bring one or not? I hope you have been writing me regularly. (over)*

Fragment, the rest is missing.

157.

[September 19, 1918]

MY DEAREST:

Just a note to tell you I am still loving you and wanting you home, it may be because I am sick of restaurants! I am that unromantic! But I do want you just for your dear little self. I am really dreadfully lonesome for you even though you think I have been very bad to you – which I haven't. I am enclosing a letter from Mrs. Blake which I opened and read and if you don't like it

Written on ARC letterhead.

you can jump in the East River and die of the smell –
Here's an old one: "Mary had a little lamb its etc. etc.
and everywhere etc. etc. that lamb would H2O."

This is 10 am on a busy morning so I stop here. All
my love to you and the baby.

HARRY

158.

[September 21, 1918]
Saturday

Written on ARC letterhead.

MY DEAREST:

Persons wires me to be in St. Louis Oct. 1 which
means I will have to be away from Sept. 29 to Oct. 3 –
ain't it hell! I think you had better come down anyway
arriving here if possible on Oct. 1, because the other
people will not be out until then. I will see that some
food is in the place and Miss Villere will look after you
for a day or two. I am dreadfully sorry dearest but it
can't be helped in these war times. Be sure and let me
know just what your plans are after reading this. I don't
think I'd come by boat if I were you. It takes too long. I
don't think it's dangerous and if you like it, come ahead
– it certainly would be a lovely ride.

It's cold as blazes here today and I have nothing but
a "fram beach" – am going up to Villere's to dig out that
suit I didn't take to Wash. Or rather the one *you* didn't.

I leave for Birmingham tomorrow night and go to
Meridian Miss. On Tuesday. I have to speak across the
river here on Wednesday and in N.O. Thursday. I'm
that popular.

I can't tell you how much I want you sweetheart because I love you a great deal.

A big warm kiss for you and David.

HARRY

159.

[September 22, 1918]

MY DEAREST ETHEL:

I am leaving in a few minutes for Birmingham. I will arrange with Owens to meet you when you arrive on the first. You can wire him here. His name is James M. Owens.

Don't postpone your trip until I get back unless you think best. I love you very much my dearest and send you and the baby a big warm kiss.

All my love.

HARRY

Written on ARC letterhead.

160.

Tuesday evening
Sept. 24 [1918]

DEAREST BOY:

After a perfect famine – as regards mail from you, your 3 letters reached me today postmarked as mailed on the 19th, 20th and 21st – respectively. I tell you it was good to get them and also Mrs. Blake's letter, which by the way is very interesting – and that wonderful clipping which is good enough for a tombstone inscription. I'm not going to jump in the East River and I wouldn't die of the smell because I'm too used to it – having lived within smelling distance of it for at least one third of my existence. There's a lady calls here who used Mary Garden perfume and I'm much more likely to pass away if I have to whiff that much longer.

You precious darling – I'll bet you've had a miserable time of it – living around at restaurants and hotels – I want to hear about every single experience – I've tried not to think about things that might have happened – my mind runs mostly to laundry, and holes in everything.

I'm aching to get back to get my hands on our things – and on you. Of course I *know* you haven't charged up on your expense account half the things you should – but that proves again that you need me at your side!

Now, I am not going to send you a night letter as I should to tell you when I'm coming. I shall put a special on this instead. I am going to begin economizing here and now. I am taking the train from Pa. Station Sunday at 1:08 p.m. for Washington and I shall reach N.O. Tuesday morning, October 1st. I shall go right up to Carondolet St. I don't know the address of our new home but I've an idea where [the] Villeres live and I'll take a St. Charles car & get out at Jackson Ave. I'll have 2 suitcases, a bag and David – but perhaps I can get someone to help me on and off cars. Will you be home in N.O. on October 3rd? I hope so. You had better leave me about $5 with Miss Villere if you have it. I ought to have some money left when I arrive – but one never can tell. I know you will think I have been very extravagant – but I really haven't. I've led the simple life ever since I came – but even the barest necessities cost so much here. I have allowed $10 for meals on the train (of course I won't use that) and $10 for cash on the trip (and I hope I won't have to use all of that) so I ought to be all right when I arrive until you come home – but one can never tell.

Goldie tried to change my ticket for me today. She stood in line for a long time only to be told that I can have it changed the last minute before I go on Sunday. You see I bought it for Friday the 27th. I hope I won't have any trouble. I don't anticipate any from what Goldie said they said. If there is any change in my plans, I'll telegraph you.

So – I'll see you on Thursday, October 3rd – and you keep in touch with me wherever you are. Send me a letter so that I'll know just what time you will reach home on Thursday.

Much love to you dear – just ever so much love – I won't ever go away again – if only I ever get back to you – I love you very much to-night and I want you – oh, so badly – take good care of yourself till I come – I can't wait until you see David – You will hear lots you've never heard before – and I hope there's lots of room around our new house – he needs it.

All my love to you sweetheart – and a great big warm kiss – from me and a wet sticky one from David. He's been eating jam.

Ever your devoted

ETHEL

Chapter Three

Marital Tensions:
The 1920s

DURING THE DECADE OF THE 1920S, Hopkins became a nationally known social worker. In March 1921, the family relocated to Atlanta, when Hopkins
was named head of the ARC Southern Division. Their second son, Robert,
was born there in May 1921. In October 1922, they returned to New York
and Hopkins took a job first with the AICP and then almost immediately after as head of the New York Tuberculosis Association (NYTBA). The family
first rented a house near Columbia University and then, on Gross's insistence, moved to Westchester county, eventually settling in Sparta, a section
of Scarborough near Sing Sing prison. The community had been developed by architect Frank Vanderlipp as affordable housing for professionals
like Hopkins. Vanderlipp also founded the very progressive Scarborough
School where the Hopkins placed sons David and Robert. In 1925, a third
son, Stephen, was born. The family spent summers, at Byrdcliffe, an artists'
colony near Woodstock, New York, where, for three summers, Gross studied art with William Schumacher.

In 1926, Hopkins met and fell in love with Barbara Duncan, a member
of his staff at the NYTBA. In many ways Gross's opposite, Duncan was from
an upper-middle-class, Protestant family from Michigan and had been
trained as a nurse at New York City's Bellevue Hospital. Hopkins conducted
an ongoing affair with Duncan, and in 1927, in response to growing tensions in their marriage, suggested that Gross take a trip to New Orleans in
order to give the couple some time off from each other. When their relationship did not improve, Hopkins first sought help from psychoanalyst
Dr. Frankwood E. Williams and then, decided that he, too, needed some

distance from the marriage. In 1928, he traveled to Europe with colleagues to attend the first International Conference of Social Work in Paris. Despite his apparent desire to mend his marriage, Hopkins continued his affair with Duncan, and in September 1929 Hopkins and Gross officially separated.

161.

My dear:

We went sight seeing in Washington – Phila – and Atlantic City all in one day! I always was fast. But this Hotel* is fierce! In fact it is on the burn – so tomorrow morning bright and early – I go to look for another room – that's me all over! Comfortable.

The ocean is too cold so no one will have the pleasure of seeing my wonderful form for some time. I walked on the Board-Walk but no one seemed to recognize me. I felt rather put out about it but then you know I'm older than I used to be.

Our ride over here was both uneventful and uninteresting. I won three cigars from Leffert the poor fish!

My pen is too stubborn to write more.
Much love,
Harry

Written on Hotel Absecon letterhead.

*The hotel was in Atlantic City, N.J.

162.

[probably April 1919]

My Dearest

The days are passing very fast but I am getting a bit bored anyway. It looks as though we are slated for Chicago – Deacon* practically insists on it.

I am on the program this morning acting as Chrmn. of the Home Service committee, by the way Mrs. August Belmont attended our rehearsal last night.

Am feeling fine – swimming every afternoon. Got your note yesterday – was glad to hear from David.
Much love and a big kiss,
Harry

Written on Hotel Absecon letterhead.

*J. Byron Deacon was the Assistant Director of the American Red Cross in 1919 and then director of the New York Tuberculosis Association until Hopkins took over in 1924.

163.

[October 21, 1920]

Written on Hotel
Bentley letterhead. The
Hotel Bentley was in
Alexandria,
Louisiana. This
undated letter was
probably written on
October 21st, which
would have been their
seventh wedding
anniversary. The
Hopkins had a baby,
Barbara, who was
born April 30, 1920,
and died of whooping
cough on May 25,
1920.

MY DEAREST:

I shall think of you every hour on Thursday and wish so much I were at home. Life has really been rather good to us so far – for we have lived seven very perfect years together and I love and care for you more than anyone else on this earth. No one could have been finer than you and we shall work out a useful and complete life together. Thru every crisis you have been perfect – while I am fully convinced we shall never have any money – I am equally sure that the finer things in life will be and indeed are ours. I am genuinely and very greatly proud of you – and David he has been adorable hasn't he? And so today if this should come on Thursday – I kiss your warm lips and dream of many more happy years together.

HARRY

164.

[probably early 1921]

DEAREST ETHEL:

I seem to be getting very little out of the meeting, although the chapter conference was fine. The consolidation of divisions seems to be held up until Persons committee reports – it is quite unsatisfactory although I feel headquarters can do nothing else.

*Frederic Munroe was
the general manager
of the American
Red Cross. As part
of the postwar
reorganization
of the Red Cross, the
Gulf Division and the
Southeastern Division
merged into the
Southern Division,
headquartered in
Atlanta.*

I am having dinner tonight with Mr. and Mrs. Rule – am sick of traveling – and how are you – I haven't heard a word so am going to try to phone you after my night if it isn't too expensive. I do hope everything is alright.

Persons' committee want me on the grill Friday and Saturday – hence I must stay on.

I have just this minute talked to Munroe* – he tells me that in all probability the divisions are to be consolidated soon and their present plans are for me to go to Southern and handle it. I am not enthusiastic. What shall we do?

I wish I were home very much at this moment – kiss David for me and a very warm one for you – dear.

HARRY

165.

[probably early 1921]

MY DEAREST ETHEL:

I am leaving Washington tonight for Atlanta. I want to get a good look at the Southern Div. and spend a day or two with Joe Logan. Will surely be home Saturday morning. Conference has been fine.

Much love and big, warm kiss.

HARRY

DEAREST ETHEL:

166.

[probably early 1920s]

DEAREST ETHEL:

I saw Rome this morning – he is doing exceedingly well – making some money.

Written on Tuberculosis Association letterhead.

Have been traveling all day through Minnesota & N. Dakota – miles of wheat fields and a train full of interesting people. When you talk to the office ask Miss Long to send news of my [undecipherable] to Denver.

There is quite a thrill in these beautiful spacious wheat fields. There are a few things going on outside of N.Y.

Much love,

HARRY

167.

[probably early 1920s]

Tuesday

*Written on
Tuberculosis
Association letterhead.*

DEAREST ETHEL:

Tal cannot come out until Saturday but Jane is going to drive me out Friday so you will not have to meet the train.

I went to the Lindbergh dinner last night – very exciting giving me at any rate a real thrill. Over at 1 o'clock.

B[undecipherable] can't come out – but will come later – I am seeing [undecipherable] in a few moments and will talk to him about [it]. Wish Friday would hurry. Am terribly busy – seeing Miller tonight. David was delightful in town.

HARRY

168.

[probably early 1920s]
Tuesday

*Written on
Tuberculosis
Association letterhead.*

DEAREST ETHEL:

I am coming home on Wednesday to be with you for a month and nothing I have done in years is looked forward to with more real delight by your permanent guest. I want to be with you and the children for days. Will you be reasonably nice to me. For I love you.

HARRY

169.

[probably early 1920s]

DEAREST ETHEL:

I sold the shawl yesterday for $100 and am enclosing a check for it today. Have had no word from Adele nor from Christine but may hear from both of them today. I cannot get away until Saturday now because of a committee meeting but will be out on the two o'clock train, West Shore, which arrives at 5. Have been working at the library and believe I have some very interesting stuff, although I am afraid some of the numbers are missing. I will make no appointments until Tuesday afternoon so that I can leave on the late train.

Raining hard here this morning. Don Luke has asked me out to spend a night next week and I want to spend another with Don and Eunice. No exciting news – many people back from vacation and I am snowed under with work.

Ben, by the way, has offered to buy Robert a pony and possibly a cart so look around!

Much love,
HARRY

Written on Tuberculosis Association letterhead.

170.

[probably early 1920s]

DEAREST ETHEL:

I want you to know how much I appreciate your asking me out last week end. I had a perfectly gorgeous time – the children *are* adorable and you were rather nice yourself. Will you ask me again? Would you mind turning the mattress and can't you fix the geography of that darn bed so that more than one and not more than two can sleep with reasonable comfort. This may not

Written on Tuberculosis Association letterhead.

seem important to you but the books lay great stress on it especially for week end guests! Have you kissed anyone this week and just what did he say and were you facing north or south.

I love you very dearly and can hardly wait till Friday but then you know I will.

HARRY

Will let you know later what time Phil and Phyllis and your star guest will be in.

H.

171.

[probably early 1920s]

Written on The Tuberculosis Sanatorium Conference of Metropolitan New York letterhead.

DEAR ETHEL:

I hope Christine arrived alright. I should think she could be a lot of help. Do try to get some stuff off by express so that our car may not be too full. I talked with Mrs. Rowtjohn today – they are leaving Saturday. She will leave an order for ice and milk. If you want groceries, will you write to Mrs. Slater.

I have $70 more available for bills although we should pay the school $50 of it. If you feel we must pay the lady that, go ahead and do it *now*.

Terribly busy but alright – met Ben Webster and his wife on Broadway – result two drinks! Am going to try to see the tennis matches on Thursday or Friday. Am lunching with Ben Webster Thursday.

Much love,

HARRY

172.

[probably early 1920s]
Sunday Morning

DEAREST ETHEL:

This is the Sabbath morn – Drolet said some beads for me at church and I am about to have a swim at the Athletes' Club for it is hotter than hell out here. I am $14 to the good – several friends contributed $10 at bridge on the train and the rest at poker last evening. I would be $20 but an unfortunate bid of 5 diamonds doubled and redoubled ended in a genuine disaster – down five – figure it up! (1/4 of a cent a point)

Basil just told me he won $25.15 at poker – the fifteen cents he won honestly and the $25 he expected to lose – hence $25.15!

I have made two speeches both of them busts – they should let me give my little talk on "Happy Childhood the World Over" – there is an emotional affect in that more in harmony with my nature. Instead of that I talk about "Membership Campaigns" and the "Rising Tide of Seal* Costs" which gives very little opportunity for my histrionic abilities.

Am having tea with the Borsts this afternoon and will of course tell them that you wished to be very especially remembered to them.

And how is the dog – poor thing – I can scarcely wait. Much love – will be home Saturday,

HARRY

Written on The Claypool Hotel, Indianapolis letterhead.

*"Seal" could refer to Easter Seals sold by NYTBA.

173.

[probably early 1920s]
Monday

DEAR ETHEL:

Be sure and prepare that statement for the insurance co. and send it to me and be sure it agrees fully with my statement a copy of which you have. Also be sure and keep me posted. If you want to reach me

Written on Hotel Claridge, New York City, letterhead.

after five better wire me at the Claridge 44 St. & Broadway because I don't know just what day I am going to Bob's and Fannie's.

Also be sure and bring my license when you meet me this week end – it may be in my knickers rear pocket.

I am going to try and see one or two other possible maids this week in spite of my protestations but don't count on too much. Will not do any thing until I have talked to you.

The week end was delightful in fact I don't recall our having such leisurely times together – the sooner the next one comes the better and August should be lovely.

The children are too adorable.

Best of love,
HARRY

174.

[probably May 1925]

Written on New York Tuberculosis Association letterhead.

DEAREST ETHEL:

I haven't been able to get you on the phone and may not be able to. I love you very dearly – and wish I were not going away, do take care of yourself.

HARRY

175.

[probably May 1925]
Wednesday

Written on New York Central Lines letterhead.

DEAREST ETHEL:

I managed to get off after a strenuous day in the office. I tried to get you on the phone several times but there was no answer. Adah came to the train to see me off and up to the present all goes well. We left Cleveland on time so I should make my connection at Chicago alright. By the time you get this I should be well into Canada. I believe I forgot nothing but the gin!

I hated to leave the yard in its present condition but Micky can fix it up. Be sure that he puts in the rest of the corn and the tomatoes.

We are just pulling out of Toledo O. Will wire you from Chicago this afternoon.

Much love,
HARRY

176.

Tuesday, June 2, 1925

MY DEAREST ETHEL:

If Sinclair Lewis ever gets the complete history of the Hopkins family, he will make "Main Street" look like ten cents. I wouldn't have missed it for the world – Rome engaged to Follies girl who happens to be Catholic and divorced – the hero selling alcohol a shade or two inside the law – Lewis flat on his back practicing the "healing art" and thoroughly disillusioned – and Emery, the 100% American selling baggage in a department store at $35 per. Rome smiles – plans matrimony and looks for bigger things – Lew smiles a little pathetically – changes the babies diapers and looks for a better practice from now on – Emery reads of heroes in the American magazine – begets a healthy child – and plans to make more money soon. All are broke – complain but little – have no alibis – are securely nailed to females who think they could have made a respectable living had they been wearing the trousers.

I have already acquired some family gems with which I can only do the justice they deserve, after three drinks and yourself and Frank and Adah as an audience. They better wait.

Lewis children are perfectly adorable – Blayne* a bit better but I fear will never be well. All are on the tag end of whooping cough.

I am leaving for Spokane tonight so you see I am really on the way home. The trip has been a bit tedious but the scenery quite beyond my expectations and the family visits pleasant thus far.

*Born in 1915, Blayne was the daughter of Lewis and Bessie Hopkins. She was lame in one leg and wore a brace for a time.

I am anxious to see mother – indeed until now I have scarcely realized how much I wanted to see her again.

Tell Adah that in spite of mad rushes to the hills every five minutes or so – the mountain to Tacoma was not out. I am sure it is there however because people in these parts speak of little else. This is a boosters paradise and a great he-man country.

Emery – who by the way is known as Jack hereabouts – has the afternoon off and we are taking the bus up the Columbia river to Multnomah Falls.

I hope I will have a letter from you at Spokane.

[†] *Gross was pregnant with their third son, Stephen, who was born in July 1925.*

How does the garden grow and yourself[†] if that be not impertinent. Kiss the children for me and remember that I love you more dearly than anything in this world. And of course I don't believe in the next.

Yours,
HARRY

177.

[June 4, 1925]
Thursday

Written on Davenport Hotel, Spokane, Washington, letterhead.

DEAREST ETHEL:

I am enclosing some clippings that will interest you and show as well what a first class publicity man the old gentleman is. Dad's business is only fair but by great economy. – they just manage to pull through. By the way I checked out $50 on the June 1 check and $75 on the June 15 check.

I am feeling fine and am enjoying my visit immensely. Mother is in much better condition than I ever expected to find her. She gets out in the garden – sleeps a great deal and keeps the house spic and span.

The social workers club here are giving me a lunch this noon and the Sec'y of the C.P.S. has just come in to get me. More later.

Best love,
HARRY

178.

[June 8, 1925]

DEAREST ETHEL:

I came down from Spokane last night to catch the train for Denver at 5 this afternoon.

Mother and father are both situated much better than I expected though that isn't saying a great deal. Dad probably has an equity of about $8000 in the alleys and the house so that he is about $5000 poorer than when he landed in these parts.* This is all due to the fact that he paid much more for the alleys than they were worth. Fortunately he is very well and never misses a day at the shop. Mother gets outdoors a great deal but as a rule is contented to stay quietly at home. She of course longs for the time when she can be at home near some of the children preferably Adah.

Dad makes about a $100 a month but the payments on the house about $50 a month must come out of this so you can see that they are pretty well broke. They need now a little extra money each month.

I am writing David today about the country.

By the way can I have $100 instead of $75 out of this check (June 15)?

I am glad to be on the way home – in two weeks I will see you.

Much love.

HARRY

Written on Hotel Pendleton, Pendleton, Oregon, letterhead.

*Hopkins's father and mother had moved from Grinnell, Iowa, to Spokane, Washington, where Al Hopkins opened up a bowling alley.

179.

[August 23, 1927]
Tuesday

DEAREST ETHEL:

I am enclosing a letter to David – I am totally depressed over the Sacco–Vanzetti affair.* Ben is coming out with me. Going to Fannies tonight and tomorrow and to a friend in the United Hospital Fund – New Rochelle on Thursday.

Best love my dearest one.

HARRY

*Sacco and Vanzetti were executed on August 23, 1927.

180.

Written on New York Tuberculosis and Health Association letterhead.

MY DEAREST ETHEL:

The household is still intact with the housekeeper carrying the banner and you're truly doing his best to keep in step. The children are fine – no complications whatever and David full of wise cracks. I had supper with the Evans on Sunday – much food and conversation – and last night to bed at nine after reading Oscar Wilde's Salome – which was illustrated by my friend John Vassos.* I had very interesting lunches with Williams and Miller this week – there is a board meeting this afternoon when many of our troubles will be ironed out and the Association gain further right to its title of a "friendly octopus".

*John Vassos was an artist/illustrator and friend of the Hopkins's. Significantly, Barbara Duncan had posed for one of the pictures in Wilde's Salome.

If the weather on the boat was as glorious as it has been here – you must have had an altogether delightful trip.† Fanny is still a bit bewildered but as usual smiles happily and hurries home to her Bennie – Ben I imagine is back though I haven't had time to see him but may lunch with him tomorrow.‡ I have written to him.

†As a result of marital tensions, probably due to the fact that Hopkins had met and fallen in love with Barbara Duncan, Gross had taken a boat trip down the Mississippi to visit her friend Mrs. Paul Winchester in Covington, Louisiana.

Mrs. Weber runs the car like a breeze – has had it fixed and seems very happy – runs your typewriter by the hour. She asked me this morning if she might have a guest for dinner and I told her by all means. She is fine with the children.

The office is running like a steam engine but I am in first rate form and quite capable of bearing up under it.

‡"Ben" refers to Gross's brother Benjamin Gross while "Bennie" refers to Benjamin Kohn, Gross's brother-in-law.

Now Ethel – do have good time – there is nothing to worry about so far as the children are concerned. And I am alright – this is the best move we have made in years and is sure to help. *And don't worry about it.* I will write you as soon as I get back from Columbus.

Best love,

HARRY

181.

Western Union Telegram
November 7, 1927
Mrs. Ethel G. Hopkins
Care Mrs. Paul Winchester
Covington, La.

Family including head of house who ever that might be is all right having dinner with Brewers tonight. Went to Princeton game Saturday. Mailing necklace. Cold and disagreeable weather.
Much love,
HARRY

182.

Covington
Nov. 8, 1927

DEAR HARRY:

I had a letter from Eunice* last night in which she said that you and she were agreed that it would be much better if I could stay away longer than November 21st.

I can't stay away from home any longer visiting friends. To be a guest beyond two or three days takes faculty which I don't possess. I met a professional visitor on the boat. He told me he spent most of the year visiting friends in different parts of the country. And he told me how he worked it. And I have no desire to go in for that sort of thing.

In other words, in my present mood, I can't go and visit Adele for 2 weeks after I get back.

As far as I am personally concerned, prolonging my absence from home won't help me to solve my problems. I can only learn by doing, as I said to you before I left home.

But if you think I should stay away longer I can do it by doing one of two things – one is to get a job and the other is to start on a mad career of pleasure. I find I can still give pleasure to certain types of people. Especially men – and

Written on The St. Charles Hotel, New Orleans, Louisiana, letterhead.

*Eunice and Donald Armstrong were close friends and Scarborough neighbors of the Hopkins family.

I'd get a real kick out of seeing how far I could string it out. If I could use my powers in this direction it would be sufficiently interesting and diverting so that I would worry less and less about getting back to the children.

I think too that in this way I could develop a hard-boiled quality that is quite an asset in many ways and that I could never develop living with someone I love.

I could get a little work to do on the side – just enough, and I think I could be clever enough to keep out of trouble.

I have a sense of power today because yesterday, a man flattered my vanity.

I think Ben would send me some money for clothes if you continued the little legend about my nerves, but I don't want to do anything to tie me down to my family too much. I want to be free.

I'd like to come home to the children as I planned on November 21st. But if you are not ready to have me come I can make very definite plans along these lines and stay away one month or even two months longer.

This kind of life might make me very unfit to take up my duties at home again – but that is the chance we take and I don't think I do that kind of job particularly well any way. Let me know about coming home so I can make my plans. I must go now because Belle's† waiting. ETHEL

†*Belle Pike was a young social worker whom Gross and Hopkins befriended during their time in New Orleans.*

183.

Western Union
November 12, 1927
Mrs. Harry L. Hopkins
Care Paul Winchester
Covington, La.

All your letters have been received. Everybody fine at home. Have never even discussed with Eunice time you should come home. Am expecting you twenty-first. Had dinner with Ben and Albert last night. Going Army Notre Dame game today.
Love,
HARRY

184.

[postmarked July 2, 1928]

DEAREST ETHEL:

This has been a heavenly trip* – the sea smooth as glass – not a moment's sickness and rested as never before in my life. I have slept hours on end – eaten every meal and partaken temperately of wines and liquors that I thought were for the Gods only.

You were right about student's third – pretty terrible but not because of the cabin. I have two nice boys, neither of whom are in evidence – the bed is comfortable and the shower's next door. But the food and general lack of elbow room completely upset my plebian ideas and the second day I went first class: Don't laugh, John and Jean, Homer and his wife, Louise Dublin, and 18 yr. old daughter[†] – another friend of theirs and Kenneth Widderman and his wife, were all up front – with table together. For $100 – I live up here and sleep below and I never spent money better in my life. I have been altogether comfortable – have read half dozen books including A & E (both of whom are pretty terrible especially Adam).

But of course the sea overshadows anything else – it cannot be described – I watch it for hours from early morning to the last thing at night – ever changing and ever more wonderful. It is the most restful and peaceful experience that could be imagined.

The trip has been quite uneventful and no one interesting on board outside of our own crowd. The pace was far too swift in third – hundreds of young things – beautiful smart and plastered. – the line of conversation was too much for me. I simply can't make the grade. My autumn is not spring! I saw little of the Bements – the two daughters became famous largely because of drinking proclivities.

As to my plans – I had bought a ticket for Paris and planned to get off at Boulogne but John spilled a pitcher of hot water on his foot and is laid up completely. No one seems to be able to stay with him so I am elected. I want to do it though. So John, Jean and I are going to Rotterdam arriving July 3 – and stay there

*Hopkins took this trip to Europe to attend the first International Conference of Social Work in Paris. He was also motivated to take this trip because of emotional troubles related to the dissolution of his marriage.

[†]*John Kingsbury (with his daughter Jean), Homer Folks (vice-president of the Tuberculosis Association) and Katherine Lenroot (head of the Children's Bureau) all accompanied him to the conference.*

until John is better or can go on to Paris. This I trust will be Thursday or Friday. I want to stick by John but if I am to be reasonably truthful I must admit that vacationing as nurse for John and guardian for Jean is not exactly my idea of a happy holiday. Jean has been difficult but the details cannot be related here. John is fine – a great friend of mine – and I like him enormously.

I stayed up to see the tender take the passengers off at Plymouth last night. Very thrilling. All of our crowd went to London from there and nearly everyone else is getting off this afternoon at Boulogne. I will cable you at Rotterdam.

The leaving was thrilling but more of that when I see you. I heard Stephen's good by, and saw and kissed you all good bye. I hope you have written me so that I will know of your plans this summer. Will write from Holland. And don't worry – best of love to all of you.

HARRY

185.

[postmarked July 5, 1928]

Postcard mailed from Rotterdam.

DEAR ETHEL:

Jean and John and I have had a delightful boat trip to some fishing villages today. Very different from last Fourth. I am seeing Ed's friend tomorrow – also the famous Rembrandt's in the gallery. Leaving for Paris at noon.

HARRY

186.

Friday July 6 [1928]

Written on Hotel Astoria letterhead.

DEAREST ETHEL:

Paris at last! Arrived from Amsterdam last night and am living in a beautiful room here in the shadow of the Arc de Triumph. Through the help of the Rockefeller Foundation – I got a room and bath for $4 a day and am altogether comfortable. I feel a great relief at being quite alone – Jean got on my nerves considerably although John is a great person to be with. I am glad I went to Holland with them just because the county is fascinating but more because John needed someone. Tell Mabel his foot is much better – I am going over to his hotel and dress it now and then dine with them. Tell her if you like that John is a great person to travel with and that I am proud indeed to be a friend of his. He has certainly had rotten luck this trip.

I am going to write David all about Holland so omit three delightful days. We arrived at eight last night coming through the battlefields and the beautiful countryside of France. I got the thrill of my life at the sight of Sacré Coeur ten miles from Paris. It is wonderful. The taxi driver of course could not understand which made the arrival perfect. I decided I would not stay with John and wired ahead to the Rockefeller crowd to get me a room. With the help of the concierge – the porter – the maid – the boot boy – the clerk etc. I managed to get into my room. Very quiet and proper hotel. Then in order to get it out of my system I went to the Follies and Maxims the same night. Don't tell anybody for I don't want to appear blasé but I walked out on the Follies at the end of the first act and Maxims was very dull. Ladies of joy and expensive food neither of which were appreciated. To bed at 12 and up at 9. I went over to register at the conference and ran into Porter Lee the President of the Nat'l Conf. Of Social Work and an old friend – we decided to go the Louvre. Why didn't you tell me it was as big as all N.Y. Perfectly fascinating and I am going many times. The "Winged Victory" – "Mona Lisa" and the "Venus de Milo" – the latter perfectly exquisite.

I got your letter at the American Exp. Co this morning and will call again Saturday. I had lunch alone at the hotel – took a nap (perfect at 2 P.M.) – then a walk in the Champs-Elysées with a delicious Italian vermouth at the Café Neapolitan while the world went by.

It is nearly seven and I must go over to John who lives but two blocks away.

Am feeling fine altogether rested – and having a gorgeous vacation. Will leave here about July 15 for

London so write me in care of the Am. Exp. Co there after you get this letter.

I hope you and the boys are all well – will write you again on Sunday – not as a sense of duty but because I want to.

Good by dear till then.

HARRY

187.

[*July 8, 1928*]

DEAREST ETHEL:

This is Sunday morning in Paris – I got up at eleven – coffee and rolls in bed and this written in my gorgeous bath robe and this is written with the sun streaming in amid the faint tootings of a thousand taxis in six minor keys on the Champs-Elysées.

Friday night John and Jean and I had dinner at the Boeuf a la Mode and then to see Notre Dame by moonlight. Perfect. John and I had a great argument on the purposes of this life which will have to wait. I am terribly bored with Jean – she is not my idea of a Parisien companion! John is up to his old tricks – he makes an engagement and then Jean must be looked after – really very amusing yesterday but it would take too long to write. Suffice to say I took her to the races at St. Cloud (lost $5) and to dinner last night.

There are two people in the crowd that are perfect to bat around with – Porter Lee and a Miss Lenroot. The latter is the daughter of Senator Lenroot of Wisconsin and the asst director of the Children's Bureau in Wash. She is the gov't delegate. About 40 – a little fat – but never in Paris before – ready to see everything and insists on going "dutch!" Perfectly safe but nice – pleasant and somewhat like Florence Kerr.* She blew me to the opera last night. We saw "Louise" at the Opera Comique – perfectly heavenly and an altogether interesting audience. Then coffee on the street.

Today I haven't a thing to do until the conference opens at 4:30 – I am going for a stroll and find a quiet place for lunch.

Florence Stewart Kerr and her husband, Robert Kerr, were both classmates of Hopkins at Grinnell College and remained friends of the Hopkins family.

Paris is beyond all expectations – am thrilled with every bit of it. As you may suspect the idea of going where and when I like pleases me enormously – I am taking it easy – getting plenty of sleep and feel completely rested. The restaurants are perfect – I haven't been even remotely lit – a little white wine with fish – red with meat and a liquor. Haven't tasted scotch or a cocktail

I bought a beautiful little Dutch suit for Robert in Haarlem in Holland and had it mailed. The card is enclosed showing that it cost 17 fl. or about $7. I paid the postage but you will probably have to pay more postage. If it doesn't arrive soon – write them and remind them it was purchased on July 4 to be sent to Robert Hopkins – Scarborough N.Y. Wooden shoes and all. I think I will buy a coat for David in London. What shall I get for Stephen.

I bought a cunning little table bell in Holland. Everything is very expensive here.

I doubt that I shall take the trip down the Rhine because I can't bear the thought of three or four days with Jean. Very funny. I shall go to London about the 16th or 17th and then some real work which doesn't please me any too well at present.

I can understand how you raved over Paris. It is all true. It pleases me immensely to learn that I am not blasé and still capable of real enthusiasms. Does it please you? I am feeling fine and am going to enjoy every minute of Europe.

I think of you and the children often and have the children's picture in front of me. But love to you all. Will write David this afternoon.

HARRY

188.

[postmarked July 19, 1928]

DEAREST ETHEL:

This trip seems to move in blocks – first the ocean – then Paris and now London. I am writing David about the last days in Paris, so you will get the news of that from him. They were hot, but very interesting, while at

Written on The Royal Palace Hotel letterhead.

the time, I was glad to get away, I should be very happy to go back and may a few days before I sail.

I arrived here yesterday and went to work immediately and am just back from my second day's look at the school medical service. Today I spent in the heart of London's East End – the poorest dock workers – miserable poverty – dirty-rotten slums, but magnificent school health work under the direction of skilled and devoted doctors and nurses. It was thrilling. We are amateurs indeed! I am spending the week looking at the school work, the administration of which is complicated and extensive. Next week, the t.b. service and then the district health service – it would take six months instead of weeks to do this adequately. I am being royally received and the whole works is open.

Harry Day was a British social worker.

I had dinner with Harry Day* last night at this very sporty club – a heavenly swim first. We sat on the veranda talking over a stein of beer and cigarettes and then for a long walk thru Hyde Park where dozens of speakers harangued a friendly and intelligent crowd.

Wednesday, July 18

I took Harry to dinner last night on Piccadilly Circus and he had seats to the musical comedy "This Year of Grace" – said to be the best show in London and coming to N.Y. next winter with Beatrice Lillie. A very sporty and altogether English audience – I saw no Americans – everyone smokes throughout the play, including women – the bar presided over by a pleasant matron. We got perfect bacon & eggs later. I have never tasted such bacon!

My day was somewhat like yesterday; reported at 9:30 at the London County Council – a perfectly immense building on the Thames just across from the House of Parliament. Visit with various people who tell me, at great length, of their work – lunch with a half dozen of the medical officers and then in the field from 2 until 5. Tonight I am thoroughly tired and am going to a quiet dinner with a bachelor doctor who will be in N.Y. this fall. He looks like a tramp, but is president of a learned medical society and in charge of all the backward children of London.

I have had no time for sight seeing and am going to put that off till I learn the town better. I am going to the seashore Sunday and next week end (the 28th). I am invited down to Harry Day's country place. I like him very much. Unless you object strenuously, I am going to buy you a damn fine Scotch tweed sport coat instead of a Parisian dress. I looked in Paris – the good ones are terribly expensive and I can buy a coat, which would cost $150 in N.Y. for about $65 here. They are stunning and perfect for the fall and spring.

Later on Wednesday

I have your letter forwarded from Paris, telling of the mumps – what rotten luck – I hope it will be all over by the time you get this and assume that nothing serious has happened or you would have cabled. They should be alright by the time you get ready to go to Woodstock. *Don't give that up.*

I am unbelievably well – sleep a lot and don't eat too much. Kiss all the boys for me – I will write you Monday and tell you all about my seashore trip.

London is big – old and stolid and no stranger can ever get on the inside. Best of love – think of you every day. Don't worry.

HARRY

I have seen a great deal of Porter Lee[†] – they are giving a tea for him tomorrow and I am going.

HLH

[†]*Porter Lee taught Family Welfare at the New York School of Philanthropy (later School of Social Work) and was a longtime friend of Hopkins.*

189.

Wednesday night
July 18, 1928

DEAREST ETHEL:

I must write you again tonight because I have just had the most exalting experience. Having had a real English dinner with a delightful physician in his very English home, he took me for a tramp over Hampstead Heath – a great park on the outskirts of London – we

Written on The Royal Palace Hotel letterhead.

were discussing the Mental Deficiency Act of England or some equally uplifting subject, when we suddenly came on a lonely path upon which was a very impersonal sign called "Keats Walk"! Upon inquiry, it developed that here Keats walked with Fannie Browne and over this very Hampstead Heath – Keats had roamed for hours and it is just the same now as then. Imagine my feeling! The doctor, not knowing Keats, could not share my enthusiasm, but that didn't restrain mine for at least I was in Keats country and every memory of the years I have known him (how long has it been – I think it dates from the time I was ill in N.Y. Hospital about eight years ago) swelled to my imagination and I saw his red head and proud step sauntering through the green – it was though I could reach out and touch him – quite like a dream. But it was not – for not two blocks away was his home where he lived for three years and where the Ode to the Nightingale was written and other heavenly music. I saw his very house and his garden that he sat in for hours on end. It is now state property and of course was closed but is open during the day and I am going back soon. Isn't it perfect? I know you will be glad to hear of this and as the only one who will fully understand what this incident is to me. That it was accidental, made [it] all the more delightful. I fairly walk on air and wanted you to know – good night dear.
HARRY

190.

July 19, 1928

The Hopkins lived in Sparta, a community in Scarborough, a New York City suburb in Westchester County. Frank Vanderlipp developed Sparta as a community of affordable homes (near Sing Sing prison) for professionals who did

DEAREST ETHEL:

As I write to the boys tonight, I want to write to you and get something settled or at any rate pass on my advice about the school next year. I think we better send them to Scarboro – they want to go – it is a great school – you want them to go and so do I – I promise not to bring it up in case we are broke next year which we won't be.* But you better save this letter to be on the safe side.

I had an interesting day – at E. Stepney, a poverty borough of London. I saw the finest school work I ever hope to see – was entertained at lunch by the social workers of the neighborhood – visited some miserable tenements and arrived here thoroughly tired out. I had dinner alone and lingered over it for two hours and am getting to bed at ten just as you are getting back from the tennis courts. I am terribly sorry about the mumps, for that will keep you pretty much tied up for a couple of weeks. They must be about over them now.

You can imagine how I feel with Luckies at 40¢ a pack – I smoke something else.

There hasn't been a day of rain since I landed, but I am told to look for aplenty. They are complaining of the heat here but it is nothing compared to New York.

This is a great experience here and I am already filled with bright ideas. I was going to the theater tonight, but am too sleepy, and must appear in some outlandish part of London at 9:30. I am taking Sat. off and with one bag am going for a swim in an English ocean.

Do take care of yourself – if you need any more money get it from the office and get to Woodstock somehow. Give my love to our Spartan friends – if you see Don[†] tell him Harry Day and I drank a bumper to his health.

Good by till Monday – I think of you often Ethel and have wished many times you were with me. If it interests you at all my virtue such as it is came through Paris intact!

Best love,
HARRY

not make a great deal of money. He also founded the progressive Scarborough School, which David and Robert Hopkins attended. The tuition was scaled to each family's income.

[†]*"Don" probably refers to Donald Armstrong.*

191.

July 22 [1928]

DEAREST ETHEL:

This is an altogether quiet Sunday afternoon and the end of my first week in London. I went to the sea shore for a day beginning late Friday afternoon, but had to come back last night because of very bad train

Written on The Royal Palace Hotel letterhead.

connections on Sunday. The countryside of Devon is lovely and the sea and rocky cliffs lovely beyond words –I should like to spend a week there, but that is a bit difficult.

I finished the school work Friday and am beginning on their t.b. stuff tomorrow. Sightseeing is not fun alone and apart from visiting all Keats' haunts I shall not do much. I think I told you that Harry Day has invited me out for the week end this coming Sat. and I am looking forward to it eagerly – he is very good company and I expect to see a lot of him for he takes his vacation in the winter.

I am going to try to do some writing this summer and will let you know later how that works out. My job is altogether interesting and I am seeing and learning many things.

I tramped all over London today – this letter is written in two jumps – and took in a movie tonight which was very fair.

It is amazing the way everyone – women as well as men catch these buses on the run – women smokers everywhere – on buses – hotel lobbies – theaters but God how homely and badly dressed.

In spite of Bob's misgivings I have received all of your letters and you should be hearing from me with some regularity now for I have written about three letters a week which you must admit is almost perfect. I shall be glad to hear that the mumps are all over and certainly hope nothing new of that sort turns up.

The news about Frank's night out is very amusing – I think he just saved himself from being ruined or whatever you call it. Has Adah recovered – I must write her – I haven't done any letter writing and an S.O.S. or two from the office remain unanswered but the damn fools should know what to do.

I am not going to worry about money, but just charge up the whole trip to the office including Holland. How glad I am the K's have gone in a different direction. I am a selfish soul as you know so well but Jean was too much for me. You would have handled it much better.

Folks – the Dublins and Widdeners were fine and I enjoyed them all immensely. John will be coming back soon and you will hear all about it.

I am going to sleep reading Lewisohn's book which started off in a pretty dull fashion. London is hot but not dirty, and I think a very dull place – Paris does the trick and any place after that would be an awful comedown.

Good night Ethel – take care of yourself and don't spend too much time on the children.

Best love,

HARRY

192.

[postmarked July 24, 1928]

DEAREST ETHEL:

I am writing this hurried note to catch the Majestic to let you know that I have decided to give up the Liverpool trip. In that case I shall be home about Aug. 20 or perhaps a few days earlier. Does this news please you. Everything going fine here – am perfectly well – working hard but will be glad to back home. Better not send me any mail after you receive this because it probably won't reach me.

Best of love – in haste,

HARRY

Written on The Royal Palace Hotel letterhead.

193.

July 24 [1928]

MY DEAREST ETHEL:

London *can* be hot, but I have taken it rather easy today looking over the work in Kensington Boro. – the same row between local and centralized authority seems to go on the world over.

I have bought a coat for you – which I trust will please you – one for David – and a little Eng. sports coats for all three – a brilliant one for Steven* – I will get through by the seventh of Aug. and am trying to get a passage back about the 9th – I probably will get one on the fly, as they are very crowded and I must take what I can get – I am not coming back third.†

Written on The Royal Palace Hotel letterhead.

*Hopkins misspelled his son's name, "Steven" instead of "Stephen."

†Hopkins returned earlier than the date he gave Gross so that he could meet with Barbara Duncan.

Last night I saw one of the finest shows I ever saw in my life – "Many Waters" a review of which I shall try to find and enclose with this.

I will have to give up Harry Day's week end because I want to see some [undecipherable] of the work in Brighton – he planned my buying tour today. I had rather planned to go back to Paris – so don't be disappointed, because I bought nothing there.

I shall be glad to get home and if you are in Woodstock I might come up there, but don't change any of your plans for me because I may not arrive until the 20th.

It is 6 in the evening and I have ordered some cold beer! I may run into Adele – if you can, tell her to get in touch with me at the Am. Exp. In London.

I haven't been even really tired for a day and will come back feeling fine.

Best love to you all,

HARRY

194.

July 26 [1928]

Written on The Royal Palace Hotel letterhead.

DEAREST ETHEL:

The days move along here very much as though I were in the office from 9 to 5 – but it is all new and therefore intriguing. I took a long walk in Kensington Gardens last night – fascinating, but they threw me out at 10:30.

I hope Robert's Dutch suit arrived – and wait till you see Steven in his new layout! They will knock Sparta dead! I decided yesterday after a conference with the health officials here to go to Birmingham for a week after all and cut London that much – I will go as soon as I get back from Brighton. It is going to mean hard work to crowd it all in but I can rest on the boat and after I get home. While the trip has been recreation – it has been anything but a lazy time – on the jump every minute – still I am not tired for strange as it may seem to you (or perhaps not) I have slept nine hours every night and am feeling very fit.

Europe can be done very cheaply but not by me! It takes all the edge off – I like a bath room and they are not to be had – even in London. And in spite of all that they say about these quaint, cheap eating places – they are a bit lousy – still $15 a day does nicely including a good room – 3 square meals – taxis – theaters etc. As you no doubt surmised I have been comfortable and much cheaper than N.Y.

It is hot as the devil but I will survive and see you soon.

Best of love to you and the children.

HARRY

195.

Western Union
4 Church St. Ossining, N.Y.
N1 Cable London 18
NLT Mrs. Harry Hopkins
Ossining (NY)

Arrive home about August fifteenth feeling fine. Address everything American Express.

Love,

HARRY

DEAR HARRY:

196.

[December 20, 1928]

<u>copy</u>

Dr. Brieant made an examination yesterday. He says conditions in the uterus are not as they should be. There is still a bloody discharge. That accounts for the slowness of my convalescence and for my continual backaches. This condition combined with a very low blood pressure and anemia makes me for all practical purposes an invalid.

I am writing you this because I don't want you to be at the disadvantage of not knowing the true state of affairs.

I think what you said about Eunice about our settling our personal problems between ourselves, is a splendid idea, but the facts of the matter are that you have completely cut off all communication between us except through Mrs. Mathews. Please spare me the humiliation of having her call me up any more to ask me what you shall do for the family for Christmas.

Chapter Four

Divorce: Diverging Lives, the Great Depression, and World War II, 1929–1945

IN FEBRUARY 1931, GROSS divorced Hopkins on charges of adultery, and Hopkins married Barbara Duncan the following June. From 1929 to 1945 the letters are mainly concerned with the children and finances. In 1931, Gross and the three boys, then five, nine, and fifteen, moved to Scarsdale, New York, where they lived until 1937. During this time Gross ran the Children's Theater Arts Workshop and taught art to children at the Scarsdale Home School. From 1937 to 1940, Gross and her sons lived in East Northfield, Massachusetts, where she rekindled her interest in social welfare, working for the American Youth Hostel Association and for a committee that provided care for refugees. At the onset of World War II, she applied for a job with the American Red Cross and was assigned as senior recreation officer at the New Station Hospital in Fort Devens, Massachusetts. In 1942 she was assigned to Newport, Rhode Island, and worked at the U.S. Naval Hospital there.

During the 1930s, Hopkins rose to national prominence, first in Governor Franklin Roosevelt's administration as head of the Temporary Emergency Relief Administration (TERA) and then as President Franklin Roosevelt's federal relief administrator, the Federal Emergency Relief Administration (FERA), the Civil Works Administration (CWA), and the Works Progress Administration (WPA), the so-called "alphabet agencies." In 1939 FDR appointed him secretary of commerce, and when World War II broke out, Hopkins acted as FDR's emissary to Churchill and Stalin and as Lend-Lease Administrator.

All three of Hopkins and Gross's sons served in the military during World War II. After Pearl Harbor, David enlisted in the Navy and was stationed on the West Coast. Robert went into the Army and served in the

Signal Corps. As soon as Stephen graduated from high school in 1943, he signed up with the Marines. In February 1944, at eighteen years old, Stephen was killed in the Marshall Islands. That same year, Gross was granted a transfer to California to be near her son David and his growing family. She worked for the ARC until 1946.

197.

DEAR ETHEL:

I stopped over here last Saturday to spend the week end and landed in bed with a rotten cold collected on the train – a little fever has kept me in bed until today. I am coming down Sunday night and will call you up on Monday.

Dad made the trip alright but is considerably weaker and losing weight every day.

I am feeling fine today and know this cold is finished.

HARRY

Written on Hotel Saranac, Saranac Lake, N.Y., letterhead.

198.

Monday
March 11, 1929

MY DEAR ETHEL:

I am enclosing a note at the bank for you to sign. Will you return it with all the bills which you *have* to have paid out of this because I want to clean them all up. I hope you can mail it back on Tuesday because these bills are getting on my nerves.

HARRY

Written on New York Tuberculosis and Health Association letterhead.

199.

[April 1929]

DEAR ETHEL:

I am returning the enclosed bills because I simply cannot pay them – the rest are paid. It won't do any good to borrow any more money because I couldn't pay it back. As a matter of fact, I am financially bankrupt. On the fifteenth after I give you $200 – I must pay for

Written on New York Tuberculosis and Health Association letterhead.

219

the auto $65 – bank $85 – your dentist $50 – leaving me $70 until May 1 – then on May 1 I will give you $300 more and pay $60 insurance and $50 to the school – leaving me in all $140 to live on for a month. I have only one suit of clothes and am not spending a cent that I don't have to.

I telephoned to Tacoma on Wednesday – father is very low and Lew thinks he will die before another week. He is with Lew.

HARRY

P.S. I wrote this last night and it sounds pretty bad – I guess it is.

H.

200.

Tuesday April 23 [1929]

Written on New York Tuberculosis and Health Association letterhead.

DEAR ETHEL:

Thanks so much for your note about father – I have a very interesting letter from Lew which I will send on as soon as Adah returns it. I want David to see it. His note and Robert's were sweet and I shall answer them both in a day or two. Tell Robert I cannot come out on Sunday. I have a letter written from mother after father died but she says very little.

So far as Mrs. Janeway is concerned or any one else like her, I would prefer that you tell her that you cannot accept – if you do not care to give a previous engagement as the reason then I think the thing to say is that we are not accepting social engagements together at this time. I hope you will not give my father's death as the reason because I have accepted other engagements here and on Staten Island that would preclude that.

HARRY

201.

[July 1, 1929]
Monday morning

DEAR ETHEL:

I borrowed $300 and paid the school bill in full – I have also deposited your check for $300 for July 1 – I can more conveniently come out this week end than any other but if you have other plans let me know and I can make it later in July. Wire me in any case. I can come out Friday night and back on Sunday.

The picture enclosed is pretty terrible. Played golf all week end.

HARRY

Written on New York Tuberculosis and Health Association letterhead.

202.

[September 1929]

DEAR ETHEL:

I find my lawyer is to be out of town for a week or ten days which means he will not be back until Sept. 5th or 6th.

My own suggestion is as follows that inasmuch as you are convinced you must have a better financial protection if you go abroad that I deposit notes with your bank promising to pay $500 a month – some such plan should give you complete financial assurance. While so far as I am concerned this is totally unnecessary but it would put the whole matter on a formal basis. I have no reason to believe that my attorney will change his point of view – but if you really want to go abroad it seems absurd to me to have lawyers with no sense of the human equations to be guiding the picture. In the last analysis you will have to do just whatever you wish to.

I had a talk with Brown who lived in the south of France last year and he tells me that a family could live exceedingly well there with nursemaid and tutor for three or four hundred dollars a month.* This is the

Written on New York Tuberculosis and Health Association letterhead.

*Gross had thought about moving to Europe and applied for passports for herself and the children but apparently changed her mind.

center of the artist colony – on the Mediterranean – warm – near Italy etc. Brown says Paris expensive and impossible. He would be glad to tell you all he knows and introduce you to some of his friends including very good school people. His name is Edward F. Brown and can be reached at the Health Dept. 505 Pearl St. He is in charge of the diphtheria work.

I hope David has had a fine and profitable week end. Give my love to the children.

HARRY

203.

September 6, 1929

Written on Saul J. Baron, Counselor at Law, 214 West 42nd Street, New York, letterhead.

MY DEAR MRS. HOPKINS:

I am in receipt of your letter of September 5th, together with its enclosure-letter from Mr. Hopkins. I have read it and am herewith returning it to you in accordance with your request.

Keep this letter, as it may be a very valuable document to have at some later date. It clearly indicates that Mr. Hopkins is most anxious to get you out of the country for reasons satisfactory to himself. I am still of the opinion that your place is on this side of the water until your domestic affairs are more firmly and satisfactorily established.

In your answer to Mr. Hopkins, I would tell him that as you are being advised by me, you feel that it would better serve both your purposes if upon his lawyer's return from out of town we were placed in communication with each other. I note in his letter to you that he says "He will not be back until September 5th or 6th". By the time your reply reaches Mr. Hopkins, his lawyer should be at his office.

With kindest regards, I am,

Very truly yours,

SAUL J. BARON

*Gross and the children were spending the summer in Byrdcliffe, an artist community near Woodstock, New York. The family spent the summer months there from about 1925 to 1931.

Mrs. Harry L. Hopkins
Byrdcliffe,*
Woodstock,
Ulster County, N.Y.
SJB:K

204.

[undated]

DEAR HARRY:

I regret very much that I could not produce myself at the hour you set this morning, but I am writing to Dr. Burnett by this same mail telling him exactly why I did not come so you will have no embarrassment.

It's my party, my pain, my operation and my risk, and [crossed out: "it will have to be done at my convenience"] I'm going to be selfish even at the risk of your displeasure.

I took no offense at anything you said over the telephone this morning. Obviously you're much more excited about this than I am. [crossed out: "and I am constantly finding myself in the position of having to say things to you to calm you down."] I realize that the lack of sympathy and the brutality are not a part of your real personality and that therefore it has nothing to do with you and me and I shall forget it.

E.

Written on Mrs. Harry L. Hopkins, Scarborough, New York, letterhead. Gross wrote this letter in pencil, and it is probably a draft of the original letter.

205.

Western Union
1931 Dec 25 AM 8 51
Mrs. Ethel G. Hopkins
317 West 93 St.

Regret impossible to accept invitation breakfast.

HARRY

206.

November 3, 1932

MY DEAR MRS. HOPKINS:

Here is a check for $200. Mr. Hopkins asked me to tell you that the balance would be forthcoming in a few days.

Hope this finds you and the children in good health. Very cordially yours,

ADELAIDE A. MATTHEWS

207.

April 8, 1933

DEAR MRS. HOPKINS:

Mr. Hopkins has asked me to tell you that you will receive $500. this month; to that end I am enclosing a check for $250 and I understand that your next check for $250. will be forwarded to you on the 15th.

Yours very cordially,

(ADELAIDE A. MATTHEWS)

208.

[date uncertain]

DEAR ETHEL:

My salary here* is $8500 – which is $10,000 less 15%. We are hoping to get the cut back but that is uncertain. I therefore get $345.16 every two weeks and will send you half of it each time. There is enclosed check for $177.08.

I am not sure when I shall be in N.Y. again but will want to see the children then.

HARRY

209.

March 20, 1934

Unsigned, typed carbon copy.

DEAR HARRY:

There is a balance of $177.08 due on the months of January, February and March, and I have not written you before because I expected that you would send it on the 15th of the month. I have had checks from you as follows:

January..................$177.08
February................354.16
March....................354.16

Leaving a balance of $177.08

I have accumulated bills which are becoming very embarrassing and which I cannot delay paying any longer. I am very much worried over this state of affairs and wish you would give this matter your immediate attention.

P.S. I have signed all the papers in connection with David's scholarship and loan at Alfred* and have notified them to refer all such matters to me hereafter.

Their then twenty-year-old son, David, was attending Alfred College in western New York.

210.

[postmarked May 19, 1934]

DEAR ETHEL:

I am leaving checks to be mailed at the new rate – I think about $197.50 while I am away.

HARRY

Written on Federal Emergency Relief Administrator letterhead.

211.

[May 19, 1934]

Written on Federal Emergency Relief Administrator letterhead.

DEAR ETHEL:

This represents one half of April 1 ($177.08) and the 5% raise dated back to Feb. 1. It will mean twenty one or two dollars a month more from now on – and July 1 – as much more.

HARRY

212.

[July 2, 1934]

Written on Federal Emergency Relief Administrator letterhead.

DEAR ETHEL:

The children's report cards are fine and I am ever so delighted to know they are getting on so well.

I am telephoning David today not to come down on Monday because I will be in N.Y. within 10 days and in the meantime will do everything I can about a job for I know how important it is. Tell him too that I will send him the twenty five dollars in a day or two – I would have sent it sooner but haven't had it to send.

HARRY

213.

July 3, 1934

Unsigned, typed carbon copy.

DEAR HARRY:

I wish to acknowledge the receipt of your letter the other day and your letter and check this morning.

It is terribly important for David to get a job this summer not only because he needs to earn something for college expenses next year but because he needs to have something definite to do. He needs to work under supervision and where definite things are required of him. Last summer his camp job was very informal; they apparently assumed that all the camp counselors knew what to do and how to do it. It was a new experience for David and being the youngest one there, he picked up what he could by observing the others. He needs training that goes with a job under supervision. I should be very glad indeed if you could get him a job this summer.

I note what you say about checks being forwarded during your absence at the new rate. Does this increase date back to Feb. 1st too? It is a very great help to receive this additional help now. I thank you for sending it and wish you Bon Voyage.

214.

[date uncertain]

DEAR HARRY:

I am sending you herewith Stephen and Robert's final marks for the year. I thought they might interest you. You will see that Robert just gets by in History and Math. But he is working for a while each day this summer in the hope that he will work next year. The physical ed mark is low because he did not pass his tennis test. He has been swimming a great deal this summer at the Rye Pool and is about to take his Junior Life Saving Test after working for three weeks with the instructor there. Both Stephen and Robert swim quite well and I am counting on the swimming summer to develop Robert's chest and arm muscles. He is growing very fast and I have had to guard against exercise that was too vigorous during the winter. He now measures 5 ft 8½ inches. I am sending you herewith a rough draft of one of his history papers so that you will see the way he writes.

You will see by Stephen's report card that he does not have any problems as far as his work at school goes. He is very quick and energetic and work is very easy for him.

David is working at the office in New York as you probably know and he seems to get a great deal of satisfaction out of doing it. I think whether or not David goes back to Alfred or whether he transfers his credits to another school is a matter which should be given very careful consideration. I think it has been very good for David to be there these two years because he was far enough away from home to be on his own, completely; because the boys who go there don't have much money to spend; and because there is neither the need nor the opportunity to spend a great deal.

David has worked very hard and his marks have been better this year than they have ever been. He received a certificate the other day of the fact that he had a 2.0 index for the second semester (which means that his marks averaged B and better). I think the fact that his scholarship and loan would be discontinued if his marks fell below a certain average, has something to do with it, but in justice to David I think he has worked harder because he has matured enough to appreciate the importance of it and because he has a genuine intellectual interest in the subject matter. I am enclosing one or two of his papers which I think may interest you. Will you please return them because I am keeping all of the things he writes. It makes an interesting record which he may want to see when he is older.

I think it is tremendously important that David finish his four years of college. I don't think there is any argument any other way, and I hope it is going to be possible for him to do it. Whether it is wise for him to continue at Alfred is a matter for consideration. I think Alfred is definitely limited when compared to other colleges, when you consider its faculty and from the point of view of social contacts for David, but I think you are in a better position to judge all these considerations than I am. David needs your advice and council at this time and I hope you will arrange to see him and talk all these matters over with him in time for him to make his plans for the fall.

We are spending the summer here, but there is a possibility that Stephen, Robert and I will go away for a while in August. If you would like to make a plan to see Stephen and Robert some time during the rest of their vacation, (they go back to school September 9th), I shall be glad to arrange anything you may suggest. They would love to see you.

I am sending all this material at this time because I think you will want to know how the children are developing. I should welcome suggestions. I wish I could think of something interesting to do with them some time this summer before they go back to school.

215.

Sept. 26 [1935]

DEAR ETHEL:

I am leaving tonight with the President to be gone till late in October – here are the checks properly dated. Don't cash them before that time or there won't be any money!

There is $30 enclosed for David. Tell him not to worry and if he gets in any jam at all – see Frank Bane* or write a personal letter to Williams† – I will be in Chicago early in November.

Give my love to Robert and Stephen and I will surely see them as soon as I get back.‡

HARRY

Written on Federal Emergency Relief Administrator letterhead.

*Frank Bane was head of the American Public Welfare Association.

†Aubrey Williams worked with Hopkins in NYC at the AICP and then as head of the National Youth Administration (NYA) during the New Deal years.

‡FDR, Hopkins, Harold Ickes (head of the Public Works Administration) and several other guests went on a three-week fishing trip aboard the USS Houston. Part of FDR's agenda for this trip was to ease the tensions between Hopkins and Ickes. Frank Bane and Aubrey Williams worked for Hopkins in the FERA.

216.

March 28 [1936]

DEAR HARRY:

Check for Mar 15 has not yet been received. Am very much in need of it.

The children's Easter vacation begins April 8th and continues until the 20th. They are expressing a desire to go to Washington some time during that period. How does that fit with your plans? David writes that he is not coming home for Easter vacation this year.*

ETHEL

*David Hopkins was attending the University of Chicago.

217.

[date uncertain]

Written on Harry L. Hopkins, Washington, letterhead.

*Cherry Preisser was David Hopkins's girlfriend whom he married in June of 1937. Preisser was a professional dancer, and she and her sister danced with the Ziegfield Follies.

DEAR ETHEL:

I am enclosing check for the first and the fifteenth but don't deposit it until Friday because I want to be sure its good.

Cherry Preisser* is here this week. I am going to see her this afternoon and will let you know later how it stands but from what I hear it looks serious.

HARRY

218.

Western Union
Harry L. Hopkins, Personal
Care Walker Johnson Bldg.
June 23, 1937

Robert completely recovered appendix attack. Doctors advise operation within week. Surgeons fee prohibitive. Can you arrange Dr. Johnson look after Robert or can you suggest alternative. Answer Scarsdale address.

ETHEL G. HOPKINS

219.

Western Union
Harry L. Hopkins, Personal
Walker Johnson Building
New York Avenue
   Robert operation today one thirty Booth Memorial Hospital. Please notify David return home.
ETHEL

220.

September 30, 1937

DEAR HARRY:
   My new address, beginning October 1st will be #5 Highland Avenue, East Northfield, Mass.
   Robert is at Mr. Herman and Stephen is at the Bement School in Deerfield. I have been able to find a furnished house to live in at a very low rental which makes the above possible. The children are both day students. Deerfield is 14 miles from Northfield but the transportation is arranged for because of other children who go from there. I am storing my furniture because I think we all need this kind of change.
   I am at present moving out of 17 Innes Road and would very much appreciate if you could send check for October 1st just as soon as possible to my new address because moving and having to start in a new place involves some immediate expenditures that cannot wait.
   David is very much absorbed in his new job and very happy in the prospect of his new home and the excitement of buying household equipment and furniture.* I only hope all will go well with him.
ETHEL

*David had married Cherry Preisser the previous June and the couple was living in New York City.

221.

Aug. 3 [1937]
East Northfield, Mass.

DEAR HARRY:

Enclosed is a copy of a letter I received from Grace Bement as a supplement to Stephen's report. I am sending it on because I think you may want to see it. The enclosed report card is the one which is usually sent to you – a duplicate is always sent to me, which I sign. I think you are expected to sign the enclosed as an acknowledgement of its receipt.

I consider Stephen has had a very valuable year at Grace Bement's and he has made many fine friends among the children. Grace's influence has been very good for Stephen and he and all the other children in the school are very fond of her, even though it is necessary for her to discipline them quite severely sometimes.

She is very anxious to have Stephen stay and finish the 8th grade next year which is the last grade in her school. If I could just stick it out up here another year. I know Stephen would have a splendid foundation for his Preparatory School or High School. Northfield with its conferences and hymn-singing is beginning to get me and I don't know how much more of it I can take.

It is very beautiful up here this summer and the boys are having a very good time – swimming and playing tennis and golf. Robert is at present at Meredith, N.H. for one week.

Is there any chance that you can come up here any time this summer? It would mean a great deal to Stephen and Robert if you could and it would give me an opportunity to talk over with you a matter of business which I have been turning over in my mind. For once I have plenty of accommodations for comfort.

*Diana was the five-year-old daughter of Hopkins and Barbara Duncan Hopkins.

Thank you for check just received

ETHEL

I hope Diana* is enjoying her summer.

222.

Jan. 15 [1937]

DEAR ETHEL:

Here is check for one month. My salary has been raised as [of] Jan 15 so the next check will be larger.

HARRY

Written on Works Progress Administration letterhead.

223.

[postmarked September 17, 1937]

DEAR ETHEL:

I am enclosing a check for $400 which pays the alimony through Sept 15.

The idea of staying in Northfield sounds fine to me. I know Mrs. Bement has a grand school – and Robert can do as well in Northfield as anywhere else. I am all for it. I am terribly sorry I missed them this summer but it couldn't be helped.

David's ménage sounds a little absurd but there is nothing for it but to let him manage his own affairs.

HARRY

Written on Works Progress Administration letterhead.

224.

#5 Highland Avenue
East Northfield, Mass.
Nov. 20 [1937]

DEAR HARRY:*

We are pretty well settled at the above address.† Robert and Stephen are very pleased with their respective schools and Robert is actually on the honor roll for this six and a half week period at Hermon. I am enclosing his report card and also Stephen's. The country is very beautiful and both Stephen and Robert take long trips on their bicycles and hike with their

*Gross wrote "Copy" above the salutation.

†Gross moved to Northfield on October 1, 1937, and worked at the American Youth Hostel.

groups from school and sometimes with groups or individuals from the American Youth Hostel Headquarters which is about a mile away. My job with them did not work out, because I found I could not live at the Headquarters with the children. It was much too hectic and would have interfered with their regular habits and their school work. That is the reason I took this house which I was able to rent furnished at a very low rental, so that even with the heating of it, it is a great deal less than renting and living in Scarsdale. The house is very comfortable – full of good books – in a beautiful location, and furnished very completely and beautifully. It is the home of Dr. Cutler, President Emeritus of the Northfield Schools who is at present studying medicine abroad and who is very glad to have someone in his house, heating it and using it. I have shut off all but the rooms we need – because it is quite large – but I have loads of room and a very comfortable guest room. David and Cherry were here over last week end. We are right next to the Northfield Hotel, where people come for winter sports. The ski run goes right through the grounds – there is a pond right out in front of the house where they skate – a place for tobogganing – and the children are looking forward to an exciting winter.

I should like you to feel that you can come here at anytime you want to make such a plan. I can always go somewhere and visit. The children are devoted to Diana and I think she could have a very jolly time. Could something be planned over the Christmas holidays? Stephen and Robert both have 18 days.

I have made many unsuccessful attempts to write to you in the past month. Words are so inadequate to express my deep sympathy for all that you have been through, all that you are going through.[‡] Is it any comfort for you to know that Robert and Stephen have a very deep affection for you and that you can count on them for loyalty and devotion?

We are driving down to New York to spend Thanksgiving with David and Cherry, returning Sunday.
ETHEL

[‡] *Hopkins's second wife, Barbara Duncan Hopkins, died of breast cancer in early October 1937.*

225.

5 Highland Avenue
East Northfield, Mass.
Dec. 17 [1937]

DEAR LEWIS:

I have just had the news about Harry from David.* I am so glad to know that you are going to be with him.

Is it too much to ask you to send me word of the result of the operation and how Harry is afterwards?

Stephen and Robert are very anxious about it all and we would be very grateful to you.

We are here for the winter. Stephen and Robert are day students at schools near-by –

Robert at Mt. Herman – Stephen in Deerfield. More of this later. If there is anything I can do, I hope you will let me know.

ETHEL

*Hopkins was diagnosed with stomach cancer in 1937 and on December 20th had two-thirds of his stomach and part of his duodenum removed.

226.

Dec. 17 [1937]

DEAR HARRY:

I have just had the news from David about the fact that you are about to have an operation. Please know that you are in our thoughts and that if there is anything that I can do that I am most anxious that you ask me to do it. Here's for good luck and a speedy recovery.

ETHEL

227.

[May 26, 1938]

Typed carbon copy. Gross handwrote at the top of the letter: "Copy of letter written to H.L.H. May 26, 1938 East Northfield."

DEAR HARRY:

I have got to see you. How can it be arranged? Matters of great importance to you and to me, concerning the children and my own personal affairs, must be cleared up, in order to take the awkwardness out of situations. The passage of time has made me completely aware of my own position. A little intelligence, and a plan, could simplify matters.

Could you stop by here on your way back from the west? I should prefer to see you here, although I could come down to New York. If you came here you could take Robert on to Washington on the date you planned. Stephen's school is over on June 3rd.

I am addressing this letter to Washington and I should appreciate hearing from you upon its receipt. My telephone number here is Northfield 312.

228.

August 15, 1938

Written on Harry L. Hopkins, Washington, letterhead.

DEAR ETHEL:

I don't know what my plans are going to be, because I am having to work all Summer. If I can, I want to take Diana to James Roosevelt's for three or four days at the end of the Summer, and I am going to try to get up to see her for three or four days in the next week or so. However, I will let you know as soon as I can about plans, because I am anxious to see you, Stephen and Robert.

HARRY HOPKINS
Mrs. Ethel Hopkins,
5 Highland Avenue,
East Northfield, Massachusetts.

229.

DEAR HARRY:

I have your letter of August 15th and we are looking forward to the possibility of a visit from you. Is Diana's camp near here so that you can combine the two visits? I hope that you will let me know before you come so that we shall be sure to be here.

We went to Woodstock over last week-end to look things over, since you suggested it as one of the places to establish a permanent home for myself and the children. Byrdcliffe was beautiful as always, and we had a very nice week-end. If the schools were better I should be strongly tempted to try it. I don't like the general instability in family life that seems to abound. Nearly everybody seems to have changed partners since I was there six years ago. Ben Webster has three children by Joya Stellforth, and he is actually getting heavy. We stayed in Carniola.

Robert is thrilled over the new camera you sent him and he is going to fix up a dark room and learn to develop his own pictures. Stephen is caddying on the golf links everyday and playing golf too.

I am making notes of the things I want to discuss and I hope you will be able to come before too long.

ETHEL

230.

DEAR HARRY:

One of Robert's classmates brought to Robert a copy of TIME magazine of July 18th which contains an article about you under the title RELIEF. Mention is made in this article of David as your son but no mention is made of Stephen and Robert.

This has happened on several occasions. The last time it happened I wrote a letter to Aubrey Williams,

Unsigned, typed carbon copy.

because you were at the Mayo Clinic (just before or just after your operation). In your absence I called Mr. Williams attention to it and asked him to instruct the publicity department or whoever was responsible, to give out more complete and more careful information in the future. There was no reply to my letter, but I did hope that something would be done about it.

It must be obvious to you how embarrassing this can become in time to Stephen and Robert and to me.

I am enclosing a copy of a letter I have written, *but not mailed,* to the TIME magazine. I shall hold it for two or three days until I hear from you. I do not wish to create awkward situations, and if you can deal with the matter directly and would prefer to do so, I shall do nothing more about this instance.

I understand Cherry has had to stop her work at the Riviera and June is carrying it on alone.*

*"Cherry" (Preisser Hopkins) refers to their daughter-in-law whose dancing career had taken her to the French Riviera. She apparently stopped dancing because she was pregnant with their first child, Cherry, born February 7, 1939. June Preisser, the other half of the sister dancing team, continued to dance without her.

231.

[early September 1938]
5 Highland Avenue
East Northfield, Mass.
August 29, 1938

To the Editor of TIME
The Weekly News Magazine
330 East 22nd Street
Chicago, Ill.
DEAR SIR:

I wish to correct a misleading statement that appeared in your magazine issue of July 18th which has just been called to my attention. In your article about Harry Hopkins under RELIEF, in describing his family, mention is made "of his son David, 22."

Mr. Hopkins has three sons by his first marriage, David, aged 23, Robert aged 17, and Stephen, aged 13.

I should appreciate your using this more complete information in any subsequent articles, whenever my family is mentioned.

Yours very truly,
ETHEL G. HOPKINS
(Mrs. Harry L.)

232.

[postmarked September 8, 1938]

MY DEAR MRS. HOPKINS:

Harry asked me to write you regarding your letter concerning "Time."

It was my pleasure last summer when Robt. was here to be with him and to observe Harry's evident love for the boy, and he has spoken to me often about Stephen.

The fact that a magazine fails to print the other boys' names, is of course something over which Harry has not the slightest control. I am sure that if he could he would have them spare all of the members of his family. But as is well known they do not ask you about such matters but write as they please.

I wish to be affectionately remembered to Robert and Stephen.

And my cordial regards to you.

Sincerely yours,

AUBREY WILLIAMS

Written on Works Progress Administration letterhead.

233.

East Northfield, Mass.
September 15 [1938]

MY DEAR MR. WILLIAMS:

Thank you very much for your letter. I appreciate the trouble you have taken to write and I hasten to assure you that I have never, at any time, doubted Harry's love for Stephen, Robert and David.

I, too, deplore the publicity, but since it is unavoidable, it sometimes becomes necessary to correct misleading statements or to counteract a wrong impression. It is because I hesitated about the procedure that I wrote to Harry. I should much prefer to have him handle it as he sees fit.

I value your interest and I thank you for your many kindnesses to the boys. They always speak of you with a great deal of enthusiasm and Stephen and Robert send you their affectionate greetings.

Yours very sincerely,

ETHEL G. HOPKINS

234.

Western Union
1939 Jun 20
   Necessary to make plans. Will you call me long distance.
ETHEL

235.

Western Union
June 29, 1939
Mrs. Ethel Hopkins
Hotel Wellington
55th Street at 7th Avenue
New York City
   Expecting boys either Thursday or Friday at their convenience in Washington. Advise office time of arrival.
HARRY
Personal – charge to:
Hon. Harry L. Hopkins
2821 N Street N.W.
HLH;Vm;mab

236.

Western Union
1939 Jun 29
Harry L. Hopkins Secretary
Department of Commerce
Personal
   Boys arriving Washington tomorrow morning eleven o'clock daylight time.
ETHEL

237.

[date uncertain]
Tuesday

DEAR HARRY:
We arrived here yesterday. The boys can leave here Thursday or Friday to come to you. Will you let us know at above address: destination, and what time of day you would like them to arrive. We're off to the fair.
ETHEL

Written on Hotel
Wellington letterhead.

238.

November 25, 1939

DEAR ETHEL:
I would love to have Robert and Stephen come down during the Christmas Holidays if they would like to. I think just before New Year would be best. I think they better come irrespective of my health for I could handle them here easily.

I have a letter from Robert telling me something of the things that are going through his mind about school next year but I think I could talk to him about that better than write.

I meant to write to you after the boys were with me last summer to tell you my impression of them. Needless to say I think they are both getting along splendidly. I have a feeling that Robert and Stephen see too much of each other and it would be better for Robert if he had more association with older boys. I am also disturbed about the fact the Robert has never worked. I think it is extremely important that he have some experience in working for somebody during his holiday time. Stephen seems to be well motivated on that front. I have a feeling, too, that Robert should not try the theater as a vocation but I certainly don't want to discourage that if he feels so inclined. At any rate, there will be plenty of time to talk that over with him when he is here.

Written on The
Secretary of Commerce,
Washington letterhead.

I seem to be getting better but very slowly. I have a nutritional disorder, cause unknown, which laid me very low; however, I feel very confident about the future. I have no idea when I will be able to get back to work, it may be soon but it is more than apt to be several weeks.

Sincerely,

HARRY

Mrs. Ethel Hopkins
5 Highland Avenue
E. Northfield, Mass.
Hlh:vm;him

239.

December 2, 1939

Unsigned copy.   DEAR HARRY:

Your letter received. I did not answer it at once because Stephen has been ill with an ear abscess, a very high temperature for three days which was checked somewhat by the fourth day by "sulfanilamide". He has had a normal temperature for five days now and the doctor is permitting him to get up and get dressed tomorrow, but he insisted that he stay home from school all next week because he says a slow convalescence is very important since Stephen was a very sick boy for a few days. He is however making a marvelous recovery, eating everything in sight, and I am very much relieved. He is planning to make up some school work while he is at home next week.

We are all very much disturbed over your continued illness. When you say it is a "nutritional disorder, cause unknown", it reminds me of something your mother told me once, after she heard about Stephen's pyloric stenosis operation. She said, "That must be what was the matter with Harry when he was a baby. We had a hard time finding food that would agree with him and he was very delicate until he was about three years old." I wonder if this can, in any way, be related to that early weakness?

As usual, the boys are happy over the prospect of a visit with you. Your letter came at a very opportune moment when Stephen was feeling very discouraged over the doctor's announcement that he would have to stay out of school a week longer than he expected.

The boy's Christmas vacation starts on December 14th. They can come down to you either the week before Christmas or the week after Christmas. In your letter I note that you say that "just before the New Year would be best". If they stay here for Christmas that would give them only about four or five days before the New Year. Is that satisfactory to you? Otherwise we could drive down to New York from here on the 15th of December and there would be more time.

Robert needs to definitely formulate his plans for next year. The whole question of whether or not he should go to college and if so, where, has to be decided. I too would hesitate to discourage his interest in the theater as a vocation because his interest in it is very keen. A complete theater training which includes all the elements of theater, would bring out all of his aptitudes. A college like the University of North Carolina might be the answer or Baird College. They both have a theater school. The Carolina Playmakers have produced playwrights as well as directors. Hallie Flanagan* suggests that the Group Theater Apprentice Groups is the best place for training, and has given Robert a letter to Harold Clurman.

*Hallie Flanagan, a Grinnell classmate of Hopkins, ran the Federal Theatre Project, a division of the Works Projects Administration (WPA Federal One).

I realize that the theater as a vocation is not very dependable, but his interest in the theater might lead to other things. He is very much interested in industrial design, and we have discussed his going to a school that gives a good course in industrial design, because it would include stage design. Norman Bel Geddes does both.

The fact that Robert has not worked for a wage does not, I think, mean that he would not or could not work. His ill health has kept him from working the past two summers, but he was very eager to work both times. The discipline of a job would be very good for him, although he works very hard at school, and very steadily and faithfully, his marks notwithstanding.

Stephen and Robert see very little of each other during the school year. They have different friends and go to different parties. All of Robert's friends are his age and older. However, one reason why I was anxious to have Robert complete his credit in Math. last summer so that he could enter his senior year this fall, was that he would be with older boys.

I think it is well to remember that Robert is going through a very awkward period, when he is neither boy nor man. It isn't very attractive and does not appear to the best advantage. I can remember how "raw" David seemed at this age, when he did not care enough about his finger nails or his hair or his clothes except to wear outlandish combinations. Robert's temperament is different, but he has a lot of force and strength and originality and talent, but there is no doubt he needs direction.

Stephen presents fewer problems at present. He goes very directly at the things he needs to do; has a lot of vitality and drive and is very orderly about his life. I hope this will continue.

I am very glad to have your impressions about the boys and it is very gratifying to know that you think they are getting on well. I have made many mistakes and to tell you the truth I don't feel very adequate at this point. For that reason I am very glad you are going to talk to Robert and that the visit is coming when it is.

240.

December 5, 1939

Written on The Secretary of Commerce, Washington, letterhead.

DEAR ETHEL:

I am terribly sorry to learn about Stephen's illness but I assume his recovery will be rapid now. I am having some things which Stephen might like to eat sent from New York.

I think the best time for me to have the boys would be immediately after Christmas, say about the twenty-seventh. I should be some stronger by then and they would enjoy their stay here much more after Christmas than before.

Sincerely,

HARRY

Mrs. Ethel G. Hopkins
5 Highland Avenue
East Northfield, Massachusetts

241.

April 7 [1940]

DEAR HARRY:

The doctor drained the fluid again this morning – the slight rise in the temperature and pulse in the last 3 days determined it. They drained off *55 ounces* of fluid this time. Robert was very weak after this 2nd draining – much more so than the first time which may be due to the fact that he had to sit up this time.

high I told you yesterday that they gave Robert a tuberculosis test. Today the doctor told me it was *positive*. What does that mean to you?

As I understand it the next thing to determine is whether this fluid is due to that fact, or to some other cause – I can't believe that Robert has tuberculosis – and the positive test does not necessarily mean that – they are going to take more X-rays tomorrow and they have sent a specimen of this new fluid to Boston to be injected into a guinea-pig.

The fluid was drawn this morning at about 11 a.m. it is now 4:30 P.M. and Robert's pulse is more nearly normal and he is resting comfortably. He had a 2 hr. nap this afternoon from 1 to 3.

Dr. Johnson who took care of Robert at first, had to go to New York to a medical conference and a Dr. Low is the doctor in charge at present. He is a young man – a grad. of the Children's Hospital in Boston, and Dr. Alfred Johnson thinks very highly of him.

Have you anything to suggest about future procedure?

I am pain-stricken over the whole procedure – except that Robert is so serene and smiling this afternoon – and he may stage a very quick recovery after this second draining.

The doctors tell me he will probably not be able to go back to school and that it will take him some time to get on his feet again.

The school doctor from Mt. Hermon – a Dr. Strong – comes in to see Robert every other day.

His appetite is good and he drinks 2 glasses of milk with each meal.

Written on Franklin Co. Hospital, Greenfield, Massachusetts, letterhead.

If you ever want to reach me at home in the evening the number there is Northfield 312. I am at the hospital most of the day –
ETHEL

242.

May 7, 1940

Unsigned copy. DEAR HARRY:

I should like very much to see you and to talk with you. Not about troublesome things but about matters involving immediate plans which have to made. For many reasons, I am finding it difficult to formulate these plans and your advice and guidance would greatly facilitate matters.

I have an opportunity to drive down to Washington and share expenses with someone else who wished to make the trip. I could be there Friday morning of this week, if that is convenient, or the early part of next week. I do not want to be away for Robert's birthday which is the 17th of May. Anytime before that would be possible for me.

Would you let me know about this as soon as possible?
Sincerely,

243.

May 8, 1940

Western Union Telegram
Mrs. Ethel Hopkins
5 Highland Avenue
East Northfield, Massachusetts
I can see you ten thirty Friday morning at home.
HARRY
Charge to NORTH 1744

244.

June 9, 1940

DEAR HARRY:

If you have mailed check for June 1st, I have not yet received it.

Do you still want Robert to come down to Washington with the idea of visiting St Johns after graduation, June 10th? We have just learned that he has passed in all of his subjects. *Even French* and he got an *85* in a final English IV test. David and Cherry are coming up for graduation exercises.

We all hope that you are well and I shall be interested to know what your plans are for the immediate future. I am not making plans until Commencement is over. We shall be here for the rest of this month at any rate.

ETHEL

P.S. Stephen's weight and height have just been checked at Hermon. He has gained *21 lbs* since last October and grown *two inches*. Isn't that amazing? He got his Junior Varsity letter in tennis and is third man on the team.

. . . at this moment Robert with his trumpet, another boy with a clarinet and another at the piano are having a "jam" session in the living room . . . the war is never out of anybody's thoughts for very long but I think it's important to engage in normal activities as much as possible.

Written on Mrs. Ethel G. Hopkins, East Northfield, Massachusetts, letterhead.

245.

rec'd Aug. 26, 1940

DEAR ETHEL:

I am resigning here within the next ten days – the going is too tough and if I am to ever get really well again – I must take it easy for a year or two. As yet I am not sure what I am going to do but I am on the track of something that will pay $5000 a year and be not too exacting. This much I feel pretty sure can be counted on but no more. So all our plans will have to be adjusted accordingly.

Written on The Secretary of Commerce, Washington, letterhead.

I should think if Robert had $35 to $50 a month that he could easily get himself through a place like North Carolina – perhaps Stephen would require somewhat more. I don't think you should plan on more that $2100 from me during the coming year.

I rather think that I shall get a room in N.Y. and put Diana in boarding school this year.

My own feeling about Robert is that he has pretty much made up his mind about North Carolina and that he better not be dissuaded. The University has a first rate standing – and an excellent president, Frank Graham, whom I know very well.

The going will be a little difficult for everybody for a while but I feel sure I am going to get better.

No matter what you may hear – be sure that everything is well between the President and me.

HARRY

246.

August 1940
East Northfield, Mass.

Unsigned copy.   DEAR HARRY:

I have your letter and I am trying to make plans accordingly. It is clear that I shall have to get a job and I am looking forward to the prospect.

I have tentatively reserved a place for Stephen at Hill School and they have agreed to renew their offer of a scholarship, by telegram. The details in regard to the amount that I am to pay will be settled when the headmaster returns on September first. Stephen is a good enough athlete to be considered from that angle. I find, on my return, that he has definitely set out to gain weight in order to make the football team, and he now weighs 160 lbs.

Robert will return by September first and I shall go on with plans to send him to North Carolina, since that seems best. I hate to have the boys so far away but I realize I should not be too dependent upon them.

I think you are very wise to get out of Washington and take life more easily for awhile. The important thing, after all, is for you to get well. Diana seems very young to send away to boarding school, but under the circumstances I suppose it is the only thing to do.

Until I locate a job I shall get myself a tiny room in New York. After that I hope to get a place large enough for the boys to come to during vacation. A home base is important. I shall stay here, probably, until I get the boys away to school, and that may necessitate my keeping the house for the month of September.

If you know anybody who needs a secretary, I can still do shorthand and typing. I prefer however, to establish an art center, somewhere, near New York; a place where children and adults can come and work in various art mediums, and pay so much an hour, in studios equipped for the purpose.

247.

August 18, 1940

DEAR HARRY:

As you probably know by this time, Robert has been accepted at the three colleges where he made application, Grinnell, University of North Carolina, and St. Johns College. It is necessary now to send in the Registration Fee, and before doing so, I should like to have your advice about the final decision.

"c/o Hans Hoffman School of Fine Arts, Miller Road, Provincetown, Mass." typed at the top right.

In view of the present situation and your own plans for the immediate future, where do you think that he should go?

Because of the great distance, I should much prefer not to send Robert to Grinnell, unless you feel very strongly that under the circumstances, that is where Robert should go.

The tuition at St. John's is $1000 a year (that is supposed to include everything). In view of what you said, I did not ask for a scholarship there, or anywhere else.

The tuition and expenses per year at the University of North Carolina amount to about $550 a year, as far as I can figure out. Robert's reason for choosing that school is because of the Drama Department.

David feels very strongly in favor of St. John's and whenever he expresses his views, Robert decides to go there. If I thought that Robert could make the grade at St. John's, I should have no hesitancy in sending him there.

The more I think about it, the more convinced I am that if the boys are to have a college education that the course that is open to me is to go and live in a town where there is a State University. The possibility of my getting a job in or around New York does not seem very hopeful at present. I am here studying at the Hoffman School (Hans Hoffman) in the hope that after this intensive course, I shall be better equipped to hold down a job teaching in an art department in one of the progressive schools.

Stephen preferred to stay at home because he was having such a good time. A friend is keeping check on him and Lena is there of course, keeping house for him, in my absence. He is caddying for a portion of each day. If I cannot get Stephen in to Hill School, what do you think about his going to Hermon as a boarding student next year?

With both boys away at school, I could explore the possibility of getting a job in or near New York, and get settled before it is time for them to come home for their Christmas vacation.

I realize that you are very busy, but I do not wish to take the full responsibility for these decisions, as they affect you as well as they do me. Besides I need any advice and help that you can give me.

You had a birthday yesterday. Please accept my best wishes for the coming year. I am so glad to hear from David that you are better.

Yours very sincerely,

ETHEL

248.

September 18, 1940

DEAR ETHEL:

I know that I am going to earn enough between September 1, 1940 and September 1, 1941 so that your share would be $170.00 a month. I am very confident that I will increases this income somewhat, and if I do, I will make appropriate adjustments in these payments.

I am, therefore, sending you a check for the September 15th payment for $85.00.

Sincerely,

HARRY

Mrs. Ethel G. Hopkins,
5 Highland Avenue
East Northfield, Massachusetts.

Robert came by yesterday – he is going to stay with the Pres. of the Univ. until he can get in a dormitory.

H.

Written on The Secretary of Commerce, Washington, letterhead.

249.

[date uncertain]

DEAR ETHEL:

I am enclosing my check for $85. – While I am hoping that I will make some more money – there is no assurance of it – and as I wrote you before it will be necessary for you to make your plans on the basis of this amount. I of course have no objection to your trying to get a scholarship for Robert – though I think working on his part would be better. Nor have I any objection to your getting any job from Florence that you can.

HARRY

Written on Essex House, New York, letterhead.

250.

172 Fifth Avenue
New York, March 4, 1941

Unsigned copy.

DEAR HARRY:

The enclosed check was returned this morning. It speaks for itself. As I have drawn against this amount quite heavily, I hope you will mail your corrected or duplicate check by return air mail

I have avoided writing you, knowing how hard you are working and how keyed up you must be, as we all are, over the situation in Washington.*

*Hopkins had just recently returned from a mission to London to meet with Churchill to discuss U.S. aid to England in the war effort. The Lend Lease bill had just passed the Senate.

But things are going very badly because I cannot manage on the $170 per month which you send me. School expenses for the boys come to almost that amount and there is nothing left for maintaining a home and taking care of the boy's vacations. The fact that I do not have enough to live on is not so important, though it is at times uncomfortable and embarrassing.

I have not been able to land a job although I am still seeing people and following leads.

I am now faced with the need for finding an apartment large enough to take care of the boys when they come home for their Easter vacation. I am anxious to take the furniture out of storage and establish a base in or near New York, but it is difficult to make plans when things are so uncertain.

I have been drawing on my reserves but they are fast diminishing and soon there will be no more.

Is there any immediate prospect of a change in this state of affairs?

If I could see any other way out, believe me, I would not write to you at this time.

P.S. *You may be interested in these figures:* – Stephen's and Robert's school expenses, beginning in September and through March (6 months) have come to $128.00 per month. (This does not include the amount spent for clothes before they entered school. They were each completely outfitted. Nor does it include added rent and expenses while they were at home during Xmas, or doctor's or dentist bills, and other incidentals.) The balance of $42 has to provide these last named items, as well as rent and my maintenance. Needless to say it is not enough.

251.

March 6, 1941

DEAR ETHEL:

I am returning the check. I am terribly sorry it was made out improperly. I see no prospect in the immediate future of my changing my plans, which means that I will have no more money to send you than you are receiving now.

I have told you several times you should organize your life to live within that and not assume that I am going to do something else to earn a larger income later. I can see no possible solution to this except your going to work. An alternate to that would be, of course, for you to take Robert out of school and let him go to work. But, as between those two, I think the former is much more preferable. I simply am not in a position to handle your personal affairs beyond the responsibility I have assumed.

HARRY

Mrs. Ethel G. Hopkins
172 Fifth Avenue,
New York City, N.Y.

252.

172 Fifth Avenue
New York, April 15 [1941]

DEAR HARRY: *Unsigned copy.*

Thank you for check received this morning.

I sent you a wire yesterday because I have been having trouble with my mail. A new superintendent has been delivering it to another apartment. Since the occupant of this apartment has been away, my mail has been accumulating there for several days.

When I discovered this yesterday, I thought your check might have been lost, and if that were the case, payment should be stopped on it as quickly as possible. That was the reason I worded my telegram as I did.

I am very much discouraged over Stephen's failure to pass his Math. re-examination. He studied on an average of two hours a day, during his spring vacation, after he was notified that he had a condition in Math. And would have to take another examination when he got back. I had a tutor for him, after he had covered all the material, who went over all of the work with him. He assured me when he left that Stephen was ready for the exam.

In Stephen's letter to me he says he did not work hard enough on logarithms and that 45% of the exam was on logarithms. He will have to take the examination again next fall.

He seems to be coming along all right in his other subjects.

I have several applications in for a job and I hope something will develop soon.

253.

May 24, 1941

Written on The White House, Washington, letterhead.

DEAR ETHEL:

I think the plan for Stephen's summer is fine.

Cordially yours,

HARRY

Mrs. Ethel G. Hopkins
172 Fifth Avenue,
New York, New York

254.

July 28, 1941

DEAR MRS. HOPKINS:
    I am enclosing Mr. Hopkins's check for $316.66. I have drawn the check to cover the amount due you on both the 15th of July and the 1st of August, as I have a limited number of signed checks.
Very sincerely yours,
LOIS M. BERNAY
Secretary to Mr. Hopkins

Mrs. Ethel G. Hopkins,
American Red Cross,
New Station Hospital,
Ft. Devens, Massachusetts.

Written on The White House, Washington, letterhead.

255.

June 12, 1942

Mrs. Ethel G. Hopkins
New Station Hospital
American Red Cross
Fort Devens, Mass.
DEAR MRS. HOPKINS:
    Ben was in to see me today and brought with him a copy of your letter to him of June 9th last. If you will refer to my letter to you of February 16, 1939 you will note that I advised you that in my opinion, the only contingency upon which Mr. Hopkins can deduct $125. per month because of the attaining of the majority of any of the children, is your death or your-marriage. I am still of that opinion.
    However, as I stated to Ben, and as I now state to you, in my opinion Mr. Hopkins is doing such great and magnificent work in connection with our war effort, that I feel that he should be not annoyed or mentally harassed in a matter of this kin and at this time.

Written on Saul J. Baron, Counselor At Law letterhead.

Then too, you must consider the careers of the boys. No step should be taken to feed the tabloid sheets to the detriment and harassing of any of the parties concerned. I have always felt, as I have expressed myself to you on many occasions, that Mr. Hopkins is a man of the highest integrity and I feel that if you had a talk with him a satisfactory adjustment can be made.

In my talk with Ben I furthermore suggested that at the convenience of Mr. Hopkins, if I could arrange to have a few minutes talk with him, not as an aggressive lawyer asserting a legal right, but in a friendly capacity, that some modification and clarification of the existing terms could, and should be made to both your satisfaction. My only hesitancy in having such a talk at this time is that I feel that he should not be upset nor diverted from his many arduous and important duties. On the other hand, he may be most agreeable for a conference of that character.

Ben is writing to you today and if, after you receive this letter and your communication from him, you would like to come down and have a personal talk with me, I think that such a talk would serve a useful purpose. If you decide to do so let me know when you are coming down and I will arrange a meeting with you at our convenience.

With kind personal regards, I am
Sincerely yours,
SAUL BARON
SJB: DB

256.

July 4, 1942

Unsigned copy. DEAR MR. BARON:

The enclosed is a copy of a letter I have today sent to Mr. Hopkins. I misplaced your outline, but I tried to cover all the points as I remembered them. Please ac-

knowledge receipt of this and let me know if you think it is all right.
Yours very sincerely,

To
Mr. Saul Baron
551 Fifth Ave.
N.Y. City.
Enclosure

257.

July 4, 1942

DEAR HARRY:

I have received your three checks in reduced amounts of $108.33 for June 1st, June 15th and July 1st.

I wish to call your attention to the fact that according to our agreement it is only in the events that I die or remarry that such reductions are in order.

This matter was brought to my attention when you made such reductions before, but because you were having many troubles and illnesses, I did not wish to disturb you further at that time.

I refer you to paragraph 3 of the Agreement. I have no doubt that this is an oversight on your part.
Yours very sincerely,

To
Mr. Harry L. Hopkins
The White House
Washington, D. C.

Written on American Red Cross, New Station Hospital, Fort Devens, Massachusetts, letterhead.

258.

July 7, 1942

DEAR MRS. HOPKINS:

In reply to your letter of July 4 Mr. Hopkins has asked me to tell you that it is his understanding that when Robert reached 21 years of age you were to receive $50 a month less alimony.

Written on The White House, Washington, letterhead.

This $50 a month is represented by the reductions in the last three checks sent you.

Very truly yours,

LOIS M. BERNEY
Secretary to Mr. Hopkins

Mrs. Ethel G. Hopkins,
American Red Cross,
New Station Hospital
Fort Devens, Massachusetts.

259.

July 8, 1942

Written on Saul J. Barron, Counselor At Law letterhead.

Mrs. Ethel G. Hopkins
American Red Cross
Office of the Assistant Field Director
Fort Devens, Mass.

DEAR MRS. HOPKINS:

While your letter to Mr. Hopkins is not as I outlined it to you, I think that it covers the situation satisfactorily.

Will you advise me as to the reply you receive, if any.

With kindest regards, I am

Very truly yours,

SAUL J. BARON

260.

July 15, 1942

Written on American Red Cross letterhead.

DEAR MISS BERNAY:

Please call Mr. Hopkins attention to the fact that the last three checks are bi-monthly checks, therefore the total reduction per month has been $100 and not $50, as you stated in your letter of July 7th for Mr. Hopkins.

Under separate cover I am sending Mr. Hopkins a copy
of the Agreement in case he has misplaced his copy.
Yours truly,

To
Miss Lois Bernay
Secretary to Mr. Harry L. Hopkins
The White House
Washington, D.C.

261.

December 22, 1942

DEAR MRS. HOPKINS:

I am sending the check and apologize for its being
late. I think if you will be patient with me I shall eventually get organized and especially on the financial end
of things. I have trouble enough with my own finances
and am somewhat worried about taking care of Mr.
Hopkins's [finances]. Do not hesitate to write me if all
is not as it should be. I shall appreciate it.

Merry Christmas to you.
Sincerely yours,
RUTH DAGGETT
1 enclosure

*Written on The White
House, Washington,
letterhead.*

262.

February 2, 1943

MY DEAR ETHEL:

As you know, I saw Robert in Casablanca.* He was with
me about a week altogether. I still do not know how he
happened to be there, because I did not send for him. He
landed one afternoon, however, dressed in a British uniform and thoroughly tired and worn out, having come to
Casablanca immediately from the front. He had been

**The Casablanca
conference, with FDR,
Churchill, and Stalin
attending, took place
January 14–22,
1943.*

there for three weeks and has seen all the action around those parts, which was considerable. I gather he behaved very well. At any rate, he talked very objectively and modestly about it and felt quite sure that shells did not bother him too much. By the time he got a haircut and shaved up, I have never seen him looking better. He lost two sets of American uniforms; one when a German bomb hit the hotel at Oran and the other time at the front when the Germans hit a laundry with all his clothes in. He took pictures of all the show there in Technicolor and I am going to have a copy of the film made and keep for him. We went over to Marrakech the last day and Robert left a week ago Monday. The last I saw of Robert he was getting in a plane to go to Algiers with Averell Harriman. By this time he is already at the front again. He seemed to have made a great many friends and everyone that I saw thinks that he is doing very well. Incidentally, he has been promoted to Sergeant.

I have not seen David but I have a letter from Captain Duncan of the *Essex* telling me David had reported there for duty.

As ever,

P.S. In the last couple of weeks Robert has been getting his mail. There is really no other way to get mail to him except by the regular A.P.O. It all automatically gets there unless it gets sunk, and the address you have for Robert is the same one I use here.

H.L.H.

263.

April 15, 1943

Written on The White House, Washington, letterhead.

Mrs. Ethel G. Hopkins,
53 Washington Street,
Newport, R.I.

MY DEAR MRS. HOPKINS:

Your letter of April 12th to Mrs. Daggett has come to me since I have taken Mrs. Daggett's place as Mr. Hopkins's secretary.

A check, dated March 15th, #30, in the sum of $108.33 was mailed to you on the same date. I have checked the bank today and find that it has not cleared – hence have issued a "stop payment" on it in view of your letter. A new check will be issued to you on Monday.

I am very sorry about this but the check evidently went astray in the mails.

Sincerely yours,
DOROTHEA E. KRAUSS
Secy. To Mr. Harry L. Hopkins

264.

April 19, 1943

Mrs. Ethel G. Hopkins
53 Washington,
Newport, R. I.

Written on The White House, Washington, letterhead.

MY DEAR MRS. HOPKINS:

Enclosed please find check #57, dated today, in the sum of $108.33 which is to replace check #30, dated March 15th in the same amount, on which stop payment was issued, due to its loss in the mails.

Sincerely,
D. E. KRAUSS
Secy. To Mr. Harry L. Hopkins

265.

June 2, 1943

DEAR ETHEL:

I have your note of the 25th.

I think now that Stephen will be down here sometime Thursday and should be through here Friday noon. I shall, of course, tell him to enlist from your address.

I had a letter from Robert the other day dated April 19th and he seemed to be perfectly well. I think there is very little probability of his getting home any time in the near future.

At this time I do not know where David is although I hope he is in some interesting part of the world.

There is no way that I could find of sending the package you sent me to Robert. Will you let me know what you want me to do with it?

Sincerely yours,

HARRY

Check encl.

Mrs. Ethel Hopkins

53 Washington Street

Newport, R.I.

266.

February 15, 1944

Written on Ed Gross, 480 Park Avenue, New York City, letterhead.

Marginalia: "Letter to Hopkins after my letter was published in newspapers. Written after letter to papers was published from me – stating that I wanted to be identified with my sons – in any future stories about my family. E. G. Hopkins." Gross was referring to the article in Time *magazine (February 28, 1944).*

DEAR HARRY:

I wouldn't hurt you for anything in the world, but after the heart breaking news came about Stephen I wanted to shout from the housetops, over and over again – my son Stephen was killed. I had to say it over and over again to believe it. I could not bear to be further removed from him by not being identified with him. It's terribly important to me to be his Mother at this time, just as important as when he was born.

Do you remember when he was three weeks old and we so nearly lost him after his operation? His being saved then has always seemed to me to be a miracle. He has had eighteen beautiful years since then. His development was such a thing to watch. He gave so much pleasure, continually. He was so full of the joy of life. He was so well-balanced. His sense of values were so clearly defined. Thanks to you and the security your earning have always given me, I was able to give him a normal, happy and regular existence. His life was full of all the things that boys love to do – football, tennis, skiing, skating, swimming, friends galore and girls too, when the time came. He was always beautiful to look at and everyone loved him. Through your great achievements

you were able to enrich his life with friendships and experiences with great – I want to say – all the great and
important people who belong to this era. Some people
– many people – live a whole life-time and never have
such experiences. All this was highly exciting to him,
and stimulating. It gave him an insight and an understanding, It matured him and he enjoyed life more
keenly because of it. He wanted so much to have you
love him. After his appendix operation when you visited him, he said he felt closer to you than he ever had
before. Over and over again since then he has told me
about wonderful talks he had had with you and how
easy it was to talk with you about "everything." All this is
the way I wanted it to be.

And there is one more thing I have wanted to say to
you for a long long time. As the years go by and I become more aware of the kind of person I really am, I
see more clearly why it was difficult for you many times:
and I blame you less for leaving me. You know how and
with whom you wanted to live your life and you have
gone a long way.

It does me good to say these things to you, and I hope
you won't mind.

ETHEL

267.

February 17, 1944

DEAR MRS. HOPKINS:

Mr. Hopkins asked me to send you a copy of the enclosed story concerning Stephen, which is being re-
leased by the navy late this afternoon.

Sincerely yours,

DOROTHEA KRAUSS

Secretary to Mr. Harry L. Hopkins.

Encl.

Mrs. Ethel G. Hopkins
53 Washington Street,
Newport, R.I.

*Written on Harry L.
Hopkins, Washington,
letterhead.*

268.

*This letter was mailed from the Mayo Clinic in Rochester, Minnesota, where Hopkins was undergoing treatment.

The Library here* has looked up the quotation of Churchill's.† It is in Scene 9 of the 5th Act of Macbeth.

It immediately follows the famous lines of Macbeth, saying:

'Damned be him that first cries 'hold' enough".

Ross tells Siward of his son's death in the quotation Churchill uses and what follows is interesting, and I am now quoting:

†*Upon learning of the death of Stephen Hopkins, Winston Churchill sent to Hopkins the quote referred to. It begins "Your son, my lord, has died a soldier's death." Gross kept the framed quote, signed by Churchill, prominently displayed in her home.*

Siward: Then he is dead

Ross: Aye and brought off the field. Your cause of sorrow must not be measured by his worth for then it hath no end.

Siward: Had he his hurts before?

Ross: Aye, on the front

Siward: Why, then God's soldier be he! Had I as many sons as I have hairs I would not wish them to a fair death, and so his knell is knol'd.

Malcolm: He is worth more sorrow, and that I'll spend for him.

Siward: He is worth no more. They say he parted well and paid his score and so God be with him.

HARRY L. HOPKINS

269.

Written on Harry L. Hopkins, Washington, letterhead. Mailed from the Mayo Clinic.

DEAR ETHEL:

In view of the fact that all of the children are now over 21 and self supporting, I am going to send you $125.00 each month.

It is a little simpler if I send it in one check on the first of the month, so I am enclosing the check for this month with this note.
Sincerely,
HARRY
Encl.

Mrs. Ethel G. Hopkins,
53 Washington Street.
Newport, R.I.

270.

June 14, 1945

DEAR ETHEL:
I talked to Robert on the telephone in London while I was in Paris. There was not time for him to come over to see me. He tells me he is to stay in London rather permanently but I fancy he will be home before long. I don't believe anyone with his long record will be used in the occupying forces in Germany. He sounded in good spirits and very pleased with himself that he could see something of Brenda.*

David is here with me and I gather he is expecting to be sent to the Pacific at once.
Sincerely,
HARRY L. HOPKINS

Mrs. Ethel G. Hopkins
Pasadena Regional Hospital,
American Red Cross,
Pasadena 2, Calif.†

*Robert Hopkins married Brenda Stephenson, an English woman, soon after the war.

†Gross had moved to California and was working with the Red Cross. She soon moved from Pasadena to Los Angeles.

Afterword

THROUGHOUT THE WAR YEARS, Hopkins traveled extensively and attended almost all the wartime conferences with Roosevelt. After Yalta, Hopkins became so exhausted and ill he was hospitalized. FDR died in April of 1945, and Hopkins left his hospital bed to attend the funeral. He made one more trip to Moscow, at the behest of the new president, Harry S. Truman, to try to reconcile the issue of Poland and to convince Stalin to relent on representation at the United Nations. Hopkins died soon after his return, in January 1946, just nine months after Roosevelt's death.

Ethel Gross moved to California in 1945 to be near her oldest son, David, and his growing family. With the financial help of her brothers, Gross bought a house in the West Los Angeles community of Mar Vista. She took great pleasure in her grandchildren and later, her great-grandchildren, who lived nearby. In 1949, Gross married Morris F. Conant, of Providence, Rhode Island, and they lived in Los Angeles. During this period, Gross was an active member of the Westwood Art Association, and she painted prolifically in a studio in her home, winning awards and having shows in local art galleries. She and her second husband lived a quiet and very happy life, supported mainly by social security. Conant died in 1969, and in 1972 Gross, in failing health, moved to Australia to be with her son, David, who had moved his family there in 1962. She died in Sydney in 1976, at the age of 90.

Selected Bibliography

The letters of Ethel Gross and Harry Hopkins were transcribed from the original handwritten and typed documents that are archived at Georgetown University in the Lavinger Library, Special Collections, Part IV of the Harry L. Hopkins Papers. Although the format has been standardized, the original punctuation in the body of the letters has been retained. Spelling and typographical errors have been corrected when this would not change the spirit of the letter. Where dates were not indicated on the original letter, the editors have ascertained and bracketed the date on which the letter was written.

Adams, Henry. *Harry Hopkins*. New York: G. P. Putnam, 1977.

Bacon, Samuel Frederick. *An Evaluation of the Philosophy and Pedagogy of Ethical Culture*. Washington, D.C.: Catholic University of America Press, 1933.

Banner, Lois. *Women in Modern America*. San Diego: Harcourt Brace Jovanivich, 1984.

Berry, Mary Frances. *The Politics of Parenthood: Child Care, Women's Rights, and the Myth of the Good Mother*. New York: Viking, 1993.

Blatch, Harriot Stanton, and Alma Lutz. *The Challenging Years*. New York: G. P. Putnam's Sons, 1940.

Boase, Paul H. ed. *The Rhetoric of Christian Socialism*. New York: Random House, 1969.

Brace, Charles Loring. *Hungary in 1851*. New York: Charles Scribner, 1852.

Bremer, William W. *Depression Winter: New York Social Workers and the New Deal*. Philadelphia: Temple University Press, 1984.

Carson, Mina. *Settlement Folk: Social Thought and the American Settlement Movement 1885–1930*. Chicago: University of Chicago Press, 1990.

Charles, Searle F. *Minister of Relief: Harry Hopkins and the Depression*. Syracuse, N.Y.: Syracuse University Press, 1963.

Crocker, Ruth Hutchinson. *Social Work and Social Order: The Settlement Movement in Two Industrial Cities, 1889–1930.* Urbana. Ill.: University of Illinois Press, 1992.

Curtis, Susan. *A Consuming Faith: The Social Gospel and Modern American Culture.* Baltimore: Johns Hopkins University Press, 1991.

Davis, Alan F. *Spearheads for Reform: The Social Settlements and the Progressive Movement.* New York: Oxford University Press, 1967.

Davis, Kenneth, *The New Deal Years 1933–1937.* New York: Random House, 1986.

Degler, Carl. *At Odds: Women and the Family in America from the Revolution to the Present.* New York: Oxford University Press, 1980.

Deminoff, William. "From Grinnell to National Power," *Des Moines Register,* November 2, 1975.

Dubois, Ellen Carol. "Working Women, Class Relations, and Suffrage Militance: Harriot Stanton Blatch and the New York Women Suffrage Movement, 1894–1909." *Journal of American History* 74, no. 1 (June 1987): 34–58.

Fitzpatrick, Ellen. *Endless Crusade: Women Social Scientists and Progressive Reform.* New York: Oxford University Press, 1990.

Fusco, Coco, "Whose Doin the Twist: Notes Toward a Politics of Appropriation." Pp. 65–77 in *English Is Broken Here: Notes on Cultural Fusion in the Americas.* New York: The New Press, 1995.

Gabbacia, Donna, "The Transplanted: Women and Family in Immigrant America," *Social Science History* 12 (Fall 1988): 243–53.

Gorrell, Donald K. *The Age of Social Responsibility: The Social Gospel in the Progressive Era 1900–1920.* Macon, Ga.: Mercer University Press, 1988.

Haenni, Sabine. "Visual and Theatrical Culture, Tenement Fiction, and the Immigrant in Subject in Abraham Cahan's *Yekl.*" *American Literature* 71, no. 3 (Sept. 1999): 493–527.

Holden, Arthur C. *The Settlement Idea: A Vision of Social Justice.* New York: Arno Press, 1922.

hooks, bell. *Black Looks: Race and Representation.* Boston: South End Press, 1992.

Hopkins, June. *Harry Hopkins: Sudden Hero, Brash Reformer.* New York: St. Martin's Press, 1999.

Kalman, Bela. *The World of Names: A Study in Hungarian Onomotology.* Budapest: Akademiai Kiado, 1978.

Kraus, Harry P. *The Settlement House Movement in New York City 1886–1914.* New York: Arno Press, 1980.

Kennedy, David M. *Freedom from Fear: The American People in Depression and War, 1929–1945.* New York: Oxford University Press, 1999.

Kurzman, Paul A., *Harry Hopkins and the New Deal.* Fairlawn, N.J.: R. E. Burdick, 1974.

Leuchtenburg, William. *Franklin D. Roosevelt and the New Deal, 1932–1940.* New York: Harper & Row, 1963.

Lloyd, Gary A. *Charities, Settlements and Social Work: An Inquiry into Philosophy and Method 1890–1915.* New Orleans: School of Social Work, Tulane University, 1971.

Matthew B. Wills. *Wartime Missions of Harry L. Hopkins.* Raleigh, N.C.: Pentland Press, 1996.

McBride, Paul. *Culture Clash: Immigrants and Reformers 1880–1920.* San Francisco: R and E Research Associates, 1975.

McElvaine, Robert. *The Great Depression: America 1929–1941.* New York: Times Books, 1984.

McJimsey, George. *Harry Hopkins: Ally of the Poor, Defender of Democracy.* Cambridge, Mass.: Harvard University Press, 1987.

Moskovits, Aron. *Jewish Education in Hungary 1848–1948.* New York: Black Publishing Co., 1964.

Muncy, Robin. *Creating a Female Dominion in American Reform: 1890–1935.* New York: Oxford University Press, 1991.

Polacheck, Hilda Scott. *I Came as a Stranger: The Story of a Hull House Girl.* Chicago: University of Chicago Press, 1991.

Rader, Frank. "Harry L. Hopkins: The Ambitious Crusader: An Historical Analysis of the Major Influences on His Career," *Annals of Iowa* 44 (1977): 83–102.

Rothman, Sheila. *Woman's Proper Place: A History of Changing Ideals 1870 to the Present.* New York: Basic Books, 1978.

Rousmaniere, John P. "Cultural Hybrid in the Slums: The College Woman and the Settlement House 1889–1894." *American Quarterly* 22 (Spring 1970): 45–66.

Schlesinger, Arthur Jr. *The Coming of the New Deal.* Boston: Houghton Mifflin, 1958.

Sharistanian, Janet, ed. *Gender, Ideology and Action: Historical Perspectives on Women's Public Lives.* Westport, Conn.: Greenwood Press, 1986.

Sherwood, Robert. *Roosevelt and Hopkins: An Intimate History.* New York: Harper and Brothers, 1948.

Sklar, Kathryn Kish. "Hull House Women in the 1890s: A Community of Women Reformers." *Signs* 10 (Summer 1985): 657–77.

Steiner, Edward A. *The Immigrant Tide: Its Ebb and Flow.* New York: F. H. Revell, 1909.

Trolander, Judith. *Settlement Houses and the Great Depression.* Detroit: Wayne State University Press, 1975.

———. *Professionalism and Social Change: From the Settlement House Movement to Neighborhood Centers, 1886 to the Present.* New York: Columbia University Press, 1987.

Wald, Lillian D. *The House on Henry Street.* New York: Dover Publications, Inc., 1915.

Wetherford, Doris. *Foreign and Female.* New York: Shocken Books, 1986.

White, George Cary. "Social Settlements and Immigrant Neighbors." *Social Service Review* 33 (March 1959): 55–66.

White, Ronald C., and C. Howard Hopkins. *The Social Gospel: Religion and Reform in Changing America.* Philadelphia: Temple University Press, 1976.

Zimmerman, Joan G. "Daughters of Main Street: Culture and the Female Community at Grinnell 1884–1917." In *Woman's Being, Woman's Place: Female Identity and Vocation in American History*, edited by Mary Kelly. Boston: G. K. Hall and Company, 1979.

Index

About the Editors

Dr. Allison Giffen received her doctorate in English from Columbia University. She teaches American Literature at Western Washington University, specializing in American women writers. Her work has appeared in a number of journals and collections, including *Women's Studies, Early American Literature, American Transcendental Quarterly, Genres of Writing: Issues, Arguments, Alternatives,* and *The Teacher's Body.*

Dr. June Hopkins received her doctorate in history from Georgetown University. She has taught American history at Armstrong Atlantic State University and is currently associate editor of the Eleanor Roosevelt Papers at George Washington University at Mount Vernon College. Her work has been published in *Presidential Studies Quarterly* and *The New Deal and Public Policy.* She is the author of the 1999 biography *Harry Hopkins: Sudden Hero, Brash Reformer.*

June Hopkins is the granddaughter, and Allison Giffen the great-granddaughter, of Harry Hopkins and Ethel Gross.